INSTITUTIONALISING PANCHAYATI RAJ IN INDIA

Institutionalising Panchayati Raj In India

V. Venkatesan

Published for

Institute of Social Sciences

by

Concept Publishing Company

ISBN 81-7022-984-7

First published 2002

Printed and published by
Ashok Kumar Mittal
Concept Publishing Company
A-15/16, Commercial Block, Mohan Garden
New Delhi 110059 (India)
Phones: +91 11 5351460, 5351794
Fax: + 91 11 5357103
Email: publishing@conceptpub.com

"I look upon an increase in the power of the state with the greatest fear, because, although while apparently doing good by minimising exploitation, it does the greatest harm to mankind by destroying individuality which lies at the root of all progress."

-- Mahatma Gandhi

Acknowledgements

My thanks are due to Mr. Rajan Kuttappan, Institute of Social Sciences, New Delhi for the painstaking task performed by him in formatting the manuscript in the book form and working on the index and Ms. Nasreen Faiyaz, copy editor, who went through the manuscript carefully and suggested many corrections. I am grateful to the Institute of Social Sciences for seeing through this publication. To the people of rural India and their elected representatives, I owe an everlasting gratitude. But for them, this book would never have been written.

V. Venkatesan

For
My Family

Foreword

It was in 1998 that I met Dr. V. Venkatesan. He came to the Institute of Social Sciences in connection with a World Bank programme: expert consultation on decentralised rural development. We had several meetings and I was greatly inspired by his commitment to decentralisation and Panchayati Raj and his extraordinary insights on the subject of local governance in the country. My association with Dr. Venkatesan resulted in a work "*Decentralised Institutions: Governmental and Voluntary Sector*" (*Economic and Political Weekly*, Vol. XXXIV, No. 9, February 27, 1999) which otherwise I would not have completed. When I came to know that Dr. Venkatesan was retiring from the World Bank assignment I pursuaded him to write down his insights on Panchayati Raj and rural development in India immediately after independence, his personal experiences during his active days in the Indian Administrative Service and his views on the present developments. He readily agreed. The present work "Institutionalising Panchayati Raj in India" is the hard work of Dr. V. Venkatesan in the last two years or so. This is a unique publication because very few civil servants have taken the pains to put on paper the rich experience of independent India's tryst with rural development and village self-government.

As development of Panchayati Raj is a major area of concern for the Institute, this publication combining historical development and the present day issues is of special importance for the Institute as it will greatly help the policy makers, practitioners and students of local government.

Today we need a realistic inside view of an administrator of 1960's and 70's for us to take correct and concrete steps for the future. The book fills the vacuum that now exists.

New Delhi
11 February 2002

George Mathew
Director
Institute of Social Sciences

Preface

The origins of this book go back to early 1970s when I was the Managing Director of the Maharashtra State Land Development Bank (MSLDB), and my tours took me to almost all parts of the State. Prof. V.M. Dandekar (Gokhale Institute, Pune) was advising the MSLDB on a survey of its borrowers, which MSLDB intended to undertake. His study "Poverty in India"[1] had just been published, and brought him well earned recognition both in India and abroad. Once I was travelling with him from Ahmednagar to Pune, in Maharashtra. I had already decided to be his student, taking leave of absence from the Indian Administrative Service (IAS), a decision which I was to implement ten years later. According to him, public policy making should be grounded in realities; and that its essential features should be simplicity, reliance on easily available statistics, and capability of being expressed in a language which a person with average intelligence can understand, even if it implies sacrificing some academic sophistication. He expanded on this idea in an article published in Economic and Political Weekly in February, 1979. He said that, while "academic sophistication is legitimate in academic exercises, which in their nature are exploratory", it is "dangerous" to permit too much academic sophistication in operative decisions of government (Dandekar 1979:233). He suggested that I do research on the essential elements of public policy making and that I draw upon my experience as a public policy maker. This was what I did in my Ph.D. thesis (Venkatesan 1982) a decade later. I have attempted to follow this advice here also.

This book covers a broader canvas than my thesis. Over the years, agricultural development has taken a back seat to a broad

---

1 His co-author was Dr. N. Rath, now at the Indian School of Political Economy, Pune , India. This was the first systematic study of measuring poverty in India. It was funded by Ford Foundation. See Dandekar and Rath 1971 and also Box 6.5.

rural development and poverty alleviation. There have been other developments also. Rural development and decentralisation are attracting a lot of attention from donors, international financial institutions, non-governmental organisations (NGO) and National and State level politicians in India. Decentralisation has been recognised as an important tool for bringing about sustainable rural development. There have been successful examples of decentralisation in many other countries which India can learn from. This book recognises these developments.

I retired from the World Bank in May/June, 1998 and went to India as a consultant to the World Bank in June, 1998. I helped the World Bank organise Expert Consultation in Hyderabad, India, followed by a National Workshop in New Delhi on "Decentralised Rural Development". The visit gave me an opportunity to discuss the vicissitudes of the *Panchayati Raj* Institutions (PRI), particularly after the 73rd and 74th Constitutional Amendments, with a number of my Indian friends. In November/December 1998, I also visited Orissa and Kerala as a World Bank consultant. When I was in Bhubaneshwar and Thiruvananthapuram, I took the opportunity to discuss with donor representatives, the institutional framework in donor-assisted projects, particularly those that deal with NGOs. In December 1999, I organised another workshop in Hyderabad for the World Bank, this time confined to three states only, namely, Andhra Pradesh (A.P.), Madhya Pradesh (M.P.) and Rajasthan, where the World Bank was supporting the District Poverty Initiative Projects. My visits to India in 1998 and 1999, especially my conversations with donor representatives and civil servants, suggested that despite the Constitutional amendments, PRIs in India are likely to go the way of the earlier Community Development Programme (CDP). I was in Pune, India, in January 2000 depressed by the way *panchayats* were being treated by all the actors in the drama – National and State level politicians in India, civil servants of the State and Central Governments, and international organisations. They are probably killing *panchayats* by pretending to fondle them. At this point my phone rang, and Dr. George Mathew, Director, Institute of Social Sciences, New Delhi, was on the line. He has an infectious optimism. I had already met him in the National Workshop and heard of the part played by him in the enactment of the 73rd and 74th Constitutional amendments. The suggestion to write this book came from him.

When I agreed with his suggestion I did not realise what I was in for. The book became an obsession. I visited the U.S.A. (where my sons live) in January 2000, and planned to write as many chapters of the book as it was possible to do from Washington. The library facilities in Washington, both in the World Bank and outside, were excellent. I could finish the skeleton of the book in Washington, and went back to India in July 2000, when I thought I could complete it. But my conversations with Mathew, his colleagues (particularly Buddhadeb Ghosh) and the various civil servants[2] made me re-focus my book. It was the suggestion of those whom I met in India, that the book should deal with specifics relating to India, with matters that I had experienced personally. Accordingly, the present version discusses the issues regarding decentralisation which are specific to India, such as, Centrally Sponsored Schemes (CSS), Planning process, the Centre-State financial relationship and the interaction between PRIs and NGOs. It includes the theoretical aspects of decentralisation, and what is happening in other countries, only to the extent to which they are relevant to the Indian situation. I must say the book is now more realistic, and has a distinctly Indian flavour.

In August, 2000 I visited the Lal Bahadur Shastri National Academy of Administration, Mussoorie, (U.P.). My visit to Mussoorie was in a way, a "homecoming" to me as I passed out of the Academy in 1961, after spending a year there. At that time, the original Charleville with its old world charm was still there. Since then, Charleville has been destroyed by fire, and a new building has been erected in its place. As I stayed in the new Kalindi Guest House, I could not but look at the past with nostalgia. The old landmarks had gone. Nowadays one cannot

---

2 My discussions with Messrs. N. C. Saxena (Secretary, Planning Commission and ex-Secretary Rural Development), S.S. Meenakshi-sundaram, Mrs. Rohini Nayyar, Dr. J.S. Sarma and Mrs. Sudha Pillai were particularly useful.

walk on the road from the Library Point to the Academy without running the risk of being hit by one of the "new generation" of cars. I went to the Kempti Falls, where previously one could go for some peace and quiet, but not any longer. One has to put up with noise pollution from the stereo systems of the cars. While in Mussoorie I had the benefit of discussion with the administrators there. The visit gave me a better understanding of the role of PRIs especially regarding land reforms.

Many administrators, wherever I went, spoke to me frankly. I also had the good fortune to discuss the issues involved with a number of my ex-colleagues, and a number of administrators who came into the IAS after I retired from the service. With a view to maintaining confidentiality I have not connected any specific remark with a specific civil servant. The views expressed here are my own.

There is a sudden burgeoning of literature on PRIs after 73rd and 74th Constitutional amendments[3] which were passed in December, 1992, with the 73rd amendment coming into effect on April 24, 1993, and 74th amendment on June 1, 1993. It therefore requires an explanation why one more book on the subject is necessary. There are four reasons for my writing this book. First, this book combines in itself a historical survey of decentralisation in India from Indian Independence in 1947 to the present day, and an analytical account of the leading institutional issues involved in decentralisation in India. Such a combination has not been attempted before. There are some excellent historical accounts of decentralisation and rural development in India, such as the one by F.K.Wadia (Wadia 1996), but they do not contain an in-depth discussion of the institutional issues involved in decentralisation and rural development in India. There are also a number of excellent analytical studies on decentralisation, such as, World Bank 1999a, Binswanger 1999, Ravillion 1999, Prud'homme 1995, but they are not India-specific. I thought there is need for a book which includes a combination of both historicism and an

---

3 A very interesting political and bureaucratic background to these amendments is given in Sivaramakrishnan 2000.

analysis of the institutional issues involved, that are specific to India. Many current issues relating to decentralisation have their roots in history, and I found it difficult to discuss these issues, without presuming some understanding on the part of the reader of the historical developments. So I decided to write the historical development as well, and refer the interested reader who wants to dig a little deeper into history, to other books and journal articles on the subject. Second, the book traces the connection between what happened during the period from 1947 till the early 1960s, and what is happening now on the decentralisation scene. Third, the book draws from sources not easily available to researchers and scholars in India. Fourth, it is grounded in realities and is based on my own experience as an administrator for over two decades. During my tenure as Planning Secretary in Maharashtra two important developments took place:

- The implementation of the Employment Guarantee Scheme (EGS), which was the forerunner of the Jawahar Rozgar Yojana[4] (JRY), gathered momentum, and
- District planning was introduced; this preceded the 73rd Constitutional amendment by almost 20 years.

I had the following categories of readers in mind, while writing this book.

- fellow professionals, researchers, scholars and graduate students,
- staff of donor organisations and the World Bank, who want to understand the forces that have shaped the democratic decentralisation in India,
- practitioners and civil servants in India who want to know the leading issues in decentralisation and rural development,
- policy makers in other third world countries who would want to understand the Indian situation, and
- well-informed readers.

---

4 This is the rural employment programme of the GOI and is described more fully in Box 10.1.

Having such a diverse audience has its price. It partly explains the rather extensive endnotes after each chapter. On the one hand, I am painfully aware that too many such endnotes and boxes can be very annoying, and will divert the attention of the reader from the focus of the discussion; on the other, I could not resist the temptation of some interesting information or annotation or reference. I have always been tormented by the question: whether a particular piece of information should go to an endnote or box remain in the text? Broadly, the rule I have followed is as follows: long quotations or annotations go to boxes; short comments or references go to endnotes, the endnote reference follows the word concerned. Ultimately the decision was mine, and I have tried to keep the convenience of the readers in mind. I presume that the more curious reader would find them interesting.

In this book, the terms 'civil servants', 'administrators' and 'officials' denote the same group of persons, namely permanent civil servants who are not affected by changes in political scene and do not, while in government employment, have party affiliations. At some places in the book, one term sounds more appropriate than the rest and is used. The term 'non-official' is a rather hazy one; it is commonly used in India to denote any person other than a civil servant or an elected official. A retired civil servant (the category to which I belong) is sometimes called a 'non-official' and sometimes an 'official', and the practice is not consistent.

Readers are likely to be puzzled by what may appear to be too much of capitalisation of words, which defies any style manual. I had to improvise my own rules regarding style. The letter "S" in the word "State" is almost always capitalised when the word refers to a State in India; and is not capitalised when it has a generic meaning, as in "state *vis à vis* citizen." Similarly, the letter "C" in the words "Centre" and "Central" is capitalised, when the word refers to the Centre or the Central (or more correctly, the Union) Government in India; and the letter "P" in the word "Plan" is capitalised, when the word refers to an Indian Five Year or Annual Plan, and is not capitalised, when the word has a generic meaning. The same principle applies to other words as well, where capitalisation is not called for, but are still capitalised. Some examples are: "State or Central Secretariat," "Head of the Department", "Ministries", or "Budget".

The reader may find some words in italics. Normally words in the local language, such as *Panchayat Samiti* are in italics, but their abbreviations are not. Thus "PRI" is not italics. Block quotations are indented to enable the reader to distinguish them from the text. I have included a glossary that contains the meanings of local terms. I have avoided titles, such as, "Shri" or "Mr." in the text.

There are more references to Maharashtra than to any other State. There is one overarching reason for this; I belonged to Maharashtra cadre of the IAS and I know more about the State than about any other. The second reason is that Maharashtra was one of the earliest States to decentralise, and I came to the State in 1961 from Mussoorie, when the air was thick with lofty expectations from decentralisation. The third reason has already been mentioned above, namely, I was associated with the EGS and district planning.

Finally, a word about what some of the terms used in this book denote:

- The term "donors" denotes bilateral and multilateral donors, such as USAID, European Union, Ford Foundation and FAO, and does not include international financial institutions such as the World Bank.
- The term "international financial institutions" includes the World Bank and International Fund for Agricultural Development (IFAD).
- The term "international organisations" includes FAO, ILO, the World Bank, IFAD and the Asian Development Bank. Thus the term "international organisations" includes all "international financial institutions" and some donors, such as the Ford Foundation, who are not bilateral donors.

The book bears the stamp of many who have perused the earlier drafts and offered their comments. I must particularly acknowledge my deep debt of gratitude to the painstaking reviews of the earlier drafts, done by Messrs. Baxter, Buddhadeb Ghosh, Meenakshisundaram and Oldenburg. But for the constant encouragement by Dr. George Mathew this book would never have been finished.

Pune, India
December 4, 2001

V. Venkatesan

Abbreviations

A.P.	Andhra Pradesh
ARC	Administrative Reforms Commission
BDO	Block Development Officer
BP	Block Panchayat
BPC	Block Planning Committee
BPL	Below Poverty Line
BRDP	Baroda Rural Development Programme
CAPART	Council for Advancement of People's Action and Rural Technology
CDP	Community Development Programme
CFC	Central Finance Commission
CSS	Centrally Sponsored Scheme
DDC	District Development Council
DLS	District Level Scheme
DP	District Panchayat
DPC	District Planning Committee
DPDC	District Planning and Development Council
DRDA	District Rural Development Agency
EGS	Employment Guarantee Scheme
GMF	Grow More Food
GOI	Government of India
GP	Gram Panchayat
GS	Gram Sabha
IADP	Integrated Area Development Project

IAS	Indian Administrative Service
IFAD	International Fund for Agricultural Development
IRDP	Integrated Rural Development Project
JGSY	Jawahar Gram Samridhi Yojana
JRY	Jawahar Rozgar Yojana
LDB	Land Development Bank
M.P.	Madhya Pradesh
MFAL	Marginal Farmers and Agricultural Labourers
MLA	Member of the Legislative Assembly
MLC	Member of the Legislative Council
MNP	Minimum Needs Programme
MP	Member of Parliament
MSLDB	Maharashtra State Land Development Bank
NARS	National Agricultural Research System
NES	National Extension Service
NGO	Non-governmental Organisation
NREP	National Rural Employment Programme
PC	Planning Commission
PIA	Project Implementation Agency
PMU	Project Management Unit
PRI	Panchayati Raj Institutions
PS	Panchayat Samiti
RLEGP	Rural Landless Employment Guarantee Programme
SAD	State Agriculture Department
SAU	State Agricultural University

SC	Scheduled Caste
SDC	Swiss Agency for Development and Cooperation
SFC	State Finance Commission
SFDA	Small Farmers Development Agency
SGSY	Swarnjayanthi Gram Swarozgar Yojana
ST	Scheduled Tribe
T&V	Training and Visit
TP	Taluka Panchayat
U.P.	Uttar Pradesh
UT	Union Territories
VLW	Village Level Worker also known as Gram Sevak
VP	Village Panchayat
ZP	Zilla Parishad

Glossary

Jawahar Rozgar Yojana: This was the rural employment programme of the Government of India. It has now been merged with *Jawahar Gram Samridhi Yojana* (JGSY). See Box 10.1 for more information.

Panchayat: The term refers to democratic body at the village level. Historically, the term was used to refer to village bodies headed by five persons, chosen by the villagers. In Hindi the word "*panch*" means "five." In modern times, the term refers to a democratically elected institution at the village levei. Since in due course, particularly after the 73rd and 74th amendments of the Indian Constitution (see below) there have been *panchayats* at the block and district levels, the term "*gram panchayat*" or what is the same, "village *panchayat*", is often used to distinguish the village level democratic body from those at other levels.

Panchayati Raj: Literally the term means "rule by *panchayats.*" The term was coined by Jawaharlal Nehru. It presupposes democratic decentralisation to the district level and below, which are recognised as "institutions of self government."

Panchayati Raj Institutions: These are democratic bodies at the district level and below. They have been given Constitutional status under 73rd and 74th amendments of the Indian Constitution, which came into effect in 1993.

Gram Sevak: "*Gram*" means "village," "*sevak*" means "worker." The term refers to a village level worker (VLW). The feminine gender of gram sevak is gram sevika. He/she is the person who comes into contact with villagers, and reports to the Block Development Officer (see Box 3.5).

Zilla Parishad: A local name for the district level PRI. It is also called District *Panchayat.*

Panchayat Samiti: A local name for the Block level PRI. It is also called Block *Panchayat.*

Garibi Hatao: "Garibi" means "poverty". The term means "remove poverty." A brief description of Government of India's anti-poverty programmes is contained in Box 6.5.

Swarnjayanthi Gram Swarozgar Yojana: This is the self-employment scheme of the Government of India. See Box 6.5.

Contents

List of Boxes

List of Annexes

CHAPTER 1

Introduction

The objectives of this book

This book has two major objectives. The first objective is to trace the growth and decline of decentralisation in India, particularly the developments in 1960s and 1970s. The author has personal knowledge of these developments. There is a thread running through these and the recent amendments of the Indian Constitution, and it is necessary to recognise it and appreciate the fact that the recent developments are the product of evolution. The second and a more important objective is to describe the institutional issues that are relevant to decentralisation. It is important to keep these issues in mind, if the momentum built by the 73rd and 74th amendments of the Indian Constitution, is to be sustained. History has some valuable lessons in this regard. The important lesson that history offers us is, that there are three formidable forces threatening decentralisation and PRIs, namely, political factors, bureaucracy, and donors and international organisations. We have to guard against the danger of a combination of these forces again making PRIs ineffective. With this in mind, I have included a detailed description of the early attempts at decentralisation in detail, particularly, the CDP, and the role of the above forces in undermining the effectiveness of the CDP. The essential difference between the CDP, and the present decentralisation programme, contained in the recent Constitutional amendments, referred to above, lies in the fact, that unlike in the CDP, these Constitutional amendments include political decentralisation, and envision PRIs as units of self-government.

Institutional issues addressed in this book

The following institutional issues are addressed in this book.

- The most sustainable institutional setup which is also effective in achieving better coordination at the district level and below.
- The integration of the human development and technical development aspects, in the CDP.
- The factors which led to the decline of the CDP.
- The transition from integrated administration to un-integrated administration, following the Ford Foundation Report.
- The institutional framework for District Planning.
- The institutional aspects of CSS and how they are the result of lack of financial decentralisation to PRIs.
- The existence of parallel organisations (or parallel structures) alongside PRIs.

The arrangement of the book

The focus of this book is on institutional issues relating to decentralisation. It has twelve chapters. Chapter 2 talks about the importance of democratic decentralisation for achieving better coordination in the administration of multi-sector programmes. Chapters 3 and 4 are devoted to the CDP, which was the first attempt at decentralisation on a national scale. It was also one of the earliest CSS. The causes for the decline of the programme are analysed in Chapter 4. It was felt that the main reason for the lack of effectiveness of the CDP, was the fact that people's representatives were not associated in a formal manner with administration at the local level. The setting up of the Balwantray Mehta Committee was the result of this realisation. The report of this Committee is discussed in Chapter 5. The report by the Government of India (GOI) on "India's Food Crisis and Steps to Meet It" (India 1959a), popularly known as the Ford Foundation Report, and the Intensive Agricultural Districts Programme[1] which followed, were the occasions for the State Agriculture Departments breaking away from the administrative arrangement established under the CDP. This heralded the reversing of the decentralisation process started with the CDP. The events of this period are described in Chapter 6. Chapter 7 describes the events of the mid-1970s and the early 1980s, particularly, the Asoka Mehta Committee Report, and the decentralisation experiments in West Bengal and Karnataka. The next landmark is the 73rd and 74th Constitutional amendments of the early 1990s. These have been recent and extensively commented upon. A brief description of these amendments are contained in Chapter 8 and some aspects of these amendments are discussed more fully.

District Planning has been with us since mid-1970s when Maharashtra started it. It has been mentioned in Art 243G of the Constitution after the 73rd amendment. The setting up of the District Planning Committee (DPC) has been made mandatory under Art 243ZD of the Constitution, thanks to the 74th amendment. The problems in administering a district planning process under the present framework are described in Chapter 9. The existence of a large number of CSS is antithetical to the decentralised planning setup envisioned by the Constitution. The reasons for the survival of many schemes in spite of many attempts to minimise them are analysed in Chapter 10. The growth of NGOs is a recent phenomenon. Many of them have joined the forces that have historically worked against the decentralisation process mentioned in the earlier chapters. The interaction of the latter with the forces mentioned above, are discussed in Chapter 11. Chapter 12 summarises the conclusions of this book.

Types of decentralisation

We shall now see how the term "decentralisation" is understood in India and in international circles. It is generally accepted that there are four types of decentralisation: (a) deconcentration, (b) delegation, (c) privatisation, and (d) devolution (Cheema and Rondinelli 1983b). Kurian (1999) contains the summary of the various types of decentralisation, discusses the merits and demerits of each of those, and also exhibits, in a matrix form, the characteristics of each type of decentralisation (Kurian 1999:10).[2] The Table at the end of this chapter is based on this matrix, which has been modified to suit the situation prevailing in India.

In practice, there is little distinction between "deconcentration" and "delegation." "Deconcentration" refers to administrative authority which is handed down from higher levels of government to lower ones, within the Ministries or Departments. It is an instance of administrative reorganisation, that seeks to give more freedom to field units to plan and implement projects which are suitable to local people. When the authority of a State Government in the Irrigation Department to give administrative approval or technical sanction to a project, is given to the Superintending or Executive Engineer, it is an example of deconcentration. There are different degrees of deconcentration, depending on the administrative reorganisation that the country has adopted.

"Delegation" refers to the transfer of managerial responsibility for certain functions, to another organisation, outside the regular bureaucratic structure of the Ministry or Department. For example, if the Government of Maharashtra entrusts the implementation of a programme to the District *Panchayat* (DP), or what is the same, *Zilla Parishad* (ZP) it is called "delegation". Delegation need not be to a democratically elected body; it can also be to a public sector undertaking.

Both deconcentration and delegation can be either constitutional (i.e. ordained by the constitution of the country) or statutory (i.e. ordained by law of the Parliament or the State legislature). Or, either can be covered by an executive order. Some of the enduring schemes and institutions in India, such as, the CDP, Planning Commission, or the GOI's anti-poverty programmes are created by executive orders. Planning Commission is not a Constitutional body (i.e., it is not mentioned in the Indian Constitution); not even a statutory body (i.e., it is not created by an Act of Parliament). It has been established by a resolution of the Parliament, and is a creature of the Union Government, which appoints it and has the power to dissolve it. If an institution is constitutional or statutory, it is more difficult to abolish it, and, if the powers are given to the body statutorily, that is, by an Act of Parliament or State legislature, it is more difficult to take away powers given to it. In India, after the 73rd and 74th Constitutional amendments, once a power is legally transferred to PRIs, it cannot be taken back except by an Act of the Legislature of a State, subject to the provisions of the Constitution. Crook and Manor (1994) compare the performance of decentralised governments in Karnataka, Bangla Desh, Cote d'Ivoire and Ghana. They find the responsiveness to be the best in Karnataka and this is attributed to the fact that in Karnataka democratic accountability[3] is more than in Bangla Desh or Cote d'Ivoire.

Sometimes, the term "decentralisation" is used to include "privatisation", as more and more tasks which were earlier performed by state agencies are given to the private sector. It results in the transfer of tasks outside government and political systems. As the objectives of privatisation are different from those of decentralisation, privatisation *per se* is not discussed here. The Table however shows privatisation as a part of decentralisation, because NGO sector is a part of private sector. In view of the impact which it has on PRIs, the NGO sector is discussed in Chapter 11. NGOs often provide services which were earlier being provided by the State, particularly, in education and health. NGOs are very visible in the rural scene and are very important. Many of them are also politically well-connected. They do not like being clubbed with the private sector, which they tend to treat with derision, saying that the private sector organisations exist for profit, and that they (NGOs) are non-profit organisations, who provide a service to the people. Many international organisations agree with them and give funds directly to them, often by-passing State Governments and PRIs[4].

Definition of "decentralisation"

Following the report of the Balwantray Mehta Committee let us define decentralisation, as a

> "process whereby the government divests itself completely of certain duties and responsibilities and devolves them on to some other authority within its jurisdiction, reserving to itself only the functions of guidance, supervision and higher planning" (India 1957c:I,7).

This definition agrees with that given recently by an active policy maker in the area of decentralisation:

> "Democratic decentralisation implies progressive devolution of decision making on all vital matters affecting people's lives. If the responsibility of development at the district level is left to the bureaucratic hierarchy under the control of the ministry at the state level, democratic decentralisation will remain an empty slogan." (Sab 1996:51).

Balwantray Mehta Committee report points out the distinction between "delegation"[5] and "decentralisation", saying that very often delegation of power is mistaken for decentralisation. In "delegation", the power delegated can be taken back by the person who delegates, as delegation is often done by an executive order. "Decentralisation", on the other hand, is the transfer of authority and responsibility for various government functions from higher to lower levels of government. Such an inter-governmental transfer of powers and responsibilities or what is known as "devolution", is the conventional concept of decentralisation in public administration; it involves elected local governments, which exercise significant measure of local autonomy. The transfer of authority mentioned above can be administrative or statutory; in India it is often statutory. The objective of decentralisation is to enable local governments to function as units of self-government, and to plan and implement programmes which are meaningful to the local population.

The above definition is consistent with the understanding of the term in important quarters, worldwide. For example, James Manor, in a survey of decentralisation in many countries, says that devolution or democratisation, has been the main thrust of recent experiments with decentralisation, and that decentralisation of resources and responsibilities without democratising political reforms would not be conducive to socially effective results (Manor 1999b:6, World Bank 1995: 2). Expressing itself strongly in favour of the concept of decentralisation mentioned above, the Swiss Agency for Development and Cooperation (SDC) says:

> "Following the basic arguments of the case for decentralisation, the World Bank's programme of good governance and the UNDP's human development programme have both placed emphasis on decentralisation as an effective tool for promoting economic development through enhanced local autonomy and initiative, as well as democracy through the restoration of liberty at the base". (SDC 1999:34)

Decentralisation means different things to different people. After analysing the different senses in which the term is used in many countries, Andrew Parker thinks that "devolution" is closer to the situation in India than any other term (Parker 1995:21). Unless the contrary is indicated, the terms "decentralisation" and "devolution" are used interchangeably in this book. The term "decentralisation" used in this book is consistent with the views of Balwantray Mehta, Nazir Sab, and with internationally accepted definitions of the term.

The standard arguments in favour of democratic decentralisation relate to responsiveness and accountability; that local governments are closer to the citizens and to the consumers of services and are thus better able to make choices, that reflect the needs and priorities in their jurisdiction than is a remote Central government. In contrast to the inter-governmental model of decentralisation, the decentralisation of management involves no direct political or democratic accountability to electors. Rather, accountability is upwards to decision makers who may be bureaucrats or elected representatives of people at the state or national level.

Decentralisation leads to good governance, legitimacy and transparency. In some areas, particularly human development, the closer the governments are to the people they are intended to serve, the more effective is their role in fostering human development. According to an observer of Indian political scene, "experience also shows that local governments tend to give higher priority than central governments to human development" (Bandyopadhyay 1996:3111).

Various aspects of decentralisation

The various aspects of decentralisation which are practised in many countries, are: political, administrative and fiscal decentralisation. Only when the three elements[6] are implemented together can a country create the accountability and transparency at the local level, and the local units will be capable of implementing the programmes given to them (Binswanger 1999). This was the important conclusion of the research undertaken by the World Bank recently, and presented at the National Workshop held by the GOI at the Vigyan Bhavan, New Delhi, on June 26 - 27, 1998. (see Box 1.1).

Box 1.1: Soufflé effect

The results of the World Bank research on decentralisation were presented by Mr. Graham Kerr (who was at that time a senior consultant with the World Bank) at the National Seminar on Decentralisation held in Vigyan Bhavan on June 26-27, 1998. He said that recent World Bank research has shown that in order to be effective, decentralisation must have all the three ingredients, namely, political, administrative and fiscal. He quoted Mr. Binswanger (who was the Director responsible for the research project) that just as, while making a soufflé one has to mix all the necessary ingredients, it is also necessary to mix all the three ingredients in decentralisation. Only then the results would be good. Soufflé effect is also mentioned in Parker (1995) and UNDP (1993).

In India, political decentralisation is enshrined in the Constitution after the recent Constitutional amendments. As mentioned above, Articles 243(d) and 243G of the Indian Constitution envision panchayats as institutions of self-government. Administrative decentralisation is mostly sectoral, and is covered by the terms "deconcentration" and "delegation" described earlier in this chapter. Financial or fiscal decentralisation is the most critical component of decentralisation. The two terms are often used interchangeably in development literature, but they denote different things. "Financial decentralisation" includes either certain taxes levied and collected by the Centre or the State and distributed to the various districts in accordance with a formula, or, any grants given by either of them to PRIs. Fiscal decentralisation comprises certain functional areas where the power to levy user charges or taxes, is delegated to PRIs, generally by State Governments. If the local government is to perform effectively it must have the necessary funds, either raised locally through user fees or taxes or given to it from the State or Central Government. In India[7], *panchayats* have legal authority to impose taxes, but the tax base of the *panchayats* is very weak and the scope of user charges also rather limited. *Panchayats* therefore have to depend on State Government and Central Government grants. When political decentralisation is combined with administrative and fiscal decentralisation, it is covered by the term "devolution". We shall return to this subject in Chapter 8.

Brief historical account of decentralisation in India

The reader may find it easier to follow the arguments in the subsequent chapters, if a brief description of the early attempts at decentralisation in India is given at this stage. The first attempt to introduce decentralisation in independent India on a national scale, was the CDP which is described in Chapter 3. Before the introduction of the CDP, the Constitution of India was adopted on January 26, 1950. During the Constituent Assembly debates, the question of mentioning PRIs in the operative part of the Constitution was being discussed. Ambedkar did not want to give primacy to village, and as a result, PRIs found a place in the Directive Principles of State Policy, which is not enforceable in a court of law, but at the same time reflects government's policy. Article 40 of the Constitution of India says that:

> "the State shall take steps to organise village panchayats and endow them with such powers and authority as may be necessary to enable them to function as units of self-government" (India 1999c:16).

Ambedkar said in his speech before the newly Independent India's Constituent Assembly in 1948: "What is the village but a sink of localism, a den of ignorance, narrow-mindedness and communalism? I am glad that the Draft Constitution has discarded the village."

Under List II of the Seventh Schedule of the Constitution, that is the State List, "Local Government, that is to say, the constitution and powers of municipal corporations, improvement trusts, district boards, mining settlement authorities and local authorities for the purpose of local self-government or village administration" was to remain the domain of States (India 1999c:221). In respect of matters in the State List, according to Article 246 of the Constitution, the State concerned has exclusive powers to make laws. Accordingly, measures were taken by States to bring their laws in conformity with Article 40 of Constitution. In those States, where no law was existing to provide for *panchayats*, new laws were passed. By 1951-52, there were over 70,000 village *panchayats* functioning in the country.

Box 1.2: Scheduled Castes and Scheduled Tribes under the Indian Constitution

The views of Ambedkar are understandable, coming as they do, from someone who has suffered humiliation under India's notorious caste system, and is an undisputed leader of the Scheduled Castes (SC). SCs have been the victims of caste prejudices. Gandhiji called them "harijans." Those who belong to the SC prefer increased urbanisation, as urban areas tend to be less caste conscious. I am aware of many inter-caste marriages involving SCs in big cities, something which is unthinkable in rural areas.

The terms SC and Scheduled Tribes (ST) are defined in Articles 341 and 342 of Indian Constitution respectively. According to Article 341, the President of India may notify specifying "the castes, races or tribes" which "shall for the purposes of the Constitution be deemed to be Scheduled Castes" in relation to the State or Union Territory (UT)[8] concerned.

According to the 1991 Census of India the percentage of Scheduled Castes in the country is 16.48, amounting to about 138 million people. Among the States, Punjab has the highest proportion of Scheduled Castes with 28.3 percent. The Scheduled Tribe population is about 68 million (8.08 percent).

These bodies were entrusted with a wide range of responsibilities. They were mostly democratic bodies, but not constitutional entities. They were creatures of State Acts. States could therefore postpone holding *panchayat* elections. Many States on various occasions actually did so. The *panchayat* area varied from a single village to a group of villages, depending on the population in the villages, the distance between villages, and the geographic factors. The statutory functions entrusted to *panchayats* under State Acts, included local administration. In order to enable village *panchayats* to implement the responsibilities cast on them, State laws provided for various sources of finance. The major source was grants from State Governments. The laws also gave powers to *panchayats* to introduce compulsory manual labour for purposes of public utility and to give option to individuals to render physical labour in lieu of taxes payable in cash (India 1954:iv).

Since 1950, besides the CDP, the major landmarks have been: Balwantray Mehta Committee; Ford Foundation Report and Intensive Agricultural Districts Programme; the decentralisation efforts in some States notably, Maharashtra, Gujarat, West Bengal, Karnataka and Kerala; Asoka Mehta Committee; introduction of District Planning; the proliferation of CSS and efforts to reduce them in number and contain their scope; the 73rd. and 74th Constitutional amendments; and, the growth and proliferation of NGOs, who are emerging as development intermediaries[9], and the growth of "parallel organisations".[10]

Constitutional amendments

What the Constituent Assembly did not do in 1949-1950, was rectified by the Indian Parliament in 1993, when the 73rd and 74th Constitutional amendments came into effect. By the time the Seventh Plan (1985-90) ended, it was realised that:

> "the objective of all round economic and social transformation of rural areas cannot be achieved without the active participation and involvement of people at the grass root level, both in planning and implementation of programmes of rural development" (India 1994a:2).

What the Constitutional amendments achieved was that, in addition to revitalising *panchayats,* they would make it more difficult for States to ignore PRIs as the latter have been given the status of constitutional bodies. Article 243B of the Constitution says that:

> There shall be constituted in every State, *panchayats* at the village, intermediate, and district levels ..." (India 1999c:87)

This and the subsequent Articles provide for democratic decentralisation. The significant achievement of the Constitutional amendments, is the statutory transfer of the 29 subjects mentioned in the Eleventh Schedule to PRIs. Thus the Constitutional amendments gave an operational content to the earlier Article 40 of the Directive Principles of State Policy.

Importantly, in order to give more resources to PRIs two sub-clauses were added to Article 280 of the Constitution. It was made obligatory upon the Central Finance Commission (CFC) to recommend "measures needed to augment the Consolidated Fund of a State on the basis of the recommendation made by the Finance Commission of the State" (India 1999c: 115). A similar sub-clause was introduced regarding municipalities.

Article 243(d) of the Constitution defines a *panchayat* as an institution of self-government. Article 243G says that "the Legislature of a State may, by law endow the *panchayats* with such powers and authority as may be necessary to enable them to function as institutions of self-government..." Part IX of the Constitution deals with decentralisation to *panchayats* which are institutions of self-government and this concept of decentralisation is consistent with definition of the term given above.[11] It is therefore surprising that some donors and the World Bank are supporting projects in India that are managed by beneficiaries and call them "decentralised" projects. As James Manor points out, the World Bank documents "appear to reveal a preoccupation with this sort of involvement of local people in development project cycles, rather than with the promotion of well-established, elected institutions." (Manor 1999b: 9). This point is elaborated in Chapter 11.

Table 1: Table showing the types of decentralisation and their major characteristics

(In the following matrix, the word "body" stands for the organisation or individual, to whom power and responsibility are given i.e. the recipient. For example, if the power is "delegated" to a PRI, then the PRI becomes the "body").

Type of Decentralisation (1)	Type of Power that is given to the body (2)	Location of that body (3)	Who Controls (4)	How is control exercised (5)	Sources of finances for the body (6)	Results or outcome (7)
Deconcentration	Mainly administrative	Within the same Central Ministries or State Departments	Head of the Department or Secretariat bureaucracy	Standards, rules, norms	Central or State Budget.	Avoids delays, reduces bureaucratic procedures, disposal of routine matters at lower levels, pursues national government's objectives
Delegation	Managerial	Outside the regular bureaucratic structure and includes corporate or public sector undertakings	Indirect control by the Central or the State Government. Govt. nominee Directors on the Board	Central or State Government regulations. Little control over day-to-day matters.	Through the sale of goods and services, and government subvention.	Efficiency and quick response to local demands.

Privatisation	Generally delivery of services, but in some cases can also include manufacturing, real estate development and selling.	Private sector or voluntary organisations including NGOs.	Government only controls policies through transparent regulations	Through guidelines, criteria	For the private sector: through sale of goods and services. For voluntary organisations including NGOs: The same as in private sector; in addition, grants/loans from the Centre or State, or internal or external donor.	More efficient delivery of services.
Devolution	Political, legislative, executive, judicial and financial, subject to Constitutional provisions.	Local bodies, which are generally elected; sometimes nominated.	People/voters; State and Central level politicians and political executives	Through the ballot box; in practice accountability to the Central or State level political executives.	Raising own revenues, agency fees for implementing programmes on behalf of the Central or State Government, and transfers from the Central or State governments.	Participation in decision-making, transparency, democratisation, autonomy

Notes

1. I have not used the usual abbreviation IADP to denote the "Intensive Agricultural District Programme" as I have used IADP to denote "Intensive Area Development Project" discussed in Chapter 2.
2. For various conceptual approaches to decentralisation see Manor 1999b; Cheema and Rondinelli 1983a, Rondinelli 1989a, Rondinelli and others 1989b, Baumann 2000.
3. See also Bardhan 1997.
4. Chapter 11 mentions what constitutes a "by-pass".
5. What Balwantray Mehta Committee refers to as "delegation" was referred to as "deconcentration" earlier in this chapter.
6. Manor calls this a "tripartite mixture" see Manor 1999b:7
7. The situation is not different in many other developing countries (see World Bank 1999b: 3).
8. UTs are treated like States for most purposes. They are covered by Part VIII of the Constitution of India. The National Capital Region of Delhi is an example of a Union Territory. In this book, the term "States" include UTs unless otherwise specified.
9. This term is explained in Chapter 11.
10. The terms "parallel organisations" and "parallel structures" are used interchangeably here as they mean the same. These terms include NGOs and organisations of line departments, and are dealt with in detail in Chapter 11.
11. The status of the *panchayats* under the Indian Constitution was discussed in the symposium jointly organised by the India International Centre and the Institute of Social Sciences on April 17 , 1999. The subject of the symposium was "Whither *Panchayati Raj*"? Speaking at the symposium, Dr. George Mathew, Director, Institute of Social Sciences said, "The Constitution aims at making *panchayats* institutions of self-government. The provisions are clear and unambiguous".

CHAPTER 2

Coordination and Decentralisation

The implementation of a multi-sector programme poses a problem of coordination. CDP, and anti-poverty programmes are examples of multi-sector programmes. This chapter explains the coordination problems encountered in such programmes, and concludes that democratic decentralisation offers the best remedy for field coordination problems. The problems of coordination have been engaging the attention of the administration, particularly after the Green Revolution, when people started to take interest in what administration was doing and whether their problems were getting solved to the extent and with the speed promised by politicians. The term "Green Revolution" refers to the seed-fertiliser-irrigation technology, based on high yielding varieties of wheat and rice, the major cereals of India, which was introduced in India mid-1960s. The technology for these crops were evolved at the international research institutes, CIMMYT (Mexico) and IRRI (Philippines) respectively. The team in the Ministry of Food and Agriculture in Delhi was led by C. Subramaniam (who was the Minister), B. Sivaraman (who was the Secretary in the Ministry) and M.S. Swaminathan (who was the Head of Indian Agricultural Research Institute). Interesting accounts of the Green Revolution are contained in Frankel 1978 and Chopra 1985. Green Revolution led to the creation of a large number of organisations in the public sector, such as, the National Seed Corporation, and the Food Corporation of India, increasing the problems of coordination. This chapter also contains an account of the early multi-sector programmes supported by the World Bank, and explains why they were neither sustainable nor did they address the problems of coordination.

Programmes and projects[1]

A description of programmes and projects is given below to enable the reader to appreciate the discussion in this and subsequent chapters. A programme denotes a set of activities with common objectives and strategies, and a long term time horizon for implementation. CDP is a good example of a programme. Within the framework of a common objective and strategy, the details of the programme can vary from one State to another in India, or even from one region to another within the same State. For example, the objective of the CDP is to bring into being "stable self-reliant rural communities with a sense of social and political responsibility." Having defined the objectives of the programme, the CDP spells out the strategies to attain these objectives. Agricultural extension is another example of a programme. A country can define the objectives and strategy of a programme of agricultural extension, to be followed nationwide. It can, for instance, say that the objective of the extension system is to provide extension on all crops, livestock and fisheries. As regards strategy, it can state that extension will be provided face-to-face and will have regular interaction with research. Other operational details, such as the frequency of farm visits, periodicity of training of frontline extension staff and the frequency of their interaction with research, are left for local adaptation.

A project, on the other hand, is a vehicle through which a programme is implemented and defines the area where it operates and the time-period when it is operational. To quote Uma Lele:

> "A project is generally understood to mean (a) a well defined range of activities which lend themselves to rather precise specification of objectives to planning, financing, and implementing within an organised unit and which have a clear beginning; (b) a set of targets by which to judge their performance; and (c) an orderly specified end" (Lele 1975: 7).

There can be several projects within the framework of a programme, with all projects sharing the common set of objectives and strategies outlined by the programme. For example, while a national irrigation programme could spell out the broad policies and strategies, there could be many individual irrigation projects as parts of this programme.

A programme is national if it is formulated by the ministry concerned in the country, and outlines the basic objectives and strategy for the sub-sector. Examples are: national programme in community development, agricultural extension, agricultural research, credit, roads, health and rural employment. National programmes may also be supported by different organisations and donors.

Policy and operational (field) coordination[2]

Many services in the rural sector in India are still being provided by public sector organisations. For example, extension is provided by the Extension Department, research is carried out by the National Agricultural Research System (NARS),[3] rural electrification by the State Electricity Boards and rural water supply by the public sector Water Supply and Sewerage Boards. The field functionaries remain within their own respective agencies; the village level functionary of the Irrigation Department (called *patkari*) remains with the Irrigation Department, the extension worker remains with the Agriculture Department and so on. It is expected that these field functionaries act in the interests of the clients whom they are meant to serve. But since they are governed by the rules and priorities of their own organisations, they are more conscious of these, than the needs of the clients. So their actions need co-ordination, and are in fact coordinated at two levels: at a higher level, generally the country or state level, what is possible is policy coordination; at the operational level, there is expected to be field or operational coordination, to give shape to the policy. The former focuses on coordination of policies, the latter on co-ordinating operations.

This is illustrated by three examples:

1. One of the major agricultural development efforts in India has been the encouragement to farmers to borrow for small scale irrigation facilities on their farms, generally dugwells and pumpsets. It was agreed at the State level that the Electricity Boards would give priority to the provision of electricity connections to the borrowers of the Land Development Banks (LDB), which gives long term loans to farmers for dugwells and pumpsets, so that they would be able to realise the anticipated income stream. This is an example of policy coordination. But field coordination

between the Electricity Boards and the LDB was a problem. The former have their own set of priorities and economic criteria and the LDBs their own. As a result, many farmers who obtained loans for wells and pumpsets would go without power for a long time; they could not repay their loans to the LDB and naturally became defaulters of loans. Similarly, there has always been a problem of field co-ordination between the Irrigation Department, which is responsible for the canals and the Agriculture Department which is responsible for *ayacut* development.[4]

2. Another example of the difference between policy co-ordination and field coordination is drawn from the seeds sub-sector. Policy coordination exists when import taxes on seeds are removed (coordination between the Ministry of Commerce and the Ministry of Agriculture), and national research centres conduct research on seed varieties which are in high demand and which can be made readily available. Effective field coordination involves:

    - Delivery of relevant messages (e.g., planting times, chemical fertiliser application) by the local staff of the extension service on available seed varieties;
    - Stocking of these seed varieties in local markets before the planting season; and
    - Functional rural roads and transportation which can help farmers purchase inputs and market surplus harvest.

3. The third example is drawn from the anti-poverty programmes administered by PRIs on behalf of the GOI (see Box 6.5). These have now been merged with *Swarnjayanthi Gram Swarozgar Yojana* (SJSY). In these programmes there is a problem of operational coordination between banks which are expected to provide loans to members of weaker sections of society, identified by *gram sabhas*[5] (GS). During his field visits, the author came across a number of cases of lack of coordination between banks and GS. Bank managers say that those identified by the GS are not eligible for bank loans, whereas GS say that selections were done as per the criteria given to them by banks.

Although field coordination is extremely difficult without effective policy coordination, policy coordination at the national level does not automatically guarantee field coordination. In fact, the latter is more difficult to achieve in practice. In the initial years of the CDP, the main component of rural development was agricultural development. As the process of development unfolded, there were other components also,

Box 2.1: The District Collector and field coordination at the district level

The responsibility to bring about the needed coordination between the various departments and agencies in the district has historically fallen on the District Collector. The Collector has always been the "eyes and ears of the government in a district." He was the symbol of the British *Raj.* The British civil administration in India of which the Collector was the lynch pin, is described by Peter Drucker as "the best example of a large and successful information-based organisation, and one without any middle management at all". (Drucker 1988). At present, the status of the Collector is very much diminished, but the Collector still continues to be perhaps the most influential district official. When in 1960, *Zilla Parishads* (ZP) were created in Maharashtra and Gujarat, and the development functions were transferred to the Chief Executive Officer (CEO) of the ZP, there was a talk that this person would become the most influential officer in the district, but it did not happen. The Collector does not have any department other than the Revenue Department under the person, but the halo surrounding the position has given the person influence over the district level functionaries of many departments.

In fact, coordination is a name given to a management function when the coordinator has little power to take decisions in the areas which (s)he is coordinating, but has to depend on the person's stature and powers of persuasion to ensure that those who come under the person's coordinating jurisdiction take their decisions in their areas in line with what the coordinator wants. By definition, the coordinator and the persons whose actions (s)he coordinates are of equal rank; hence the term coordination.

such as, primary education and rural health. And, as concern for the rural poor increased, many schemes providing "safety net" for the rural poor, such as the anti-poverty schemes of the GOI, came to be formulated. These latter areas are more appropriate for the government departments, than for the private sector. The need for operational coordination increased. In fact, as agriculture is increasingly taken care of by private sector, the attention of the administration is taken up more and more by the coordination problems of the broader rural sector.

Operational coordination at the district level

The District Collector is expected to convene a coordination meeting each month but very few coordination problems get sorted out at these meetings. The district officers and managers of commercial banks often escalate issues to the regional or State level. For example, suppose extension says that research is not undertaking research on a specific problem relevant to the district, and the researcher concerned pleads inability to undertake the research because of want of funds. The problem gets escalated to the State level. Each side assigns the responsibility for causing a shortfall in meeting the programme targets on the other; such blaming wars used to be (and are) very common. Recently there was a case of land acquisition for a dairy. The Revenue Department which is responsible for land acquisition could not complete the proceedings in time and the district officer of the Dairy Development Department was not sure of the funds needed to build the dairy when the land was given to that department. When funds were available, the land was not in the possession of Dairy Development Department and when the land eventually came to the Department's possession, funds were not available. The ultimate sufferer was the farmer whose milk could not be purchased by the Dairy Development Department. The coordination problems in the health sector range from land acquisition matters to the non-availability of medicines when needed. The fact is that Collector can do neither policy coordination, which is settled at the State or Central level, nor field coordination. (S)He can at best bring the personal stature of the person to draw the attention of the departments or organisations concerned, to the problem.

In many meetings at the State level attended by the author, whenever difficult coordination problem arose, there was a tendency to give it to the Collector. For instance, there was a complaint that the local manager of a commercial bank in a district, did not "care for the poor." This meant that the person did not sanction loans to those identified as belonging to "below poverty line" (BPL) category. The GOI undertook a survey in 1997 to identify families below the poverty line. The persons so identified are eligible for benefits under the anti-poverty programmes of the State and Central Governments (see also Box 6.5). Under the circumstances, there was not much which a Collector could do, beyond lending to the issue the weight of the authority of Collector's office, and persuading the commercial bank manager concerned to have a talk with the ZP president regarding the criteria for bank loans, and how some of the BPL population did not meet the criteria. But still the decision was to give it to the Collector. Collector has almost become the "default" option, to use the computer language.

Coordination, privatisation and decentralisation

Problems of coordination are not peculiar to government. They are present in every organisation which is more rule-oriented than client-oriented. Such organisations are called bureaucratic organisations and the concept is discussed in Crainer 1998. The originators of the concept were Weber and Taylor who laid the foundations of modern organisation. Weber's conclusion was that the most efficient form of organisation was mechanical, characterised by "precision, speed, unambiguity, knowledge of files, continuity, discretion, unity, strict subordination, reduction of friction……" (Crainer 1998:9). In the kind of organisations envisioned by Weber and Taylor, rules and procedures become ends in themselves. The words used by Weber were "command and control", and he dealt with organisations as if client did not exist. The defenders of bureaucracies contend that such systems are essential for expediting large scale operations, but the public generally associates "bureaucracy" with red tape, indecisiveness and exorbitant paperwork. Any major system of administering large organisations that are authoritative in nature and have installed clearly defined set of regulations as is the case with governments, is likely not to have a client focus.

Role of the client in coordination

It is now accepted in many quarters that, the management style needed, in areas where client focus is critical, does not come naturally to government organisations. It is very tempting, with hindsight, to criticise the organisational development that led to large bureaucratic organisations, but the problem was not with organisations themselves, but with the expectations from such an organisation. The importance of the concept of organisation by Weber and Taylor needs to be recognised. The organisation as conceived by Weber was perhaps appropriate when it was formulated, but now that both in the public and the private sectors, client plays a critical role, it is no longer relevant. Henry Ford is supposed to have said: "The customer can choose a car of any colour, as long as it is black". But modern management has moved quite a bit since Henry Ford. It is significant that Matsushita, the successful Japanese businessman derided the Western management philosophy and said that "We (Japan) are beyond the Taylor model."

Client plays a crucial role in coordination. This principle is realised more in private sector organisations than in public sector ones. For example, let us suppose that the client wants a car with a particular combination of colour and other features. The car company either satisfies the requirement of the client or loses the person's business. In this example, the client not only expresses a wish but also puts pressure on the various actors (including the car company and it suppliers) to coordinate. Thus clients exercise the necessary pull towards coordination. To use the spatial analogy, coordination is seldom achieved from "above"; but always from "below." This concept is elaborated below, in the context of "integrated" vs. "un-integrated" administration.

In modern management, the organisation is designed to serve the client. The closer the organisation is to the client, the less is the response time, and the better the chances of co-ordination. In democracies, the elected persons represent the clients and the closer they are to the people the better the co-ordination. That is why democratic decentralisation is critical for achieving better coordination. Research shows that decentralisation in smaller groups is more effective from the point of view of coordination. In smaller groups individuals are better able to coordinate because of better communication and because of increased transparency.[6] The less the number of persons, the greater are the chances of coordination. The only arrangement which ensures transparency, democracy and co-ordination, is democratic decentralisation.

Minimising problems of coordination

Problems of coordination in administration cannot altogether be eliminated; they can at best be minimised. The first step towards minimising problems of coordination within government is to reduce the involvement of government in services which can be provided by private sector. But there is a limit for privatisation. It is very difficult to privatise primary education or rural health in a developing country. Second, the closer to the people the centre of decision making is, the less the problems of coordination. In the case of the BDO setup under the CDP, the block was given a specific grant, and the BDO was the ultimate decision making authority. It was working fairly smoothly, at least to the extent of BDO's decision making territory. Problems arose only when circulars from Delhi and the State headquarters started pouring in, telling the BDO how the grant had to be utilised and when the BDO machinery came to be used as an implementing agency for many development programmes, rather than a decision making agency. This was a problem of excess vertical communication, and led to co-ordination problems, because these circulars often meant that the BDO had to interact with other line departments, over which (s)he had no control. Problems of coordination are bound to occur whenever an agency is used purely as an implementing agency, and too many instructions are issued from the State headquarters, or the Centre. The field staff would spend more time on interacting with the district and the State headquarters, and the Centre, than with the clients, namely the people. Unfortunately, PRIs which, according to the Constitution have the status of governments, are being increasingly used as implementing agencies of programmes of the Central and the State Governments. Instead of learning lessons from history the latter are committing the same mistakes.

The early multi-sectoral anti-poverty programmes supported by the World Bank[7]

In 1973, McNamara (who was then the President of the World Bank) announced in Nairobi, that the World Bank would be taking the lead in poverty alleviation and rural development. Before this, the World Bank was supporting large scale infrastructure, irrigation and power projects. This shift was reflected in the Bank's *Rural Development Sector Policy Paper* (World Bank 1975) which described the operational goals of rural development as "improved productivity, increased employment, and thus higher incomes for target groups, as well as minimum acceptable standards of food, shelter, education and health." Since 1973, many more countries have come under the active care of the World Bank, with varied social, economic and political situations. The World Bank lending for rural development increased from $218.1m between 1965-66 to $2976.6m between 1974-86 (World Bank 1988:11).

In the 1970s, when following McNamara's Nairobi speech, the World Bank financed a large number of programmes in rural development, the two main vehicles for implementing the rural development programmes were the "Integrated Rural Development Project" (IRDP)[8] and the "Integrated Area Development Project" (IADP). A Project Management Unit (PMU) is an umbrella or integrating agency, usually established outside the relevant government ministries as an independent agency to manage and integrate development activities in a geographical area defined by the project. PMU is a project-based unit and is an example of integrated administration, but it is outside the regular administrative framework.

Integrated Rural Development Project

An IRDP covered a small geographical area (usually a district or a region) and typically included components, such as agricultural extension, research (if technology was lacking), marketing, input supply, credit, rural roads, water supply, rural electrification and small-scale irrigation, which are relevant to rural areas. Some IRDPs also had social infrastructure components such as primary schools and health centres. In most areas, the project staff were different from the mainstream government staff. This dual and parallel setup in most IRDP areas has been deplored by many writers[9]. The arrangement of maintaining a separate identity for the "project staff" tended to breed jealousy and envy among the ordinary government staff who resented the special status enjoyed by the "project staff.."

Integrated Area Development Project

IADPs were similar to the IRDPs and were located primarily in areas of low agricultural potential, which, according to the countries concerned and the World Bank, have not participated in the development process to the extent of the other regions of the country concerned, owing to their being handicapped by unfavourable climatic factors. The logic behind such projects was that since those who inhabit such areas were generally poor, a strategy of poverty reduction should include projects to serve them. These projects, like the IRDPs, were multi-sectoral, providing services largely through heavy reliance on foreign technical support in agriculture, water supply, health, rural infrastructure, and small-scale, off-farm enterprises. The World Bank's Operations Evaluation Department (World Bank 1988) has drawn attention to the failure of the IRDP to offer a sustainable tool for poverty alleviation. The IRDP approach has been considered by the Operations Evaluation Department to be defective, as it lacked institutional and financial sustainability, beneficiary participation, linkages with technology and capacity building. The term IRDP hereafter includes IADP also.

The rationale for the decision of the World Bank to adopt IRDP management model, was the belief that: (i) agricultural development should be regarded as part of overall rural development and agricultural services should therefore be delivered as part of a more comprehensive package of rural development services; (ii) since several facets of life of the rural population are integrated, services for the development of these facets should be provided by the same agency which is located close to the population which they serve; (iii) since the real problem was one of field coordination, the best way to achieve it was through delivering these services by the same field agency. IRDPs were regarded by the World Bank as effective instruments for the purpose. However, coordination of services never occurred to the extent intended. PMU of IRDP was neither sustainable nor effective in bringing about the needed coordination. Both in the IRDP and the IADP it was assumed that delivering the services in an integrated manner would automatically ensure coordination, but that was not so.

Reasons for the failure of IRDP

Further, the essential element in IRDP, namely, integration, became a victim to the urge to spend the project funds. Any saving on extension or on-farm research, which were "slow spending", tended to get diverted to roads or purchase of machinery which were "quick spending", upsetting the integration envisioned when the projects were formulated. With neither coordination and nor integration, the most important *raison d'être* for the IRDPs ceased to exist. In addition, four major factors rendered these projects unsustainable.

1. After these projects ended, the operation and maintenance of the assets created under them, posed a problem. In India too, a similar problem exists in multi-sector projects. Maintenance of the assets created, has always been a problem, even when the projects are planned and implemented by line departments. This is a general problem of low priority being given to non-Plan expenditure, and maintenance has been categorised as non-Plan. This problem is more pronounced in any project which seeks to create a special project-based management unit; and the fact that the IRDP was not anchored in a national (or where relevant, State) institution in the functional area concerned, further compounded the problem. Line departments are often reluctant to spend their insufficient non-Plan budget on maintaining assets planned by "special projects." For example, there has been a problem of maintenance of the roads and other assets created under Maharashtra's EGS, which is a multi-sector programme, implemented by the line departments concerned, but planned by the Collector in each district. For example, the EGS works could be part of the soil conservation programme (implemented by the Agriculture Department) or a road work (implemented by the PWD). The line department concerned never "owned" them and never came forward to maintain them out of the maintenance grants sanctioned for that department. It is a bureaucratic fact that the line departments do not recognise any activity not "sired" by them. The GOI has recently woken up to this tendency. The recent JGSY programme is being implemented through *Gram Panchayats* (GP) and the

work is being undertaken only after the GP passes a resolution that it would undertake the responsibility of maintenance. Till now, the fact that the beneficiaries were not associated with either project formulation or project implementation was given as the main reason for the assets created under the project not being maintained. Now that the beneficiaries are associated with project formulation and project implementation, albeit the fact that they do not have the freedom to divert the funds for any other purpose, we shall have to wait and see the effect on maintenance.

2. PMU was not a sustainable management entity, a fact mentioned earlier. The Bank staff while responding to McNamara's call for rural development did not address the institutional issues adequately. Even in Maharashtra, which had democratic institutions in rural areas, such as ZPs and *Panchayat Samitis* (PS), they persuaded the State Government to setup a special project office for the Drought Prone Areas Project (DPAP). It is not surprising that many of the IRDPs were neither managerially or financially sustainable. In fact in Africa, where a large number of IRDPs were setup, there is now no trace of these.

3. The IRDPs tended to create a closed 'universe', with their components not having linkages even with the national programmes, not to speak of linkages with international institutions. For instance, project-based agricultural research had very little to do with the Central or State agricultural research organisations. In Maharashtra, where DPAP (which was a typical IADP), was being implemented, the project contained a dairy development component which had no linkage with the State Dairy Development Department. The latter did not take much notice of this component. The project had a grass seed component which had nothing to do with the State-wide seed distribution network. It is not therefore surprising that IRDPs are often referred to as 'enclave projects'. When there was need for more technology, for example, the remedy was to include project-specific research components, rather than build linkages with national agricultural research systems (NARS). Such a

"closed universe syndrome" accentuated the problem of maintenance mentioned earlier.

4. It was not realised that there are limitations to the bureaucracy bringing about rural development. This is particularly relevant to the CDP. Both the IRDP and the CDP depended on the bureaucracy to bring about rural development. The situation was sought to be remedied by Balwantray Mehta Committee, but not till the recent Constitutional amendments, was the basic legal structure created nationwide, for the involvement of the local elected office-bearers of PRIs with rural development.

"Integrated" and "Un-integrated" administration

When different departments interact with people, it was thought at the time the CDP was formulated, that the best way to achieve a coordinated delivery of services, was to bring the field functionaries of the ministries (or departments) concerned under the administrative control of some person, who is close to the people. The rationale is similar to the one for IRDP given earlier. The BDO's establishment (shown in Box 3.5) came close to this objective. Briefly, BDO was assisted by a team of officers, (called extension officers) drawn from the relevant departments, who interacted with rural people through a *gram sevak.* It was an example, like PMU, of integrated administration, where the field officers are the supporting technical staff of the BDO, and are under the administrative control of the latter[10]. For technical matters they are accountable to their respective technical departments. The other administrative model is un-integrated administration. We shall see in Chapter 6, that State Agricultural Departments were the first to have their own extension staff by-passing BDO. They were followed by other departments who started their own "State Sector" schemes, which were parallel programmes implemented by the State Government line departments, also by-passing BDO. They created what is known as un-integrated administration. In un-integrated administration, each technical officer is responsible to his own ministry, with no coordinating authority (like the BDO) close to the people and each line department has direct interaction with people. There is nothing basically wrong in this kind of arrangement, provided two conditions are satisfied: (i) the population which the different departments are serving can exercise the necessary coordination from "below"; and (ii) the departments have a transparent management system which is known to the clients of the departments (Cheema and Rondinelli 1983a). Un-integrated administration is managerially more sustainable, but requires a population well aware of their rights, and capable of putting pressure on the line departments or what is the same, sector departments, to act. It is very difficult to achieve in practice, particularly in India, with its age old tradition of "*ma-baap*"[11] government. Actually, coordination can be achieved even without integration, if every participating ministry has a well understood and transparent management system. After a survey of many IRD initiatives, Hayami and Ruttan postulate five generalisations, of which the first one is:

> "Rural development program activities must be organised around activities and services that have relatively well-defined technologies or methodologies and objectives. It is important to rural communities that the technologies, methodologies, and services needed to improve rural welfare become simultaneously available *but not necessarily administratively integrated.*" (emphases added). (Hayami and Ruttan 1985: 413).

Table 2.1 at the end of this chapter, shows the salient features of the integrated and un-integrated administration. It indicates that in the case of un-integrated administration the pre-conditions of successful coordination is more difficult to achieve in practice. In the case of integrated administration, (such as the BDO's establishment), field coordination is done from "above" and the beneficiaries are not associated with the planning and implementation of programmes. The only feasible way to achieve a combination of the positive aspects of un-integrated administration, particularly, coordination from "below", the positive aspects of the CDP, and the association of beneficiaries with the planning and implementation of programmes, is through democratic decentralisation and to create a political marketplace, that is, to have elected representatives, at the local level. In that case, the elected representatives of the beneficiaries, can not only coordinate the various line departments which are administratively responsible to them, but also act as the necessary "pulling force from below" to coordinate actions of the line department functionaries who are not responsible to them. There is need for operational co-ordination at the district level and this need was felt recently during the earthquake in Gujarat, when several NGOs from all over the world converged on one district with huge funds, creating the need for coordinating their activities. Entrusting this coordination with PRIs would have eliminated a lot of mis-matching of the needs of the people and what they got.

Box 2.2: T&V system of agricultural extension

Training and Visit (T&V) system of agricultural extension was perhaps the first national programme in recent times, with a transparent management system. The programmes of other departments did not have such a rigid and well known structure. It was a well known example of un-integrated administration. In due course T&V also lost its field orientation and the structured field visits for which it is well known. Experience with T&V shows that in India co-ordination is better achieved through "spokespersons" of the people, who are the elected persons at the local level.

Summing up

Coordination is of two types: policy coordination and operational (or field coordination). Integrated administration typified by the BDO's establishment came close to tackling the problems of field coordination. IRDP is also an example of integrated administration. In both, the problems of coordination have remained untackled. The other model, namely un-integrated administration where each line department interacts with its beneficiaries, is not suitable for India, for two reasons: (i) many line departments lack transparency, and (ii) effective field coordination requires a population well aware of their rights and capable of putting pressure on line department to act. Rural population in India require "spokespersons" for their causes, such as PRIs, who provide democratically elected spokespersons close to the population. Association of beneficiaries, through their elected representatives, with the planning and implementation of programmes therefore offers the best chance of field coordination, provided PRIs are not used as mere implementing agencies but as decision making agencies by the State or Central Governments. Herein lies the rationale for democratic decentralisation.

Table 2.1: Table showing the features of integrated and un-integrated administration

Types of administration	Examples	Salient Features	Advantages	Disadvantages
Integrated	BDO's Establishment	The field functionaries are in their own respective departments and are administratively under the BDO but for technical matters report to their own departmental superiors.	Managerially sustainable	➢ The urge to spend project funds by the end of the year results in uneven development and there is a lot of difference between what the project planned to do at the beginning of the year and what it ended up doing. ➢ Bureaucracy was engaged in doing social development, which they were not by temperament and training equipped to do. ➢ Maintenance of the assets created under the project posed a problem. ➢ Field co-ordination was attempted from above, and neither beneficiaries nor their representatives were associated with the planning and implementation of programmes.
Integrated	IRDP/IADP	The field functionaries are both administratively and technically under the project manager, who is	Manageriably unsustainable	- do -

		very often a foreign technical assistant (TA). The IRDP is not anchored in any line ministry of the government. Some States in India (e.g. Maharashtra) or countries in Africa (e.g. Kenya) try to overcome this problem by placing special projects under the Planning Ministry but that is not the same as keeping it under a line Ministry.		
Unintegrated	➢ T&V extension ➢ State sector schemes which are implemented by the departments.	The field functionaries are under the departmental heads and do not come under any "umbrella organisation" such as the BDO or the IRDP management.	Manageriably sustainable. Field coordination from "below" namely the beneficiaries.	In addition to the first three disadvantages outlined above, preconditions for successful coordination are difficult to meet, namely: ➢ Transparent management system ➢ Beneficiaries who can take upon themselves the responsibility of field co-ordination.

Notes

1. This section is based upon Venkatesan and Kampen 1998.
2. See Mukerji 1961: 122.
3. Either Agricultural University (as in many States) or a public sector research institute.
4. This is the development of the command area and includes land shaping and grading, and the development of roads and market yards in the command area.
5. This is a body consisting of all the registered voters in a village. See Chapter 8.
6. This has been discussed in Olson 1965. Also see Oechssler, Jörg, 1997. The latter paper addresses the relationship between the degree of decentralisation in a population and the probability of coordination.
7. I have relied heavily upon Venkatesan and Kampen 1998 while writing this section.
8. This should not be confused with the Indian IRDP which is a part of the anti-poverty schemes of the GOI. In order to distinguish this from the latter, the Indian programme is spelt out in full, in this book, and is not denoted by abbreviation.
9. The institutional approach to rural development in these projects was considered unsustainable, and in due course, the World Bank gave up the approach contained in IRDP and IADP. The "IRDP" approach is intensively critiqued in Lele 1975 and Ruttan 1984.
10. While both PMU and the BDO's setup are examples of integrated administration, the essential distinction between them lies in the fact that the PMU, being a project-based unit, is wound up when the project is over, whereas the latter not being project-based, is more sustainable.
11. The term literally means "mother-father". What it conveys, is that India has a long tradition of paternalistic governments who think they know best what people want.

CHAPTER 3

The Growth of the Community Development Programme

The first nationwide decentralisation programme which was introduced in Independent India was the well known CDP. It contained only administrative decentralisation and offered very valuable lessons regarding decentralisation. It contributed substantially to institutional development in rural areas. Above all, it underscored the difficulties involved in achieving decentralisation in a complex, democratic country like India. This chapter surveys the growth of the CDP, and its achievements.

Different meanings of the term "Planning"

Soon after its independence from Britain in 1947, India adopted planned development. India was fortunate to have had legendary leaders committed to her development. The innovations conceived during India's early Five Year Plans, and which were reflected in the Plan documents, introduced some of the ideas currently being used in developmental arena, such as, participation, responsiveness to community demands, emphasis on women and accountability to beneficiaries. Even though the terms 'planning' and 'planned development' have lost the lustre which they once had, particularly after the collapse of the former Soviet Union, they are still valid for countries such as, India, where many services in the rural sector were (and still are) being provided by the government. It is desirable to plan for investment in these services and to address issues such as, (i) the most cost effective manner of providing these services; (ii) the most appropriate institutional framework and (iii) the administrative structures and management systems that are needed. There are thus two kinds of planning. The first kind of planning comprises government planning for others, such as, farmers and the private sector. This is generally referred to as "central planning"; and it is this kind of planning that has, justifiably, fallen into disrepute since mid-1980s. India's Second Five Year Plan (1956-61) contained many elements of this kind of planning. The second kind of planning comprises planning public sector investment and services, and addressing the kind of issues mentioned above. It involves governments planning for what they should do. It is the kind of planning which all governments should be encouraged to do, and do better.

Community Development

India achieved independence in 1947 and the planning era started in 1951, with the launching of the First Five Year Plan (1951-56). From the beginning of the planning era, rural development was sought to be achieved through the Community Development Programme. Community development, as the term implies, means the development of all the facets of the entire community. Under the programme, the community was expected to address their common economic and social problems in a democratic manner. CDP was a national programme implemented by the Central Ministry of Community Development through the States. The Centre gave financial assistance to the States for its implementation, prescribed the staffing pattern for rural development for the entire country and specified the goals and objectives of the programme.

The term "community development" was first officially used in 1948, at the British Colonial Office's Cambridge Conference on the Development of African Initiative. The conference defined community development as a movement to promote better living for the whole community, with the active participation, and if possible, on the initiative of the community. It was conceived as a means to enable the British colonies in Africa to prepare themselves for independence "by improving local government and developing their economies." (Holdcroft 1984:47). According to the GOI's Guide to Community Development (India 1957a:2) the objective of Community Development and National Extension programmes was to assist each village in planning and carrying out an integrated family and village plan directed towards increasing agricultural production, improving existing village crafts and industries, and organising new ones and programmes in health, education, housing and for women.

As stated in the beginning of this chapter, CDP contained only administrative decentralisation and did not include political decentralisation. It was administered by the Central Government through State Governments. The political executives of the Centre and States and civil servants at all levels were involved with its implementation. Detailed guidelines regarding the manner of implementation of the programme came from the Centre.

Decentralisation

Decentralisation is not new to India. The institution of panchayats has been in existence in the country since ancient times. Sir Charles Metcalfe, a British Governor in India during the 19th century, called the village panchayats "little republics having nearly everything they want within themselves and almost independent of foreign relations. They seem to last when nothing else lasts."[1] But with the advent of the British *Raj* and the centralisation which came with it, the village institutions which supported *panchayati raj* atrophied in most parts of the country. There had been several attempts by the British to introduce administrative decentralisation on a limited scale. One of the earliest such attempts was by Lord Mayo, the then Viceroy of India; the administrative decentralisation envisaged by him is contained in his Resolution dated December 14, 1870, and consisted principally of the allocation of financial powers and responsibilities to the provincial governments. This was followed by Lord Ripon's Resolution of May 18, 1882, which introduced local self-government in major municipal areas. This was the first attempt at political decentralisation, albeit limited, and confined to major municipal areas. In September 1907, a Royal Commission on Decentralisation was setup, with the objective of instituting administrative re-organisation at the grass root level. The Commission approached its tasks from the point of view of management and administration and not development. Its report sought to answer the question "what is the most effective administrative setup"? and not "what is the most effective setup for achieving development and involving people"? This was followed Government of India Resolution of 1915 and Government of India Act, 1935. For a detailed account of the developments during this period see Wadia 1996.

Precursors of the Community Development programme

There were many instances of Community Development being tried on a modest scale in various parts of India prior to the launching of the countrywide CDP in independent India.[2]

Mahatma Gandhi

The inspiration for CDP was provided by Mahatma Gandhi and his contemporary and Nobel Laureate, Rabindranath Tagore. Gandhiji started village upliftment programme based on his 18-point village development plan, which included the use of khadi, promotion of village industries using the locally available raw materials; basic and adult education; rural sanitation; uplift of backward classes; welfare of women; removal of untouchability; economic equality and so on. Some of them were social programmes, and some economic ones. He started his initial experiments in Sabarmati and Wardha in 1929 and the concept gradually spread to other centres in the country. The movement started by these experiments was known as the Sarvodaya movement.

Rabindranath Tagore

Tagore started the Sriniketan scheme of rural development in 1921 (Mukerji 1961:16). It "sought to make villagers self-reliant and self-respectful, acquainted with the cultural tradition of their own country and competent to make efficient use of modern resources for the fullest development of their physical, social, economic and intellectual conditions". (Bhattacharyya, 1970:21). Sriniketan programme of rural reconstruction soon extended to other villages. This programme included both social and economic components.

Marthandam, Travancore

At the other extremity of India, in a place called Marthandam in the then Travancore (now Kerala) Spencer Hatch of the YMCA started a village development programme based on the Christian ideals enshrined in Ruskin's "Unto this Last". The emphasis here was more on economic programmes though there were some social components like adult education. The basic tenets of this rural reconstruction programme, or the "pillars of policy" as Hatch called them, comprised: building on what the village and people have, making certain that they 'own' the programme, helping people to help themselves, including all people in the programme without caste or religious barriers and reaching the poorest. By 1940, there were about 1300 volunteers who were engaged in the implementation of the programme.

Baroda

Another early rural development programme worthy of mention was the Baroda Rural Development Programme (BRDP), started in the 1930s. V.T. Krishnamachari (who was the *Dewan* or the Prime Minister of the then princely state of Baroda from 1927) was the moving spirit behind this programme and he later occupied the important position of the Deputy Chairman of the Planning Commission. He enjoyed the confidence of the British administrators and of Jawaharlal Nehru. He was the Chairman of the Grow More Food Enquiry Committee and in that capacity he had the opportunity to study the role of agricultural development in a predominantly rural economy such as India. He knew that the pathway to increasing rural incomes in India was through agricultural development. In BRDP, he laid more stress on economic programmes, particularly agricultural programmes. The social programmes in BRDP comprised "adult education, development of community sense and a feeling of solidarity in the village" (Bhattacharyya, 1970:26). The BRDP did not depend upon government machinery for undertaking people's development. There was no generalist worker (multi-purpose *gramsevak*)[3] as was provided in the CDP. The main reason for this was the existence of *panchayats* and schools in all the villages of Baroda and cooperatives in most of them. These organisations had whole time functionaries accountable to them. The extension officers of the various technical departments could establish contacts with all the families through these functionaries (see Box 3.1).

Much thought was given to the administrative framework and sustainability of the programme. There are many dimensions to the concept of sustainability of a programme – financial, technical (importantly environmental) and managerial. The broader concept of "sustainability", must, as was the case with the BRDP, include all the three. In order to increase the managerial sustainability of the programme, the normal development administration of the district was made responsible

Box 3.1: Diagram showing the interaction of the technical departments with the people through Panchayats/Cooperatives

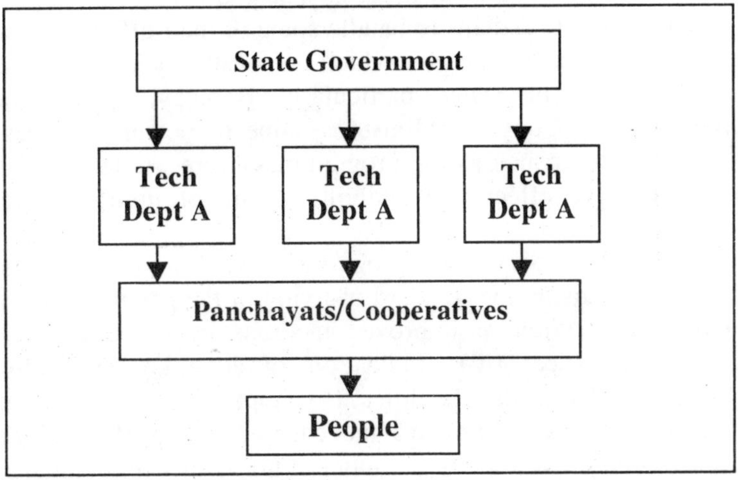

for all development programmes. Translated into to-day's terms, the most sustainable arrangement would be for all development programmes in the district to be with PRIs.

British India

Gurgaon: At the peak of the nationalist movement, the *Raj* came under criticism for neglecting the welfare of the rural people. Government therefore launched a scheme of their own. Brayne,[4] who was the Deputy Commissioner of Gurgaon (then Punjab, now Haryana), was entrusted to do the planning and implementation of a rural development programme in Gurgaon. This was the first time when government machinery was employed for doing rural reconstruction. This was also the beginning of the Deputy Commissioner of a District, who was the symbol of the *Raj* in the District (see Box 2.1), being drawn into the developmental arena, a process which has not so far stopped.

Brayne also introduced the concept of a "generalist" extension worker, one man for a few villages, to do the work of various departments of the government, importantly, agriculture and public health. This aspect of the Gurgaon experiment anticipated the multi-purpose *gramsevak* or village level worker

(VLW) of the CDP, who was trained to cover the important fields of activity in the village.

Bombay, Madras and Uttar Pradesh: The 1935 Act of India gave limited powers to Indians to handle some of their affairs. Rural development was an area for which responsibility was given to Indians. In some States, particularly, Bombay, Madras and Uttar Pradesh, Congress Ministries came to power. In these States, rural reconstruction programmes were started, which sought to give effect to Gandhiji's dream of uplifting rural masses.

In Bombay Sarvodaya programme was started with the objective of raising the standard of living of the people through: (i) the introduction of improved methods in agriculture; (ii) cottage industries; (iii) eradication of illiteracy and adult education; (iv) health facilities (v) improvement of village records. All these were to be achieved, consistent with Gandhi's idea of *Sarvodaya*, through simplicity, non-violence, dignity of labour, and reconstruction of human values.

In Madras C. Rajagopalachari was the elected Chief Minister of the then Madras Presidency. He started rural development programme which was later on (in 1946, after the end of the Second World War) known as the "*Firka* Development Scheme". *Firka* is a geographical area consisting of about 5 to 10 villages; in some states it is called a "circle". Asoka Mehta Committee (see Chapter 7) would call it a *mandal.* This scheme sought to attain the Gandhian ideal of *gram swaraj* by bringing about all round improvement to the village, revitalising the spirit of the people and making them self-confident and self-reliant. The literal translation of *gram swaraj* is village independence, but the word means a lot more than political independence; its meaning includes economic independence, and ability to stand on one's own legs. As in Gurgaon, government machinery was used to bring about rural development. By 1952, the programme covered seventy four firkas. The District Collector was made responsible for the implementation of the programme in his district. At the State level, a State Rural Welfare Board comprising heads of the departments concerned, and some non-officials, was constituted for advising the government on how to "organise the villagers for a happier, more prosperous and fuller life to which the individual villager will have the opportunity to develop both as an individual and as a unit of a well integrated society." (Bhattacharyya, 1970:30)

In Uttar Pradesh (U.P.), a separate Rural Development Department was made responsible for executing a programme of rural reconstruction throughout the state. After an inter-regnum due to the Second World War, the programme was started in right earnest in 1947. Etawah district was selected for implementing the pilot programme, in 1947. Government machinery was entrusted with the task of rural reconstruction. The specifics of the Etawah programme included increasing agricultural production and many other economic programmes, and social programmes such as adult education, provision of reading room and drama competition. In the economic literature of the period, Etawah district planning was often cited as a model.

Nilokheri

Nilokheri scheme was initiated at about the same time as the Etawah programme. It started as a transit camp for the refugees from West Pakistan after the partition. S.K. Dey, who was to play a crucial role in the formulation and implementation of the CDP, became a voluntary worker in this camp, after giving up a lucrative job in the U.S.A. In February, 1947 a vocational-cum-production centre was setup near the camp at a place called Kurukshetra. Nilokheri township grew near Kurukshetra on a marshy land given by the government. What was impressive about the Nilokheri township was that it was built entirely by the trainees at the vocational training centre and by refugees. It was an example of peoples' efforts to build their own future. Nehru who visited Kurukshetra in 1947 was impressed by the high quality of work that was going on there. He invited S.K. Dey to join his Cabinet as the Minister for Community Development, and Dey agreed. Dey took charge of the Community Development Programme first as Administrator. He later on became a Minister when the Community Development Ministry was created.

Nehru era

In independent India, especially till the mid-1960s, the thinking of Jawaharlal Nehru (1889-1964) regarding most aspects of the economy was dominant. When he was a student at Cambridge, England, he imbibed the tenets of Fabian socialism and came to believe in the responsibility of the governments for correcting market forces. The economic theories of the 1920s and the 1930s, which were popular with the intellectuals of that era, and the post-war economic theories, were supportive of India's post-independence socialist policies. The middle class intellectuals of India, from whom most political leaders and senior civil servants were drawn, were not friendly towards the capitalists and the unbridled market forces. They were supported in their belief in state activism in economic policy, by Keynes and the New Deal economists, or socio-political activists, such as David Lilienthal, Eleanor Roosevelt, William Douglas, Chester Bowles and Kenneth Galbraith.[5]

Nehru visited the then Soviet Union and was struck by the material progress he saw there. He was impressed by the central planning matrix, and the large scale manufacturing enterprises in the public sector. He selected Mahalanobis for India's Planning Commission and gave him prominence. Mahalanobis, also Cambridge-educated like Nehru, was an economist with leftist leanings, who provided the intellectual underpinning to Nehru's ideas on economics and planning. He played an active role in formulating India's Second Five Year Plan (1956-1961), and favoured like Nehru, a high level of state activism in what Nehru called the "commanding heights of the economy", such as steel and heavy industry. The result was a series of public sector plants in steel and heavy industry - what Nehru described as "modern temples". But Nehru was too much of a democrat to be swayed entirely by Stalinism.

The influence of Mahatma Gandhi (1869-1948) over Nehru dates back to pre-independence days. As stated earlier, Gandhi was a staunch believer in *gram swaraj.* From the beginning there were tensions between the exponents of the Gandhian concept of small scale cottage industries at the village level, and the Nehruvian concept of large scale manufacturing enterprises.

Box 3.2: Dandekar on Gandhian Economics

According to Mahatma Gandhi, development policies of the state should be so fashioned that each village can be self-sufficient. This presumes that a village is a universe by itself and ignores the existence of markets outside. But historically the opposite has been true. The existence in India of *bazaars* from time immemorial is well-known. The *bazaar* is a trading place where all the villagers within a reasonable distance of each other, produces what (s)he can do more economically, and for the making of which (s)hc has bcttcr access to raw materials and in the making of which he has greater proficiency, than the competitor. (S)He takes them to the *bazaar* to sell. The principle of "comparative advantage" works here. The Gandhian approach tried to replace this age-old custom by village self-sufficiency. Dandekar says that in general, Mahatma Gandhi seemed to prefer self-sufficiency to efficiency. Gandhiji's apprehension regarding efficiency would appear to be that it might lead either to an unlimited and uninhibited pursuit of material wealth and comfort, or to a situation in which a few produce all the needs of a society while a large majority are denied the opportunity to work and earn their daily needs. Dandekar quotes Gandhiji on a person producing surplus to that person's requirement and says: "As we earlier said, the basic proposition of Gandhi is that "God has given everyone the capacity to work and earn his daily bread" and he wants everyone to labour for his daily bread. Now Gandhi is making a further and crucial point. He wants not only that everyone should labour for his daily bread but that no one should produce any more. Under these conditions he says, "there will be no rich and no poor, none high and none low, no touchable and no untouchable".......We do not know if Gandhi ever saw the implications of a society not producing surplus; what if the population increases? Gandhiji says proudly: "..We have managed with the same kind of plough as existed thousands of years ago..."." Dandekar continues: "How do you remove the chronic poverty of the Indian peasant? Gandhi tried to grapple with the problem but failed even in principle." (Dandekar 1996: 249). For a discussion on Gandhian economics, see Chapter 7, "Gandhian Legacy" in Dandekar 1996.

In the end, Indian planning was a combination of British Fabian Socialism, American New Deal, lukewarm Stalinism and Gandhian Economics.

Etawah and Nilokheri

The desirability of having the kind of development seen in Etawah and Nilokheri was engaging the attention of Nehru for some time. He remarked, after visiting Nilokheri: "I want 9,999 more Nilokheris...." (Dey 1962b:57). The Indo-American Technical Agreement (described below) signed in 1952 gave further fillip to Nehru's idea of scaling up the Etawah and Nilokheri experiments to be spread across the entire country. As noted earlier, Chester Bowles, the then U.S. Ambassador in India[6] was enthusiastic about the programme. S.K. Dey who, by now, was well known for the work done by him at Nilokheri, and who had become the Minister for Community Development, preferred the Nilokheri kind of development, which was based on a combination of productive and welfare services, to a purely economic programme. This question of whether the CDP was to be a welfare or a production programme or a combination of both was never adequately faced, until Balwantray Mehta Committee came to grips with the issue.

American association with the CDP

The programme attracted the attention of the United States, which in the immediate post-war era, was the only world power with a vibrant agriculture and rural development. S.K. Dey during his stay in the U.S.A. before he came back to India, was very much influenced by the New Deal. Chester Bowles was impressed by the CDP and produced a report called "The Indo American Aid Programme-the problems and opportunities". Following that report, the Indo-US Technical Agreement was signed in July, 1952. Under that agreement U.S. was to support the CDP with $50 million. As remarked earlier, those were the times when there was an immense faith, both in the Indian and the American camps, in state activism in economic and social planning. The early Indian experiments in planning and CDP received considerable attention from foreign governments and the aid agencies.[7]

Community development and agricultural development

Soon after independence, India set about making its agriculture more productive. The most urgent problem was to make the country self-sufficient in foodgrain. There were not many options then, and Green Revolution was more than fifteen years away. It was not therefore surprising that till 1970s, when the country could pride itself on the fact that it was able to feed itself, rural development was synonymous with agricultural development. There are many writers who question whether the GOI was right in emphasising agricultural development, particularly when the Green Revolution technology favoured the irrigated areas and those with assured rainfall. As this is not the focus of this book we shall not enter into this argument, but simply note that in those days (i.e. prior to the 1970s) agricultural development was the predominant concern of the GOI.

Grow More Food campaign

In April 1942, the GOI called a conference of representatives of Provinces and the princely States. It was an important all-India agriculture development programme initiated and directed by the Centre close to Independence. A detailed account of the GOI's efforts to increase agricultural production during this period is contained in Dandekar and Wadia (1989). The recommendations of the conference formed the basis of what came to be known as the Grow More Food Campaign (GMF). At this conference, three main thrust areas were identified: (i) switching over from cash crops, mainly from short staple cotton, to food crops; (ii) intensive cultivation of cultivated lands through irrigation, better seeds and manures and better farming practices, and (iii) extensive cultivation, by bringing under plough current fallows, culturable waste lands etc. This was the programme until 1946, when it was decided to continue the programme for another five years. The emphasis during the extended period was on minor irrigation, development of local manurial resources, improved seeds, tube wells, and land reclamation. By 1952, it was realised that the campaign had failed. India's First Five Year Plan was being formulated in 1950 and food production was a major issue in this Plan. Concentration of the GMF in suitable areas selectively, was discussed with States in connection with the programmes for 1951-52. According to Dandekar and Wadia, "the attitude of the States, generally speaking, was that over-insistence on this principle, was likely to lead to discontent in the areas which would be left out." (Dandekar and Wadia 1989:8). In February 1952, the GOI setup a Committee of Enquiry under the chairmanship of V.T. Krishnamachari to examine the working of the GMF. The Committee whose report was published in June 1952, pointed out that GMF covered only small proportion of the country, about three percent. It recommended (i) enlargement of the area covered by the GMF campaign, (ii) reorganisation of the administrative machinery, and setting up of an extension service. The GMF succeeded in emphasising the role of administration in agricultural development. For example, in the then East Punjab a "systematic programme of agricultural development of the State was taken up on a massive scale in the shape of GMF schemes, to be followed with (*sic*) a programme of (compulsory by law) consolidation of land holdings and augmentation of canal irrigation .....Under GMF *lakhs*[8] of uncultivated acres were reclaimed and brought under the plough"(Chopra 1985:110). GMF prepared the administration for its responsibilities under the technocratic agriculture which is synonymous with the now well-known Green Revolution. When technology arrived in mid- 1960s, the administrative apparatus was ready. This was an important contribution of the GMF campaign.

Besides emphasising the role of administration in agricultural development, the committee laid the foundations of CDP. It pointed out that "the economic aspects of village life cannot be detached from the broader social aspect; and agricultural improvement is inextricably linked with the whole set of social problems" and "that all aspects of rural life are inter-related and that no lasting results can be achieved if individual aspects of it are dealt in isolation"(Mukerji 1961:16). The recommendations of the GMF Enquiry Committee were responsible to a very large extent in shaping the extension approach under the CDP. The Committee also recommended the creation of an organisation for rural work which "would reach every farmer and assist in the coordinated development of all aspects of rural life". (Bhattacharyya 1970:44).

Community development as a means for achieving agricultural development

It was considered that the approach and methods of community development were best suited to motivate farmers to adopt better methods of farming within their capacity and with their own local resources, such as, use of better seeds which they could themselves multiply and store for the next year's sowing, use of irrigation from small irrigation works that, through community effort, they could themselves construct and maintain, the adoption of simple soil conservation and crop protection measures which they could easily adopt. Capital resources being scarce in the agricultural sector, it was thought that community development should exploit the advantage of relying on local resources, particularly on the availability of manpower. Technology would soon change many of these assumptions. In a technocratic agriculture it is not possible for farmers to produce their own seeds; nor is labour abundant as the Green Revolution would show. In the absence of technology (before Green Revolution) there was more emphasis on motivational programmes urging people to help themselves through their own labour. Community development was considered to be an appropriate vehicle for this purpose.

Agricultural development strategy in the First Plan

While the CDP was the medium through which agricultural development was to be brought about, the strategy of agricultural development, as announced in the Draft Outline of the First Five Year Plan, was to concentrate resources and extension in the most favourable areas of the country, so as to obtain a quick increase in agricultural production. The Draft Outline expressed a clear preference in favour of increasing production even if it meant going contrary to the socialistic fervour of the policy makers. It said:

> "it is essential that every State should draw up a programme of work for bringing certain areas, one after another, under intensive development, while holding the rest of the State more thinly. Since additional production is the most urgent objective, those areas should be selected where, on account

of irrigation facilities or assured rainfall, additional effort is likely to produce more substantial results". (India 1951:42).

Concern for achieving an immediate increase in agricultural production is obvious from the fact that the Draft Outline even went to the extent of advocating a postponement of land reforms (India 1951:99).

Consistent with this approach to agricultural development indicated in the Draft Outline of the First Five Year Plan, of concentration of administrative efforts in a few selected areas of promise, the first cohort of Community Development Projects was started on a pilot basis in late 1951 in 15 selected areas in each of 15 States. (Taylor *et al* 1965:230-233). These pilot projects were later on, in May 1952, increased to 55 in number, covering 27,388 villages and a population of 16.7 million (India 1957d:109). The pilot Community projects should not be confused with the CDP. The latter was a programme describing the policy goals and the objectives, and the former a project; and like all projects, it has a defined project area, and spells out various details such as administrative pattern and budget. Each pilot Community Project was placed under the charge of a Project Executive Officer, assisted by two Assistant Project Officers. For administrative convenience, the project area was divided into suitable blocks, but the unit of administration was the entire project, cutting across existing administrative boundaries. Since increased agricultural production was the most urgent objective, the selection of areas was done more with reference to the existence of assured rainfall or irrigation facilities, rather than on the basis of the existing administrative boundaries. This approach of choosing as the unit of development, an area different from the unit of administration was another innovation introduced in the initial phase of the First Five Year Plan. This anticipated the organisation of the watershed development programmes of the 1980s and 1990s, which are discussed in Chapter 11.

The growth of Community Development programme

Both the CDP and the Planning era started at about the same time. The chapter on "Community Development and Rural Extension" in the First Five Year Plan describes the organisation of the national rural extension agency to be established. The

Plan emphasised the need for ensuring people's participation, not merely in the execution of the pilot Community Development Projects but in the planning of the entire programme. After the pilot projects were launched in May 1952, the GOI decided to rapidly expand the coverage of the projects. It was also decided, that these projects should be implemented within the framework of a national programme, and that the entire country would be covered with CDP by 1953, a schedule which was considered too rapid for effective implementation. With that in view, CDP was launched nationwide on October 2, 1952 – the birthday of Mahatma Gandhi. At that time, there was a lot of discussion on the nature and scope of Community Development. The Pilot projects were area based and Community Development need not be area based, and the proponents of the latter approach including S.K. Dey, argued in favour of organising the CDP on the lines of administrative boundaries, and including the pilot projects in it. This issue of balancing the claims of area development, such as watershed development, and those of a development programme organised along administrative boundaries, is still with us, and this is dealt with in Chapter 11.

While agricultural production was the main emphasis of the programme, the idea underlying the CDP was to bring about an all round development of rural life as a whole, encompassing economic, social and cultural aspects. The essential characteristics of the pilot projects and their emphasis on achieving coordinated development remained. The two essential elements in community development are participation by the people themselves in efforts to improve their level of living with as much reliance as possible on their own initiative and resources; and the provision of technical and other services in ways which would encourage initiative, self help and mutual help and make these more effective. The core of the CDP was local participation and Government's participation was, in due course, to be reduced to no more than a catalyst to community action. The First Plan document clearly stated that "people's participation" was "the very essence of the programme" (India 1953:228). The CDP was thus an all-embracing programme with mixed objectives–partly economical and partly social–and its chief goal was the creation of stable self-reliant rural communities with a sense of social and political responsibility. About the programme Jawaharlal Nehru said:

> "All over India, we have centres of human activity, which are like lamps spreading their light more and more in the surrounding darkness ….I think nothing has happened in any country in the world during the last few years so big in content and so revolutionary in design as the Community Projects in India…. They are changing the face of rural India."[9]

Every block under the programme, was to pass first through a less intensive and then a more intensive stage of development, with additional funds provided in the latter stage, and thereafter pass into the third, normalised stage of development.

Box 3.3: The U.N. and Prof. Toynbee on CDP

CDP has been subjected to a careful scrutiny by a number of scholars. This box contains the views of the United Nations and Arnold Toynbee, the famous historian. The basic philosophy of CDP, dedicated to the well-being of the people, came in for particular mention and praise at the UN regional conference on Community Development in South and South-East Asia held at Manila in Dec 1954. According to the Conference, such a philosophy is consistent with many of the aspirations expressed in Article 55 of the UN Charter. About CDP Professor Arnold Toynbee, the famous historian, while delivering lectures at the University of Pennsylvania in 1961, observed, rather ecstatically: "Go to India; visit some of the thousands of villages there, in which the community development plan is already in operation; and you will see, with your own eyes, new hope and purposefulness and energy breaking into flower. This is, to my mind, the most wonderful sight there is to be seen in the present day world. And this revolution of the peasantry is the most glorious revolution that there has been in the world's history so far". (Quoted by Bhattacharyya 1970).

Economic development and social development

From the beginning, there was an unarticulated conflict between the those who favoured welfare programmes focusing on people, as the sole component of the CDP, and those who favoured

production programmes, particularly agricultural programmes. The approach of CDP and the perception of CDP as a bundle of production programmes has been well articulated by Mukerji.

> I am not very certain, however, that even now the idea is well understood that community development as a method and philosophy of development of an under-developed country and as an integral part of our democratic planning and development has to be a permanent feature of the Welfare State. In the common man's understanding, community development is still identified with the programme of activities, improvement of agriculture, promotion of village industries, building of school houses, roads etc. (Mukerji 1961:28).

While both S.K. Dey and V.T. Krishnamachari favoured a combination of social and economic aspects, they differed in the emphasis given to them and the manner of implementing them. The former preferred more emphasis on the social aspects, arguing that "there is a difference between community development and economic development......Material progress without developing human capacities is temporary and superficial. That is why in community development, economic programme received only secondary importance". (Bhattacharyya 1970: 2). V.T. Krishnamachari, on the other hand, would have preferred more emphasis on the economic aspects, and less role for bureaucracy in bringing about social transformation; something akin to the Baroda pattern. He felt that the economic programmes should be kept distinct and separate from community development, and should be the responsibility of the technical services. According to observers of the Indian scene of that era, there was great wisdom on the part of Indian planners, to focus as much on the development of human resources as on the development of physical and economic resources of rural areas.[10] Balwantray Mehta Study Team (which is described in Chapter 5) agreed with V.T. Krishnamachari, and in fact, went farther than him on this issue. The team said:

> "Here we would point out that the tendency in the past years has been to stress the welfare activities more than the economic development activities....We would urge that the

> emphasis should shift without delay to the more demanding aspects of economic development.... An intensive programme of economic development will generate a demand for a programme of amenities" (India 1957c:I, 4).

This matter, namely, the relative emphasis on the social and technical aspects of rural development in India, and the role of bureaucracy in bringing about social transformation, has not been successfully addressed so far. This problem of harmonising the human with economic aspects has been faced by many countries. According to Devas (1997:352), in China, decentralisation has been mainly an economic process, in which provincial and local governments have strengthened their positions by exploiting their local economic advantages, a process that has brought with it the risks of fragmentation of the national economy.

The twin goals of Community Development were economic development (which when translated into the goals and objectives of that period was agricultural development), and social development. According to the Review of the First Five Year Plan:

> "It was recognised that structural and institutional changes of a far-reaching character would be necessary if the process of development was to bring forth the desired results, not merely in terms of the increase in output, but in terms of an increase in the production potential and of the satisfaction of vital democratic and egalitarian urges within the community". (India 1957b:12).

Reliance on local institutions at the village level, like cooperatives and GPs for agricultural development, formed the core of the proposals contained in the First Five Year Plan.

Oscillation of policy between concentration and diffusion

Ever since the publication of the Draft Outline of First Plan (1951-1956), a good deal of political debate started regarding the approach to agricultural development. When quick increase in agricultural production was the immediate need, concentration of resources, both administrative and financial, over a few compact areas with promise of results, appeared to be the direct and simple answer. But, at the same time, political and social considerations tended to exert a pull towards spreading developmental efforts over all the areas.

Box 3.4: Diagram showing the revenue and rural development administrative pattern in a State during the CDP

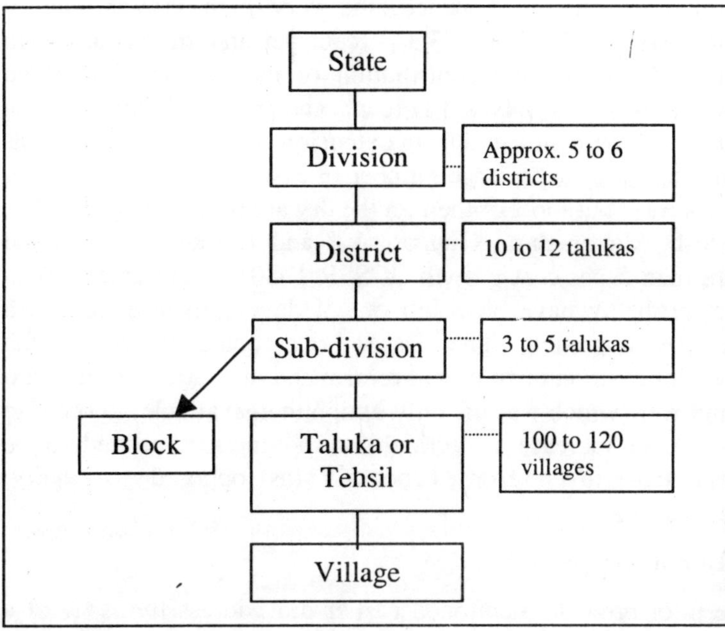

This oscillation of policy between concentration and diffusion runs through the evolution of India's agricultural development experience in the 1950s and 1960s. The interplay of forces finally settled in favour of dispersion during the First Five Year Plan and what finally emerged in the First Five Year Plan was a broad front strategy. The final version of the First Plan clearly stated that a national extension organisation, to be called the National Extension Service (NES) would be setup, covering the entire rural area within ten years (India 1953:231). Thus NES became the implementing arm of the CDP, and henceforward CDP would be implemented exclusively through the NES.

Economic soundness of the broad front strategy

Even though the adoption of the broad front approach was perhaps the result of an intense political debate, it should be noted that, at that time, there were no technological options in agriculture, and even an intensive approach in selected areas would not have resulted in quantum increases in production. A creeping increase attained over a large area would, with low technology agriculture, result in a higher overall increase in production. As it happened, the very high growth rate of agricultural production of 3.3 percent per annum was achieved in the 1950s; but the contribution of increase in yield (land productivity) was only 1.3 percent, and the remaining increase of almost 2 percent came from extension of cropped area. It has been observed that a large number of districts scattered all over the country, but most of them in the dry areas of Rajasthan, M.P, Pradesh, Maharashtra, Gujarat, A.P and Karnataka, registered more than 5 per cent growth (ICSSR 1980). These areas would most probably have been left out of development efforts in a selective approach. The lesson one could draw is that dependence upon institutional reform and utilisation of idle rural manpower (which was the only option then available) in order to achieve an increase in agricultural production, needed to be broad front even from economic (as opposed to equity) considerations.

National Extension Service

The pilot projects mentioned earlier did address the issue of a suitable institutional framework for intensive rural development. The main question, namely, the establish-ment of an extension organisation throughout the country as a permanent development structure, which has been emphasised by the Planning Commission since the First Five Year Plan, however, remained to be tackled in a systematic way. The GMF Enquiry Committee, which had gone into this question by this time, had recommended that for such an extension organisation, the *taluka or tehsil,* the administrative unit consisting of 100 to 120 villages (see box 3.4), should constitute a convenient development block, in charge of a Development Officer or an Extension Officer. The Revenue Sub-divisional Officer, according to the Committee, should perform the functions of the Extension Officer in the sub-division and the District Collector was to be the Chief Extension Officer for the district. The aim was thus to link the extension organisation with the

administrative organisation and bring about a transformation of the existing regulatory machinery into a welfare administration. According to this pattern, at the block level, the development and regulatory functions, importantly, land revenue administration, land reforms and small savings, were kept distinct with the BDO and *Tahsildar* respectively; at the higher levels of administration, namely, the Sub-division and the District, the same officer who was earlier a purely regulatory officer, was to perform both development and regulatory functions. This arrangement, with only minor changes, has continued till today in most States.

In Maharashtra (and Gujarat) after the enactment of the Maharashtra *Zilla Parishads* and *Panchayat Samitis* Act of 1960, ZPs were setup at the district level and an officer of the rank of the Collector was appointed as the Chief Executive Officer of each ZP. The development functions of the Collector were given to the CEO. In A.P the revenue functions of the Collector were separated and given to the District Revenue Officer. The main difference between bureaucracy of the A.P. pattern and that of the Maharashtra pattern was that the District Revenue Officer was subordinate to the Collector, whereas the CEO, ZP was not.

The administrative setup under the NES - the BDO

The staffing pattern under the CDP was laid down by the Centre; there was one generalist at the level of a village or a group of villages. We have already seen that he was called the VLW. He was backed by experts of the various relevant departments. This staff structure is shown in Box 3.5.

The administrative setup for carrying out the CDP was so designed as to be consistent with the core objective of the programme of bringing about an all round development of the rural area with focus on agricultural development. After some initial experiments, it was decided that the unit of development would be an NES block. The head of the block level administration was the BDO. The BDO was assisted by a team of Extension Officers for different fields of work-agriculture, animal husbandry, irrigation and works, panchayats, public health, social education, village industries and women and children's welfare. The idea of a team of extension officers from different departments functioning at the block level under the BDO was considered essential for (i) achieving the basic objectives of the CDP and (ii) to reduce the problems of coordination. It was an example of integrated administration described in the previous chapter.

While at the block level, there were different extension officers, they all functioned through the multi-purpose VLW. In fact, he was the only link between the farmer and the block administration. This fitted in with the underlying philosophy of the CDP summed up in the Review of the First Five Year Plan:

> "When different departments of the Government approach the villager, each from the aspects of its own work, the effect on the villager is apt to be confusing and no permanent impression is created. The peasant's life is not cut into segments, the way the Government's activities are apt to be; the approach to the villager has, therefore, to be a coordinated one, and has to comprehend his whole life. Such an approach has to be made, not through a multiplicity of departmental officials, but through an agent common at least to the principal departments engaged in rural work"(India 1957b:108).

It was made clear that the block level setup was not to be a sector by itself functioning alongside other sectors such as public works, irrigation and public health, but is the medium through which all the sector departments concerned would function and seek to reach the people. The relationship between the block level setup and the various sector (line) departments, and the link between the setup and the farmers are given in Box 3.5.

CDP's contribution to the institutional framework for rural development

Even though it could be debated whether its immediate contribution to agricultural production during the First Five Year Plan was significant, the CDP was nevertheless a significant step in the development of institutional framework for agricultural and rural development. For the first time, an attempt was made to have an administrative framework consistent with the objectives of the programme in the context of the technological options available at that time. To appreciate how much of a departure it then constituted, it is necessary to realise that prior to the commencement of the programme, the different line departments were hierarchically structured, each department having its own roots up to the district level or even below. This was called un-integrated administration in the previous chapter. The CD programme, for the first time, brought the line functionaries of the different developmental departments, such as irrigation, public works, public health, agriculture and animal husbandry at the block level, under the administrative control of the BDO.

Box 3.5: Diagram showing the Block Level administrative pattern

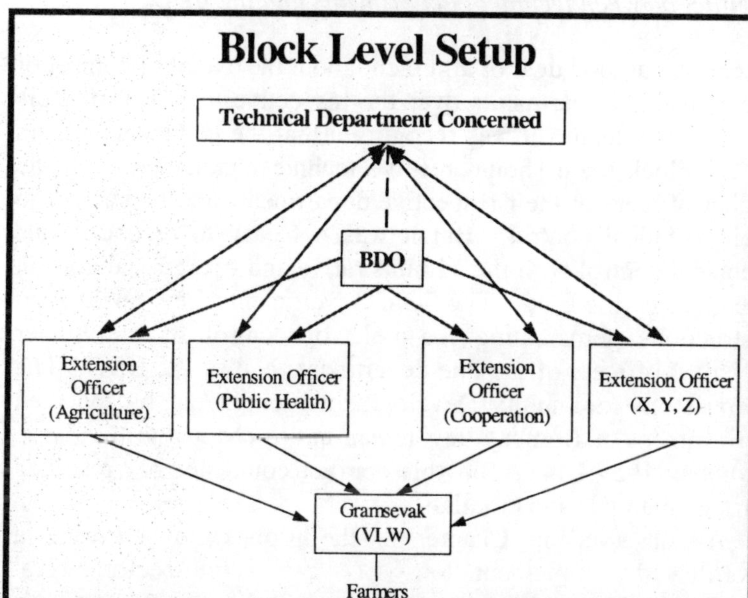

This was not achieved easily, nor did it work smoothly. The technical officers of the block team resented being brought under the administrative control of a generalist administrator (who was of the rank of a *Tahsildar*).[11] The different sector departments did not easily get reconciled to the idea of their 'base' being brought under the administrative control of the BDO. It was therefore very difficult to obtain technical officers on loan from the respective line departments to serve on the block team as Extension Officers; recruitment from the open market to these cadres of Extension Officers was not feasible. The line departments who were to provide the necessary technical support to the block level team were at best cool and at worst hostile towards the CDP. The Review of the First Five Year Plan observed:

> "Until towards the end of the First Plan there was perhaps a tendency on the part of individual development departments to consider that national extension and community project areas were in some way less their concern than other areas"(India 1957b:114).

Conflict between technical departments and the BDO

There was a good deal of argument about the extent of control of the technical departments over the respective technical officers of the block team. It was recognised that the technical officers of the block team should receive technical guidance from the higher officers of their respective departments and be subject to their technical control. But it was not easy to reconcile this technical control with the administrative and operational control exercised by the BDO. The State Governments drew up detailed instructions demarcating the field of control of the higher technical officers of the line departments and of the BDO. The Manual on Community Development brought out by the then Government of Bombay devotes an entire chapter to this issue (Bombay 1959:I;14). But this conflict could not be resolved through manuals and circulars.

As observed in Chapter 2, the problem of ensuring a coordinated implementation of any multi-sector rural development project is very formidable and has so far defied a satisfactory solution. The block level administrative setup perhaps came nearest to a solution (for the then prevailing technological options) because the different departmental functionaries at the block level were placed directly under the control of the BDO. Every such move invariably produces a pull in the opposite direction by the line departments trying to break away from such a control. The oscillation of institutional arrangement for rural development between integrated and un-integrated administration is another feature in development

administration. The history of rural development effort, is also the history of attempts to devise a suitable administrative setup which would ensure a coordinated working of the line departments connected with the different aspects of agricultural and rural development.

The impact of CDP

The CDP has many achievements to its credit and many of them have been mentioned earlier in this chapter. The CDP was the first nationwide programme to have addressed the broad issue of rural development and it has made very valuable contributions to the development debate. We will not be far from truth if we say that the rural development programmes in India since the 1950s is a series of footnotes to CDP. More specifically, the CDP: (i) gave importance to extension as a tool for rural development, (ii) recognised the importance of coordination in a multi-sector programme such as rural development, (iii) prescribed an administrative setup which was consistent with the need for coordination; (iv) provided administrative apparatus in the rural areas which played a critical role in Green Revolution. In many States, the BDO setup played a key role in increasing the area under HYV/hybrid, by supplying farmers with the needed inputs.

It is not difficult to pass judgement now, with hindsight, over the failures of the CDP. We must realise that CDP was a product of a different era. It is indeed amazing that it anticipated some of the ideas now taken for granted such as participation, and self-help. It would certainly have benefited by the association of people's representatives with administration, an idea mooted later by Balwantray Mehta Committee. On the other hand, it relied on bureaucracy to motivate people. Both by temperament and by training, the bureaucracy is not suited to the task.

One major negative factor with the CDP was its centrally driven status. In fact it was one of the earliest and certainly the most well-known CSS. These are programmes planned by the Centre and given to the States for implementation. The monthly letters of S.K. Dey (Dey 1962a) to the State Development Commissioners suggest that the CDP was mostly micro-managed by the Centre. There is an unmistakable element of pride in these letters – pride of a man who has conceived of an idea and has seen the idea being translated into action in many corners of the country. But, he was responsible for creating a huge bureaucracy at all levels; the bureaucracy did one thing they know best, that is, paper work. Its concept of accountability is the conventional concept of accountability of adherence to financial and administrative norms. When they did not deliver and were not accountable in a larger sense to the people, Dey got frustrated, and his frustration was reflected in his letters: "From my visits in the field I have an impression that our reports and returns are imposing too serious a strain on the field staff." (Dey 1962a:13)

The letters of S.K. Dey indicate his conviction that for every problem there is a bureaucratic solution. For example, when he realised that the CDP did not pay attention to village industries, he wrote: "I am working in close touch with the Ministry of Commerce and Industry to expedite preliminary arrangements.... In this connection I would like to refer to the appointment of Joint Directors of Industries and two Technical Experts ....It is essential that these functionaries be put in position before we can even begin a move forward....." (Dey 1962a:16) If the problem is to start village industries, the solution need not necessarily be the appointment of Joint Directors. In the early 1960s, (like now) there was more reliance on bureaucracy than on local politicians. But on balance, it had more positive features than negative ones.

Notes

1. I am indebted for this quotation to the presentation of S. S. Meenakshisundaram at the Fourth Annual World Bank conference on Environmentally Sustainable Development, Sep. 25-27, 1996.
2. For a detailed account of these see India 1968d.
3. *Gramsevak* is a Hindi name for a village level worker; *Gram* means village, and *sevak* denotes a person who serves the village. The feminine gender of *gramsevak* is *gramsevika.*
4. In some States the Collector is called the Deputy Commissioner. Brayne had excellent credentials for the task. He had written extensively on the Indian village scene and his work in Gurgaon attracted Gandhiji's attention.
5. I am indebted to Lane Holdcroft for suggesting that I call them "socio-political activists". I am reminded of David Potter calling the ICS and IAS officials as "India's Political Administrators." (Potter 1986).

6. Chester Bowles the US Ambassador to India twice, during 1951-53 and again during 1963-69.
7. See Klingensmith 1997. The article describes the influence of foreign advisers and institutions such as the Ford Foundation and the Rockefeller Foundation, particularly during 1950s and 1960s. These institutions were staffed by the New Dealers who were in sympathy with the state led development approach, whose names were mentioned earlier. I remember walking through the corridors of Krishi Bhavan, New Delhi, in the 1960s. From the name plates on the doors it was obvious that there were many foreign advisers. Some of them showed up in the field as well. The World Bank entered the arena in the early 1970s when McNamara was its President, as mentioned in the previous chapter.
8. A *lakh* is an Indian term for 100,000.
9. Quoted by Annasaheb Shinde in his Foreword to Bhattacharyya 1970.
10. See Taylor et al 1965:611.
11. A Tahsildar (in some states he or she is called a Mamlatdar, or Talukdar) is the Head of a Taluka (or Tehsil).

CHAPTER 4

The Decline of the Community Development Programme

In the last chapter we had mentioned the contributions of the CDP to India's agricultural and rural development. In spite of these admittedly valuable contributions, CDP declined. One of the reasons for the decline, was that after the Green Revolution, many people in the rural areas, including the local politicians, became more conscious of increasing the production of foodgrains, and started focusing on production programmes. They did not appreciate the human development aspect of CDP. Much of the reason was the growth of factors which caused its fading away. These factors are very much with us to-day. Unless they are openly addressed in national forums, there is a real danger of the fledgling PRIs, created after the recent Constitutional amendments, going the way of the CDP. This chapter contains a discussion of these factors.

Factors which influenced the decline of the CDP

Among the factors which influenced the decline of the CDP the following were the most prominent: growth vs. distribution; generalists vs. specialists; centralisation vs. decentralisation; and sociological factors. These are briefly discussed below.

Growth vs. distribution

In the early 1950s, when the CDP started, rural development was synonymous with agricultural development, and as part of a concentrated strategy, it was initially started as a pilot project, only in a few promising pockets of the country. This was soon followed by a broad front strategy, and the objective of the CDP was mentioned as equity rather than growth. There was an argument between economists and the sociologists when the programme started; the former preferred starting it in the most favourable parts of the country, and the latter, in all areas. It

was seen earlier that under the technological options available to the administration at that time, a broadfront strategy was both socially and economically desirable. Thus the CDP was started in all areas of the country. But the argument eventually settled in favour of the economists when the Ford Foundation Report (India 1959a) emphasised a concentrated approach and agricultural administration started focusing on the most favourable spots of the country.

When technocratic agriculture was adopted in the late 1960s, the question of concentrating the new seeds, fertilisers and manpower in the most favourable areas of the country once again engaged the attention of the policy makers. The policy makers preferred a policy of concentration as yield increases on an appreciable scale was possible with the new agricultural technology. C. Subramaniam, who, as the Central Agriculture Minister during the mid-1960s, was one of the architects of the Green Revolution, argued:

> "If we concentrate our efforts in a given area where we have assured water supply and we have the necessary extension services also concentrated in that area, then it should be possible for us to achieve much better results than by merely dispersing our efforts in a thin way throughout the country." (India 1965:6075).

It is interesting to note here that in the 10th Meeting of the National Development Council (NDC), held in May 1958, (prior to Green Revolution) C. Subramaniam, who was then the Finance Minister of the State of Madras (as it was known then), had observed:

> "The entire Plan depended on agricultural production and for the purpose of increasing agricultural production they had mainly depended on community development and national extension service. If before the end of the Plan (Second Five Year Plan, 1956-61) the entire area was not covered with community development and national extension scheme, programme for agriculture would to that extent be affected." (India 1958b:7). (words in brackets added).

Box 4.1: National Development Council

The NDC is chaired by the Prime Minister and has the Chief Ministers of the States and the Union Cabinet Ministers among its members. It is the highest policy making body (albeit not a constitutional body). In the initial years, it served as a sounding board for the proposals of the Planning Commission, and a forum where important proposals of national importance were discussed. It was political in nature, whereas the Planning Commission was technical.

He was actually pleading for covering the entire country with NES so that agricultural development would not be adversely affected. These two views by a person, generally regarded as the moving spirit behind the Green Revolution, indicate the appropriate strategies during the HYV and pre-HYV periods. Gradually, as the position regarding inputs improved, the challenge was to spread the HYV technology over as much area as possible and to convert as many farmers as possible to adopt HYV. Thus after the Fourth Five Year Plan (1969-74), administration had a two-fold challenge of spreading the HYV message, following it up with timely supply of inputs and credit, and providing farmers with necessary extension services. Thus in the initial years of Green Revolution, the strategy was one

Box 4.2: C. Subramaniam

C. Subramaniam died on November 7, 2000 at the age of 90. *The Economist* carried an obituary in its November 18th issue, which said: "Last year there was a lot of support for naming Subramaniam India's man of the century, even of the millennium. He was too modest, and too wise, to allow himself to be given the laurel for a discovery for which many claimed credit….Perhaps because others sought to be acknowledged as "father" of the green revolution, India was slow to acknowledge what Subramaniam had accomplished." He did not discover the miracle seed, but certainly created the institutions which were responsible for the Green Revolution. In particular, at great political cost to himself, he made the price incentives to farmers operational, by creating appropriate institutions. He manoeuvred through India's political and bureaucratic jungle and obtained a number of decisions which made life easier for scientists.

of concentration, and later, one of dispersion. In the later years of the Green Revolution, that is in late 1960s and 1970s, the approach towards agricultural development was oriented towards technology, and human development on which CDP was predicated, took a back seat.

Since the Green Revolution, and the growth of the CSS (see Chapter 10), it was felt that there was no need for CDP. In the early 1970s, the Ministry of Community Development ceased to exist at the Centre. The term "safety net" entered the development lexicon. Many anti-poverty schemes were formulated by the Centre as CSS, and these were intended to take care of those who were by-passed by the development process. The rest of the economy was, by implication, for growth. CDP was thus a victim of the dualism which found its way into the economy: growth vs. distribution. The impression gained ground that the line departments favoured growth. This impression was reinforced by the SADs breaking away from the BDO fold, following the Ford Foundation Report. This is more fully described in Chapter 6.

There was another development, which re-inforced the dualism mentioned above. After the green revolution in the mid-1960s there was a growing concern that the agricultural strategy of the country was accentuating the disparities in the rural areas. The introduction of the Minimum Needs Programme (MNP) in the mid-1970s was a response to this concern. It was not a programme as much as a means to persuade the States to provide more outlays in their Plans on certain schemes, such as elementary education, adult education, rural health, water supply, rural roads, provision of housing sites, and nutrition, which will enable those who do not have the means of production, to participate in the development process.

Generalists vs. specialists

The CDP was an administrative programme. Under the programme the BDO, who was a generalist administrator, was the head of the development administration in the Block and that person was accountable to the District Collector. The senior IC & AS officers[1] were generally in favour of the BDO's establishment. From the beginning of the CDP, the specialist departments, particularly Agriculture Department,[2] were not friendly towards it. Many States reorganised their Agriculture Departments by-passing BDOs. This started the move away from accountability of the technical departments to a generalist administrator. The heads of technical departments resented having to go through an ICS or IAS officer in the State or Central secretariat in order to get ministerial approval to their proposals. At the district level they were unhappy about being accountable to a generalist Collector. BDO's establishment thus became a casualty in the bureaucratic warfare between the generalists and the specialists. The political support to the BDO's establishment also waned in the 1970s. But despite all attempts to kill it, the BDO's establishment has still endured. In many states it has become part of the *Panchayat Samiti* or what is the same, Block *Panchayat* administration.

It is the tendency of all bureaucrats, to report to their own clan, rather than to an elected person, and the BDO is no exception. BDO would prefer to report directly to the Collector or, in some States such as, Maharashtra and Karnataka to the Head of development administration in the district, rather than to the PS chairperson who is an elected person. The solution to the problem is a two-step solution: first, to make the line department personnel in the Block report to the BDO, thereby achieving an integrated administration at the PS level; and the second, to make the BDO report to the Chairperson of the PS. In many States, the latter part is achieved, but not the former.

In the U.S.A. this generalist vs. specialist controversy was active during the early 1960s, the heyday of Community Development in India. When foreign experts (mostly from the U.S.A.) came to India, the Indian IC &A.S. officers struck a sympathetic chord in them. During the Kennedy administration the AID agency was riven by this controversy. Lane Holdcroft says: "It was an ideological battle which pitted the generalist against the specialist, the social scientist (excluding the economists) against the technologist, the pluralist against the monist." (Holdcroft 1984:52). This controversy was one of the factors which were responsible for the decline of the CDP. The battle is still raging in India, and the beneficiaries of this battle are the development intermediaries, a term which is explained in Chapter 11.

Centralisation vs. decentralisation

This closely follows the "generalist vs. specialist" debate described in the foregoing paragraphs. We saw how the specialist sector departments never got reconciled to their "base" being brought under a "generalist" like the BDO. In any kind of political decentralisation, inevitably, the local officials of the specialist sector departments will come under the administrative control of a generalist, and for this reason they (i.e. specialist sector departments) are not kindly disposed towards *panchayati raj*. They are willing to go as far as delegation of powers and responsibilities to lower levels of the same ministry or department, as long they can hold the 'purse strings'. To give a specific example, they are very comfortable with an arrangement where a sector specialist (such as the Chief Engineer, Irrigation) is directly accountable to the Minister for Irrigation, and with the former having a long tail under him comprising Superintending Engineer, Executive Engineer, Deputy Engineer and so on, ending with the last person in the field, by-passing BDO. Asoka Mehta Committee which was appointed in 1977 by the Government of India to enquire into the working of PRIs observed that the system of line hierarchy found favour with the specialist departments (India 1978a:3). Their interests coincided with the interests of the Ministers (at the Central and State level) and the Members of Parliament or those of State Legislatures namely members of the Legislative Assembly and those of the Legislative Council (MLA/MLC), who did not want to share political power with the district politicians. PRIs were the casualty of this alliance between the technical departments and the Central and State level politicians.

Sociological factors

Indian society is horizontally stratified. In almost every village there are the so-called upper castes and the lower castes (Scheduled Castes). There is more in common between the upper castes of two villages, even if they are not neighbouring villages, than between the upper castes and the SC of the same village. For example, the Thakurs of different villages have more in common between them than the Thakurs and the SC of the same village. The Brahmins of the South have more in common with the Brahmins of the North, than with SC who speak their own language. This caste factor makes it difficult to achieve community development, in the sense in which the policy makers wanted, that is, the feeling of belonging to an entire village community. The concept of community which they wanted is alien to India. There is a Maratha or Thakur community, but it is spread over several villages and is more caste based. It is significant that Balwantray Mehta Committee observed:

> "The word "community" has for the past many decades, denoted religious or caste groups or in some instances, economic groups not necessarily living in one locality." (India 1957c:I,1).

The only way in which one can achieve cohesiveness between various castes in a village, is through political decentralisation, where one has to earn the votes of all castes, which means, one has to do good work at the village level, for all castes, in order to survive in village level politics. This was the main reason why Mahatma Gandhi, who was against casteism, stressed the need for political decentralisation. Only political decentralisation would create a political marketplace in a village for the elected representatives of the people.

Targets in agricultural and rural development

Another factor which brought disrepute to the CDP was target consciousness, which all bureaucracies are guilty of. Agricultural and rural development administration in India is no exception to the rule. There are areas where targets are meaningful, and administration can be made accountable for their attainment, and there are also areas where the attainment of targets is beyond the reach of administration. The problem with CDP was that these two things were not kept distinct and separate and the programme was required to deliver results which bureaucracy was incapable of delivering. It is indeed surprising that policy makers did not display familiarity with the proper and feasible role of administration in the field of agricultural and rural development.

Role of administration in agricultural and rural development

Ever since Independence, administration has been playing an active role in agricultural development. Agricultural development in India is the end result of a number of steps to be taken by farmers, political leaders, social workers and administration and also of policy decisions of the Centre and States. It is the responsibility of planners and policy makers to clearly identify and spell out the tasks of administration, which should be within its competence to implement. In fact, with what effectiveness administration responds to the tasks assigned to it, depends very much upon how clearly its role is defined, and whether this is the role which it is competent to fulfil. Some examples of this are given in the following paragraph.

It is meaningful to talk of a target for production of improved seeds by the block administration for supply to the farmers, if the production is undertaken on government farms. It is equally meaningful to talk of a target for covering a certain acreage with appropriate soil conservation measures like bunding, terracing etc. But it is not meaningful to give a target to the agricultural administration for bringing a certain acreage under improved seeds, because this is an area where farmers' involvement is vital. Similarly, it is not meaningful to give a target to the block administration for a certain number of wells to be dug by farmers. The construction of an irrigation project can be regarded as falling entirely within the capability of administration, if the necessary resources are made available. Managing the irrigation system, and creating physical conditions conducive to the farmers' utilising the irrigation potential created, can also be said to come within its capability; but making farmers utilise the irrigation potential created lies beyond its capability. Similarly, mobilising rural manpower to construct village assets cannot be considered as falling within the ambit of administration. Organising village cooperative institutions, by its very definition a voluntary association of people, cannot also be considered to be within the competence of administration. In other words, certain activities in the field of agricultural and rural development require action primarily by administration; whereas, some require concerted action by both administration and the farmers. It is necessary to keep this distinction in mind while discussing the role of administration in agricultural and rural development. Balwantray Mehta Committee which went into the question of target-setting in governments had this to say on the subject: "During our visits to various blocks we repeatedly heard complaints that the fixation of targets has been arbitrary and unrealistic" (India 1957c:I,24). The point made above is that government should not set targets in matters the implementation of which is beyond the control of administration. It will certainly appear to be arbitrary, when it cannot relate the efforts put in, to the results achieved.

Classification of the contents of the CDP

From the point of view of implementation and the nature of administrative methods to be followed, the contents of the CD programme can be classified into the following categories: (i) matters primarily to be organised by the administration; (ii) matters to be organised by the administration but with substantial help and close cooperation of people; (iii) matters to be developed primarily on the initiative of people as their own programme, but, for which, suitable help by way of technical advice and external financial assistance is to be provided by the administration.

Among the agricultural development programmes entrusted to the block administration, while some programmes like organising soil conservation measures (contour bunding, terracing and levelling), construction of new irrigation works like minor irrigation tanks etc., could be said to fall under the first category mentioned above, most of the programmes were really falling under the other categories. Thus there were two clearly distinct aspects, namely, what the people should be motivated to do by the block administration and what the administration itself could do. But, in actual practice, these two aspects were not kept distinct and separate. What the block administration was expected to motivate the farmers to achieve, somehow became the targets of the administration itself. Thus detailed instructions were given during the Second Plan regarding the preparation of the agricultural programmes for the block, which was to be further broken into village agricultural plans and ultimately family-wise production plans. What this implied was that the administration was to prepare farm production plans, which would, it was assumed, eventually be adopted by the farmers as their own plans, and, on the assumption that all the recommended farming practices would be followed by them, detailed calculations of additional production per acre, were required to be done by the block administration. All these efforts ultimately resulted in nothing more than a considerable load of paper work and in due course the preparation of such plans became ritualistic. The real problem was that block administration had very little within its capability to see that plans made for farmers could be adopted and followed by them.

Areas where targets are meaningful

Much of the criticism of the block administration and, in fact, of the CDP itself stems from the failure to realise this basic fact, namely, that targets can be given to administration only of such things which it is capable of achieving. When targets are given to administration, which really pre-suppose farmers' involvement to a considerable degree, administration tends to adopt questionable means, which eventually would bring it discredit.

Among the different targets given to the block administration, it was but natural that it concentrated on what it could achieve, like construction of buildings, so that the target expenditure for the block could be "booked" somehow, as any surrender of unspent financial provisions at the end of the year was considered to be an index of poor performance on the part of the BDO. If, for instance, in spite of the best efforts of the block staff, enough farmers did not come forward to avail of irrigation loans, (as ultimately it is their decision whether to go in for a dugwell or not), the effort put in by the BDO would never figure in the returns to be submitted by the block administration. Inevitably therefore, there was more concentration on "visible" achievements within the capability of the administration. The Third Evaluation Report on the CDP noted this trend:

> "In the operation of the programme there has been excessive emphasis on physical and financial accomplishments-getting the targets achieved, expenditure incurred, buildings constructed etc. and not enough on educating the people into new ways of doing things, on making the NES an effective agency for carrying out the total programme of development and reform provided for by the National and State plans" (India 1956a:239).

Targets, therefore, are meaningful and relevant only in certain areas. While it is true that administration can only respond to peoples' requirement and that it is not realistic to expect administration to make people automatically respond to the targets given to administration, targets are, all the same, inevitable as means of control and supervision. Once it was accepted that it was one of the functions of the block administration to motivate the farmers to use improved seeds and adopt better farming practices, the question would arise: how can the work of the BDO be measured? What norms should the BDO apply while evaluating the work of the *gramsevaks*? In an agricultural development strategy built around extension as the key instrument, it is necessary to spell out some means of measuring the degree or the intensity of extension efforts put in. This is yet another of the dilemmas facing development administration: that targets cannot be entirely dispensed with, but, at the same time, excessive emphasis on targets could lead to unhealthy practices. The solution to this dilemma seems to lie in the field work by the senior departmental staff. An intensive field trip would make the officer distinguish between a really good BDO and someone who only writes good reports. The same is true of any other field staff. But unfortunately field trips by senior staff have become a casualty of the fast communication techniques of the present times.

Targets and decentralisation

When administration is centralised at the State or Central level, the political executives do not have either the time or the inclination to visit all parts of the State. In fact, empirical observation shows that the political executives at the State or Central level, at the most, visit their own constituencies and often forget that they are for the entire State or the country as the case may be. The practice percolates down: what is true of the political executives is true of the bureaucracy, and the so-called "field departments."[3] In decentralised administration, since the political executive has much smaller territory to cover, the chances of field orientation of administration are certainly better.

The author has seen BDOs who do not stir out of their offices, and whose reputation as a "good" BDO lies in their capacity to write good reports, and interpret rules from the State or Centre. This is another reason why the State and the Centre should desist from formulating schemes and giving them to PRIs for implementation. They should make PRIs formulate their own schemes to suit the local conditions and monitor them. Monitoring should be done in the field and not from the State headquarters or Delhi on the basis of reports; in the latter case, report writing ability will become the criterion of isolating the grain from the chaff. It is necessary to define what constitutes a "field". For a person from Delhi, the State headquarters is the "field". For a person from the State headquarters, district headquarters is the "field". The most appropriate definition of what constitutes a "field" is where service is provided to the client. In health schemes, it could be a primary health centre; in agriculture it is farmer's field. Decentralisation offers a combination of field orientation and realistic targets. Since CDP contained only administrative decentralisation, there was no political executive below the State level, who could visit villages where, in most rural development programmes, service is provided to the client.

To sum up, it is necessary to distinguish between two kinds of targets in agricultural and rural development. The first kind of targets in areas which are entirely within the ambit of administration, like construction of irrigation projects, production and timely positioning of seeds etc., have real meaning and administration can be held accountable for any shortfall. The second kind of targets, like bringing a certain acreage under improved seeds, seeing that farmers undertake spraying of their cotton crop with appropriate pesticides etc., though they are not entirely within administration's control, are nevertheless relevant. It is necessary, however, for planners to be aware of the danger of basing important plan projections on such targets. This may be illustrated from the Second Plan:

> "The targets set out at present in the plan are in the nature of working estimates indicating the increases in production potential arising from various development programmes. It is hoped that through better integration of the agricultural and national extension programme, it will be possible to fix appreciably higher targets for agricultural production. This problem is at present under discussion between Planning Commission and the authorities concerned." (India 1956a: 62).

In May 1956, NDC called for higher targets of agricultural production than those initially proposed for the Second Plan, and these targets were therefore revised upwards rather arbitrarily. The revisions made were substantial: foodgrain production from 75 million tons to 80.4 million tons; Oilseeds from 7 million tons to 7.6 million tons; sugarcane from 7.1 million tons to 7.8 million tons, and cotton from 5.5 million bales to 6.5 million bales (India 1956b: 37). But the basis on which the revision was done was not spelt out (in fact, the basis of even the original targets is not clear), beyond stressing the need for measures to secure the fullest participation of the people through community projects and NES. The NDC in the 10th meeting (May, 1958) endorsed these targets. The Council

> "stressed the fact that the level of outlay which could be undertaken would depend in degree on the success achieved

> in increasing agricultural production. Local participation and community efforts *must be enlisted on the largest scale possible* in support of agricultural programmes such as the full utilisation of the available irrigation potential and the adoption of improved practices especially in areas which have irrigation and assured rainfall and intensive efforts should be made to reach through Village Panchayats and the Village Cooperative." (emphasis added) (India 1958b:20).

Projections and hopes based on fallible assumptions somehow became firm targets.

Notes

1. The term refers to the officers of the Indian Civil and Administrative Services. Before Indian Independence in 1947, the premier service in India was the Indian Civil Service (ICS) which consisted of British and Indian officers. It was labelled as the steel frame which held the *Raj* together. After Independence it was succeeded by the Indian Administrative Service. See Drucker (1988) for a discussion of the management aspects of the ICS, and Potter (1986) for a very interesting account of the political and administrative aspects.
2. At that time the bulk of the BDO's work related to agriculture.
3. The name stands for Departments, such as the Directorate of Agriculture or Animal Husbandry; they are called field departments to distinguish them from secretariat departments.

CHAPTER 5

Balwantray Mehta Committee Report and Democratic Decentralisation

We saw in Chapter 3, how bureaucracy was involved in bringing about rural development under CDP. It was realised by the national leaders soon after the CDP was started, that bureaucracy alone cannot deliver the goods in the absence of democracy at district and lower levels. There have been several attempts in India to achieve democratic decentralisation, the recent Constitutional amendments being the latest. The earliest such attempt at the national level, was the report of Balwantray Mehta Committee, and the follow-up action. Democratic decentralisation was introduced in the States of Maharashtra and Gujarat following the reports of Naik Committee and Rasiklal Parikh Committee respectively. This chapter contains an account of the important recommendations of Balwantray Mehta Committee and the experience of Maharashtra with democratic decentralisation.

Five Year Plans and CDP

The CDP was a part of the planning process. In point of time, the First Five Year Plan (1951-56) started before even the pilot community projects of late 1951 were started. According to Mukerji (Mukerji 1961: 22), the Five Year Plans aimed at bringing about all-round development of the country in a democratic manner and the CDP was to take care of the rural sector of development. Therefore, the same basic objectives and policies used to govern both the Five Year Plans and the CDP. The fact that the CDP was a part of the Five Year Plans would seem to account partly for the greater attention given to the accomplishment of visible and spectacular physical results, than to the qualitative aspects of community development, since, as we saw in the previous chapter, bureaucracy tends to pay more attention to factors which are tangible and measurable.

Second Five Year Plan (1956-1961)

The institutional framework for agricultural and rural development during the Second Five Year Plan was mostly a continuation of that of the First Plan. CDP was implemented through the NES. The CD blocks continued to be the focal points of the strategy which, as mentioned earlier, had two main elements: (i) motivating farmers to adopt better farming practices, and (ii) mobilising rural manpower to construct labour-intensive agricultural infrastructure works. The Second Plan document states:

> "An underdeveloped economy has large resources in manpower which are not being utilised. These resources have to be used for creating permanent assets......One of the central aims of the NES is to organise the systematic use of manpower resources, particularly in the rural areas, for works of benefit to the community as a whole." (India 1956a:141).

A strategy which depended very much for its results on a continual dialogue and fruitful partnership between the administration and people at the local level could not sustain for long without the association of the peoples' representatives with administration. The need for active involvement of people's representatives in the development process was expressed in the Second Plan document (India 1956a:160). Following the Budget speech of 1956-57, the NDC appointed a Committee on Plan Projects, and this Committee, in turn, constituted a Study Team under the leadership of Balwantray Mehta. The Study Team's report is officially known as the *Report of the Team for the Study of Community Projects and National Extension Service,* (India 1957c). It is popularly known as the Balwantray Mehta Committee Report and the study team itself is known as Balwantray Mehta Committee. As a result of the recommendations of the report, many States set up PRIs.

Democratic decentralisation

The Balwantray Mehta Committee was mainly appointed to study the contents of the CD programme, and the priorities assigned to the different fields of activity in it, and to report on the system, organisation and methods of work adopted for the implementation of the programme. The Committee was also to study the intensification of agricultural production, coordination between different ministries, departments and agencies. Later on, the NDC, at its Eighth Meeting held on the December 8 - 9, 1956, requested the committee to enquire into the pattern of the existing district administration and suggest its reorganisation. The objective of such a reorganisation was to be the setting up of democratic bodies at the block and district levels which are linked with village *panchayats.* According to the Council, such an administrative set up, which would be accountable to local elected representatives, would, in due course, take over the entire general administration and development of the district or its sub-division, other than law and order, administration of justice and revenue administration. The committee submitted its report on November 24, 1957. In short the report recommended that the most efficient arrangement would be to have a self-governing elected institution at the block level, replacing the block advisory committees, which had been set up earlier to associate the non-official elements with the block administration.

Recommendations of the Balwantray Mehta committee

There were many recommendations of Balwantray Mehta committee, other than the one for which it is well known, namely, the recommendation pertaining to the establishment of democratically elected bodies below the district level. The committee recommended progressive devolution of the powers of the State Government to elected bodies at the local level. The team said:

> "Some of the Central Ministries operate their own schemes in State areas even in fields which the Constitution has left entirely to the States.....In those fields which the Constitution has assigned exclusively to the State, the Central Government should not merely not operate directly, but should not concern itself with details of a purely local nature." (India 1957c:I,29).

It would have blushed at the present number of CSS, in areas which are best left to PRIs. It also tackled questions such as: whether election to the District level body should be direct or indirect and the responsibilities and finances of the local bodies. The committee recommended: (i) indirect elections to PSs from GPs to ensure that the former are controlled by the latter; (ii) that the functions of the PS included agriculture prominently; and (iii) that only supervisory and coordinating functions should be assigned to the ZPs and not a decision making role. According to the report, decentralisation should be introduced without delay in the field of development and "it is here that we consider that the panchayat samiti should begin to operate with the least possible delay. Its function should cover the development of agriculture in all its aspects...."(India 1957c:I,11). There was a good deal of discussion at that time as to what would be the best first stage of decentralisation – district (ZP) or the block (PS). As stated above, the Balwantray Mehta Committee report favoured PS and said that the district body should confine itself to tackling the problems of coordination.

The NDC endorsed the objective of introducing a democratic structure of administration above the village level as recommended by the Balwantray Mehta Committee, but left it to the States to consider the precise manner in which the principle was to be applied. According to the NDC there was no need to insist upon a uniformity among different parts of the country. Democratic decentralisation, as the process initiated by the Team's report came to be called, took different forms in different States. Some States, like A.P. and Rajasthan, which took the lead, set up effective democratic bodies at the block level, whereas, Maharashtra and Gujarat set up such bodies at the district level, which were called ZPs.

Rationale of Balwantray Mehta committee's recommendations

The main reason for the recommendation of the Balwantray Mehta Team for bringing about popular participation in administration at the district level or block level, was that there should be decentralisation of authority and decision making to PRIs. It was not the intention to make the democratically elected bodies mere implementing agencies of the Centre or States. But that was what they, in practice, became. Since the GOI was initially bearing 100 percent and subsequently (i.e. during the Second Plan) 75 percent of the expenditure on the CD programme, the budget of the CD block handed down from the

GOI to the States tended to become rather rigid. The prescription to the block level administration that it should respond to the local "felt needs" was not really reflected in the standard "schematic budgets" of the CD blocks. Understanding peoples' needs was not as difficult as responding to them within the framework of the standard, schematic budget of the block. To give an illustration, when the author was a BDO in the early 1960s, he visited a village, where the villagers pointed out that a local *nulla,* a local term for a rivulet, needed to be deepened and trained properly as there was a serious water-logging problem. The author was indeed helpless, as he was not sure whether the block budget permitted taking up this work as part of programme of the block, to be financed from the block budget. A reference had to be made to the State Government which, in turn, referred the matter to the Centre. There were a number of such references from blocks around the country. The U.N. Evaluation Mission, which studied the CD program, had expressed the opinion that there was sometimes too much rigidity in the application of the community development programme sent out by the Centre (India 1957d). The Balwantray Mehta Team also came to the same conclusion and in fact recommended that the Central Government should only lay down the policy and prescribe the broad outlines of a scheme and then leave it to the State Governments to work out the details to suit local requirements.

The recommendation of the Balwantray Mehta Team notwithstanding, the rigidities remained to a considerable extent. This has been commented upon even as late as 1978 by the Asoka Mehta Committee:

> "Further, in the process of implementation of transferred activities, here and elsewhere, a number of orders and directions by the State Government led to a gradual development of subsidiary legislation which would tend to curtail the decision making powers of the elected bodies"(India 1978a:5).

Striking a balance between financial accountability to the authority providing funds and operational flexibility is another recurrent theme in development administration. This dilemma in development administration is faced in many World Bank supported projects which are also considered highly standardised (Brinkerhoff 1994). The detailed nature of the World Bank's Operational Directives and the internal processing of issues do not, many times, leave sufficient room for local changes. Reconciling accountability to the agency providing funds and specificity is difficult to achieve in practice.

The consequence of PRIs becoming implementing agencies

There were two issues here which were inter-related, and which affect the health of PRIs now: (i) the "rigidity" referred to by the U.N. Evaluation Mission, and (ii) that PRIs became mere implementing agencies. The main reason for both is the fact that almost all Plan schemes are prepared at the Centre or at State level, and the role of PRIs in planning is minimal. Even if people's representatives are actively associated with PRIs at the local level, unless the basic issue is addressed, namely, the role of PRIs in planning, it is unlikely that PRIs will be able to deliver what is expected of them. This was what the recent Constitutional amendments were expected to achieve. Article 243G of the Constitution refers to planning by *panchayats* at the appropriate level, but this has not yet been implemented. Planning and implementation by the same agency, which also has the funds, would appear to be a distant dream.

We saw in Chapter 3 the inherent ambivalence in the CDP in the treatment of the welfare and production aspects of the programme, and how it was addressed by the Balwantray Mehta Committee. The Committee was of the view that "material progress in the agriculture sector can be judged only by the total increase in production." By emphasising the measurable indicators of development (rather than the qualitative ones) it unwittingly contributed to the target consciousness which we referred to in the previous chapter. The Balwantray Mehta Committee's report has rightly been described as exceedingly forthright. "We know of no such analytically devastating report on an ongoing programme in any other developing country." (Taylor *et al* 1965:240). The report is a milestone in the history of development administration in India.

Third Five Year Plan (1961-66)

The Third Five Year Plan was exercised over the working of PRIs. To make their working more effective, it recommended that: (i) while developing institutions at higher levels, the greatest stress should continue to be laid on the work of the GS and the *Panchayat* at the village level; and (ii) technical officers at the District level should try to make their advice and assistance available to extension officers at the Block level and to the PSs. The Third Plan also called for rationalisation of district administration, with the introduction of *Panchayati Raj* and coordination of activities of different executive bodies in the rural sector. Accordingly, a number of study teams and working groups were set up during the Third Plan period. To name a few of them (the name of the chairman is given within brackets): Study Team on Nyaya Panchayats (G.R. Rajagopal); Study Team on Gram Sabha (R.R. Diwakar); Working Group on Panchayati Raj Administration (Ram Subhag Singh); Study Team on Budgeting and Accounting Procedures of PRIs (M. Ramakrishnayya); Study Team for a System of Audit of Panchayati Raj Accounts (R.K. Khanna, Accountant General, Central Revenues); Study Team of Panchayati Raj Finance (K. Santhanam); Committee on Panchayati Raj Elections (K. Santhanam).

The role played by Community Development and *Panchayati Raj* movement, was reviewed by the Chief Ministers' Conference in June 1968. The Conference noted that: (i) the three tier structure of *Panchayati Raj* has not been established all over the country, as expected; (ii) the resources available to PRIs, particularly at the middle and higher levels were severely limited; (iii) each department tended to form its own hierarchy, for development work in the field. None of these problems were unknown, but the Conference did not make any recommendation to remedy the situation. The administrative arrangement recommended by the Planning Commission namely, the integration of PRI staff with the normal departmental staff dealing with all the development work with purely local impact, were not acted upon either by the ministries or by the States. After the Third Plan period, there was no significant development regarding PRIs until the late 1970s when the working group on Block Level planning under the chairmanship of Prof. M.L. Dantwala, and the celebrated Asoka Mehta Committee were set up. These developments are described in Chapter 7.

The experience of Maharashtra with ZPs

As has been observed earlier, in Maharashtra and Gujarat democratically elected ZPs were formed. The then Bombay State[1] appointed a committee, known as the Naik Committee,[2] to go into the question of the appropriate model of democratic decentralisation for the state. The Committee made a bold departure from the model recommended earlier by the Balwantray Mehta Committee of a strong, democratic institution at the block level, and a ZP (at district level) assigned only supervisory and coordinating functions. The Committee recommended that the first point of decentralisation should be the district level and that there should be an officer of the rank of the District Collector, in charge of the development activities of the district. The Committee observed:

> "We therefore feel that the district body is the best operative unit of local administration as it alone will be capable of providing the requisite resources, necessary administrative and technical personnel and equipment required for a properly coordinated development at the district". (Maharashtra 1961:74).

Recommendations of the Naik Committee

The Naik Committee recognised that (i) coordination would become increasingly important as the process of development progresses; (ii) operational coordination is best achieved at the district level where the executive officers of most departments are located; (iii) for a coordinated implementation of programmes, a multi-disciplinary organisational setup is inescapable; (iv) the coordinating officer should be of a high enough status; and (v) it is not enough to build an official setup to bring about coordination; the official setup needs the backing of a strong political setup. According to the report: "all departments put together will function as one integral unit under the overall superintendance and control of the chief administrator". (Maharashtra 1961:96). The Naik Committee recommended that the CEOs of ZPs should be officers "who have already finished their tenures as District Collectors" (Maharashtra 1961:103).

The author joined the Maharashtra State in 1961 after one year at the National Academy of Administration in Mussoorie, along with his colleagues also assigned to Maharashtra. We called on the late Yeshwantrao Chavan who was the Chief Minister of Maharashtra. Just then the Naik Committee report was out and there was a lot of expectation in the air. But we were fresh from Mussoorie and had not yet gone through the "rough and tumble" of the district life. We were exercised over the fact that the Committee had recommended that Annual Evaluation Report (referred to in government circles as the Confidential Report or "CR" for short) of the CEO of ZP was to be written by the ZP president. In fact, we were so upset by this recommendation, that we thought it fit to raise it in our meeting with the Chief Minister. In retrospect, it all looks very immature and somewhat childish. Chavan smiled, when we raised this, (that inscrutable smile which became his trademark) and said that after all, he was writing the CR of the Chief Secretary and that we might object to that also. The implication was very obvious. He thought that the status of the ZP president was that of the Chief Minister of the district and that of the CEO was that of the Chief Secretary of the district.

Asoka Mehta Committee had, after observing the working of PRIs in different states and analysing the increasing complexities of agricultural and rural development also endorsed the view that the district should be the first point of decentralisation. The committee said:

> "For planning, supervising and coordinating developmental programmes, administrative and technical competence of the requisite calibre is available at this level, and not at the lower, say, sub-divisional or Block level. Some states, like Gujarat and Maharashtra have demonstrated the soundness of their choice. Apart from Administrative Reforms Commission appointed by the Union Government, a number of committees appointed by the various State Governments in the sixties and the seventies have persuasively commended the Maharashtra-Gujarat model, which has

treated the District as the first point of decentralisation." (India 1978a:37).

Setting up of ZPs in Maharashtra

The recommendations of Naik Committee were accepted by the State Government and ZPs were set up in 1962. When these bodies started functioning there was a lot of expectation from them and speculation about the attitude of the State Government towards them. The scope and the power of the ZPs was in the minds of the officials of all departments. Despite Naik Committee's recommendation, the initial batch of CEOs of ZPs were not those who had finished an innings or two as Collectors; they were mostly those promoted for the first time to the Collector's rank. But for their being posted as the CEOs of ZPs, eyeing the Collector's post, they might not have got their promotion at all. The first presidents of the ZPs (whom Nehru described as the future State and Central ministers) were new to administration and most of them were tasting power for the first time, particularly power over bureaucracy. Not all of them used this power with maturity. The situation in most districts in Maharashtra and Gujarat in 1962 was that, on the one hand, there were the (mostly young) CEOs of ZPs, for whom a ZP, CEO-ship was "a waiting room" before they became Collectors. There are many reasons why posting in ZPs is not as popular among IAS officers, as District Collector's post. The major reason is the historical halo around the latter, and the power and influence wielded by the person. On the other, many presidents of the ZPs lacked maturity and did not know how to wield power. Maharashtra was fortunate to have had a mature and dedicated minister in Abasaheb Khedkar, who was sympathetic to both sides, and handled the delicate situation with grace, humour and aplomb.

The responsibility for planning for agricultural and rural development has been statutorily cast on the ZPs under the Maharashtra *Zilla Parishads* and *Panchayat Samitis* Act, 1962.[3] The Act has classified the State's developmental activities, into state sector activities, which were implemented directly by the departments of the State Government; and local sector activities, which were implemented by the ZPs. So the local sector/state sector distinction depends upon whether the implementation is done by the ZPs or by the State Government department concerned.

Attitude of the State and Central ministers and elected politicians towards ZPs

It was seen in the previous chapter that the pull away from the control of the BDO was discernible from the inception of the CDP. The pull was even stronger in Maharashtra after the formation of the ZPs, as political forces fortified the centripetal forces already existing, mostly due to the sector departments. Strong ZPs would naturally mean strong ZP presidents. In fact, in the early years of the ZPs in Maharashtra, the power and prestige of the ZP presidents were almost comparable to those of State ministers. The members of parliament (MP) and state legislatures did not conceal their unfriendly feelings towards the ZP presidents. The way to weaken them was to weaken ZPs. In this, they were assisted by State ministers, who preferred to deal directly with the district level bureaucracy rather than with politically powerful ZP presidents. Thus the political wind was against ZP presidents. The senior officials of the sector departments, were also averse to the inter-position of the relatively junior generalist administrator (CEO, ZP) between themselves and their district staff. The staff assigned to the ZPs were also not a happy lot. They resented what they felt to be "interference" in their work by the elected PRI politicians, but what the latter felt was their legitimate duty. The ZPs were thus caught between unhappy bureaucracies, both above and below. Thus the attitudes of officials of sector departments and ZPs, and of State ministers and MPs/MLAs/MLCs towards ZPs and ZP presidents, coincided.

Increase in State sector schemes in Maharashtra

Ever since the creation of ZPs, the question of which activities should be entrusted to the ZPs and which should remain with the State sector has been debated often and many committees were appointed by the State Government to look into this question. The earliest of these committees was the Shaikh Committee set up in 1965. This Committee was required to precisely define the role of PRIs in the field of agriculture and rural development. In particular the Committee was required to examine "the mechanics for bringing about effective coordination among various institutions and agencies dealing with complementary and inter-related aspects of agricultural programmes." (Maharashtra 1966). The Committee recommended the transfer of many schemes from the State sector to the local sector. No action was taken by the State Government on the recommendations of this report. The report on the Reorganisation of Maharashtra Administration known as the Heble Commission also said:

> "Certain technical departments of the government continue to have their own independent organisations, in respect of some schemes, right down to the village level, and this is sought to be justified on the grounds that these schemes require higher technical skills not available with the ZPs. The committee is not inclined to accept this argument. The tendency to create parallel state organisations down to the village level, if encouraged, will strike at the very root of democratic decentralisation."(Maharashtra 1971:202).

This was followed by Patil Committee (Maharashtra 1986). The Committee made some important recommendations, which included, distribution of functions of government amongst the Centre, State and District. Some of the recommendations, later on, formed part of the Constitutional amendments. The recommendation regarding upgrading some posts of BDOs to Class I, was perhaps the only recommendation of the committee, which was implemented by bureaucracy with alacrity. But despite the overwhelming arguments in favour of turning over more schemes to ZPs, the State Government departments succeeded in retaining with themselves, all new schemes started since the inception of the ZPs.

Notes

1. In 1960 the States of Maharashtra and Gujarat were formed; prior to 1960 they were part of the then Bombay State.
2. Gujarat *Panchayat* Act, 1961, which introduced democratic decentralisation in Gujarat was based on the recommendations of the Democratic Decentralisation Coommittee, set up by the Government of Gujarat and headed by Rasiklal Parikh, who was that time the Home Minister of Gujarat.
3. Maharashtra Act V of 1962.

CHAPTER 6

Intensive Agricultural Districts Programme and the Beginnings of Re-centralisation

It was observed earlier that ever since the start of the CDP, the sector departments–particularly the agriculture and irrigation departments–never got reconciled to their field staff being brought under the control of the BDO. When the country passed through food shortage, this hostility came to the surface. The real reason for the food shortage was not the administrative arrangement at the block level, but the absence of technology. When the dwarf varieties of wheat came (in mid-1960s) and the farm gate prices became attractive to producers, Indian farmers ushered in the Green Revolution.

An important landmark of the period from the late 1950s to the mid-1960s, when the Green Revolution took place, was the publication in April 1959 of the "Report on India's Food Crisis and Steps to Meet It" (India 1959a).[1] This report is by the Agricultural Production Team sponsored by the Ford Foundation, and popularly known as the "Ford Foundation Report".[2] At the time of the formulation of the Third Five Year Plan, the GOI appointed this team to study India's past attempts to increase agricultural production, and to make recommendations to overcome the identified bottlenecks. The team consisted of thirteen American agricultural scientists and twelve Indian counterparts. The programme which was launched in 1960-61, the last year of the Second Five Year Plan, as a result of the above report, was called the Intensive Agricultural Districts Programme or the "package programme". The Report had a wide spectrum; its recommendations ranged from farm prices to soil conservation, irrigation and drainage. Here, the focus is on the administrative arrangement for agricultural extension and rural development. The report of the team was an important landmark in the evolution of the strategy towards agricultural development.

Important recommendations of the Ford Foundation Team

First, the report sought to increase the awareness among the policy makers of the need for a substantially increased resource commitment for agriculture. The report said:

> "It is clear to us that food production increases at the rate required ....cannot be realised unless an all out emergency programme is undertaken, and adequate resources are made available". (India 1959a:13).

The report strongly suggested that agricultural production should be given the highest priority among all categories of development, for the remainder of the Second Plan and the entire Third Plan period. It greatly strengthened the hands of the Ministry of Agriculture in its demand for higher allocation of Plan resources. This increased awareness is reflected in the fact that in the Third Five Year Plan, the share of the Agriculture Sector was increased from 6.0 percent of the total outlay to 8.49 percent (India 1962:85).

Second, the report recommended an intensive and selective development strategy based on a combination ("package") of modern practices - improved seeds, chemical fertilisers and pesticides - in irrigated areas and other climatically well-endowed areas of the country. It may be recalled that concentration of efforts in favourable pockets in the country was in fact the strategy advocated in the Draft Outline of the First Plan, and practised in the pilot Community Development projects. This was given up later in favour of dispersion of developmental efforts. As in the Draft Outline of the First Plan, the argument of the Ford Foundation Report favoured a strategy of concentration based almost entirely on the need to maximise production goals. The report said that "immediate potential" for increase in wheat and rice production lay in certain districts with assured rainfall or irrigation facilities, and where farmers are anxious to apply new technological knowledge. These districts had shown appreciable increase in yields (India 1959a:56). Intensive Agricultural Districts Programme was initially implemented in a few selected districts with immediate production potential and was, in due course, taken up in 37 districts in 14 States, in three stages.

Third, the report strongly supported the CDP's reliance on extension, and recommended a closer relationship between agricultural research and extension at the State and Central levels. The report said:

> "Unless the block staff are adequately supported by a core of agricultural subject matter specialists ... who are continuously in touch with current research developments, the local staffs cannot be expected to carry on successful extension programmes to increase crop yields by modern farming methods" (India 1959a:42).

Fourth, the report recommended that the *gramsevaks* should be relieved of the vital service functions, particularly inputs and credit. Similar recommendations were given regarding the block team dealing with agriculture such as the Agricultural Extension Officer, and the Agricultural and Animal Husbandry Officers. These latter were expected to serve as the Subject Matter Specialists supporting the Block Staff.

Box 6.1: Green Revolution

Ford Foundation Report prepared the ground for the Green Revolution, which was basically the result of a political decision. In circa 1965 when Lyndon Johnson was the President of the U.S.A. and Mrs. Indira Gandhi was the Prime Minister of India, India was opposed to the American involvement in the Vietnam war. President Johnson said that, India, which could not feed itself, had no business to oppose American involvement in the Vietnam war. When told that India was not alone and that even mainland China was opposed to it, President Johnson is supposed to have said: "but the Chinese do not eat our wheat." (This incident was common knowledge and was recently re-iterated in the Television documentary called the "Dynasty" aired in the U.S.A. by the Corporation for Public Broadcasting). This remark made Mrs. Gandhi resolve that India had to be self-sufficient in food. She gave only one goal to her Agriculture Minister, C. Subramaniam, and the goal was to make the country self-sufficient in food. Fortunately, technology was available then, and thanks to Ford Foundation, the administrative apparatus was ready. The main contribution of the Ford Foundation team was to create an environment in which Green Revolution could take place. The rest, as they say, is history.

Fifth, the report emphasised organisational problems as much as technical ones. According to the report (India 1959a: 21), the organisation problem does not stop at the State level and that appropriate changes should also be made at the district, block and village levels.

The relationship between the SADs and the block team

The report was however, ambivalent about its view of the relationship between SADs and the block team. On the one hand, it devoted a whole section on 'block level'. It cnvisioncd SADs working through the BDO and recommended that the block staff should receive greater support from SAD. It said that the "the basic idea of a block team of a group of officers having special areas of responsibility and functioning under the leadership of the BDO is sound" (India 1959a:114). On the other hand, it said that far-reaching centralised authority with a clear line of command and execution alone could meet the challenge of growing more food. It recommended a simplified administrative structure and pleaded for "clear lines of authority and responsibility established at all levels of Government, so that policy decisions are carried out to the village level." (India 1959a:21). There are parts of the report which support the view that SADs keep out of the Block setup in the interests of accelerated food production. It explained:

> "how to apply intensive, specialised knowledge effectively to particular objectives, such as increased food production is a problem of organisation and administration. It is in this context that the concept of the VLW and the block staff need to be examined and alternative patterns of organisation explored" (India 1959a:115).

It recognised the hostility between administrative and technical personnel and said:

> "A complicating factor exists in the rigid lines and status distinction of Indian public service between administrative and technical services....But it would seem desirable to make careful studies of this problem and to experiment with alternate patterns of arrangement, perhaps on a pilot basis in a number of sample blocks" (India 1959a:127).

Perhaps the team did not want to take sides in the ongoing warfare between the Ministry of Community Development and Cooperation and the Ministry of Food and Agriculture. As it had to do the delicate balancing act between the two ministries, the report was ambivalent on the relationship between the BDO and SAD. Obviously, it did not categorically say (as is generally believed) that SADs should have their own staff right down to the village level, by-passing BDO, but that was what the SADs ended up having. Their breaking away from the Block setup was the thin end of the wedge. In due course, the other departments, broke off from the block setup under the BDO.

Ford Foundation team did not say anything which was not known to the GOI. It was known that: (i) the Second Plan emphasised heavy industries in the public sector at the expense of agriculture; (ii) a strategy of concentration was necessary to produce quick results; and (iii) the technical departments resented their field staff being brought under the administrative control of the BDO. But it required a foreign, supposedly neutral umpire, to arbitrate the dispute among warring ministries (in this case the Planning Commission, Ministry of Food and Agriculture, and Ministry of Community Development and Cooperation). International politics also played a role. It is now well known that the second plan was influenced by the then Soviet Union. There were people in the GOI, who were not terribly enamoured of the idea of too much focus on heavy industries in the public sector. Nehru was a democrat and listened to them. At his instance, Ford Foundation established an office in New Delhi in 1952.

The long term impact of the Ford Foundation Team's report

The Ford Foundation Report had long term impact on the institutional arrangements for agricultural and rural development in the country. The report led to a departure from reliance on multi-purpose *gramsevaks* to attend to agricultural development in addition to other aspects of rural development. In the districts selected under Intensive Agricultural Districts Programme, special staff positions were created, in addition to the existing ones, for exclusive attention to agricultural development, and these were under the direct control of the SADs. The new staff created a parallel bureaucracy in the district, one of the earliest "parallel" structures, described in Chapter 11 which are not accountable to the BDO. This was the beginning of the view that agricultural extension should be made more professional and should not be entrusted exclusively to generalist multipurpose *gramsevaks.* It emphasised a much more direct involvement of SADs in agricultural development programmes, particularly agricultural extension. It anticipated the Training and Visit extension, which the country embraced in the 1970s and 1980s.

Box 6.2: Meeting to discuss the agricultural production in Maharashtra

The author participated in a meeting convened by the Chief Minister of Maharashtra in June 1973. The subject of the meeting was "Ways to increase agricultural production in the State." It was pointed out that Maharashtra achieved its highest foodgrain production in the 1960s, in 1960, and since then, even though the Agriculture Department bureaucracy has expanded, it has not had any impact on foodgrain production. The Director of Agriculture, who was present at the meeting, said that his department was asked to "fight the battle without resources." He expanded the statement to mean that the department had no control over *gramsevaks* who were with the BDO. This is an example of the feelings of the line departments towards the BDO setup.

Awareness of the need for professionalism in agriculture

The emphasis in the CDP was on an integrated delivery of services to the farmers through the *gramsevak* and on bringing the block level functionaries of the different development departments, both production and human development, under the administrative control of the BDO. The need for integration was reinforced by the Balwantray Mehta Team's report and the process of democratic decentralisation which followed it. The strong pull exerted by the line departments away from integration had already gained momentum during the Second Plan, and the Third Evaluation Report on the Community Development Programme had noted that the dual control of specialists concerned with different subjects at the block level, by the BDO and by technical officers at the district level, was not working satisfactorily. In many cases, departmental officers, instead of looking upon extension or community project as their own agency, tended to concentrate in other areas where they had more direct control over their specialist staffs. The Ford Foundation Report, launching of the Intensive Agricultural Districts Programme and the importance attached by the mood of the times to the creation of 'a professional cadre' of extension workers solely for agricultural development, added to this momentum. It was seen in Chapter 2 in the context of coordination that the history of rural development effort, is also the history of attempts to devise a suitable administrative setup which would ensure a coordinated working of the line departments connected with the different aspects of agricultural and rural development.

The growth of Training and Visit extension

It was felt that technocratic agriculture called for the introduction of professionalism in agricultural extension. The multi-purpose *gramsevak* was replaced by the agricultural assistant in T&V. What really clinched the issue in favour of taking agricultural extension from the VLW was the fact that (s)he was not devoting sufficient time for agriculture. (S)He was spending too much of time in fortnightly meetings at block headquarters, and in distributing supplies. Even the extension officers posted in the BDO's office seldom visited villages. This tendency was commented upon by the Ford Foundation Report, which said that general resolutions to the effect that VLWs are to devote 70 to 80 percent of their time to agriculture, for example, cannot be effective unless and until time allocations and programme emphasis at all levels above the VLW are similarly changed (India 1959a:21). It was not realistic to expect the VLW to focus on agriculture if the targets given to the BDO are different; the BDO and along with that person, the VLW, march to the beat of the drummer.

Box 6.3 : Line Departments as parallel structures

Decentralisation achieved by line departments is at best only administrative decentralisation and is more appropriately called deconcentration. There are two views regarding direct implementation of programmes by the line departments concerned, through their own field staff, by-passing PRIs. These views have been aired since CDP days, and they came into sharper focus after the Ford Foundation Report.

The *first view* is that, the best way to implement any agriculture and rural development programme, is to implement it through the line departments concerned, without the intermediary of an organisation like PRIs at the district level or below. This would imply, that every sector department must bring about "deconcentration" of its activities. Inter-departmental field coordination can be taken care of by the end-users (clients) themselves. In order to reduce the problems of coordination, every department will have a management system, which involves frequent and regular contact with the beneficiaries, and making bureaucracy at various levels accountable to them. Problems of coordination cannot be totally eliminated, but requiring every line department to have a transparent management system would tend to reduce them. No bureaucratic coordinating mechanism at the district level or below is likely to succeed in tackling individual cases.

The *second view* is, to my mind, more realistic and is based on empirical observations on the behaviour of government bureaucracies. Government bureaucracies in India do not care for the beneficiaries. They exemplify the eternal truth of the statement of the Bard: "insolence of office" (Hamlet, III, 3, 73). They have to be placed under the control of elected people, and the closer these elected people are to beneficiaries, the better will be their position to deal with individual cases. They would act as the needed pull factor, to make the line departments coordinate with each other. The elected representatives act on behalf of beneficiaries. We have already commented that herein lies the rationale for decentralisation. In the former case, we are talking of "deconcentration" and in the latter case, of "devolution". In one case, the functionaries remain within their own line departments, and in the other, they come under an elected body at the local level. Deconcentration without devolution would not work, because there will then be no accountability to elected persons at the local level. Therefore, in democratic decentralisation, the second view is more convincing.

extension (see Box 2.2) are:[3] (i) the staff deal only with extension work, and are organised to provide a unified extension service to farmers, that is the same extension agent providing extension advice to farmers on crops, animal husbandry and fisheries, with a single line of command, under the SAD, and (ii) the system is designed to transfer technology from the research stations to farmers. T&V was mainly responsible for the SADs having their own chain of command from the State Directors of Agriculture till the extension agent in the field, by-passing BDO, (a fact noted earlier), and later on, PRIs. The local extension staff are accountable only to the departmental specialists above them and not to local elected representatives. The agricultural extension programmes were followed by a number of Centrally sponsored programmes in health and education.

Box 6.4: VLW and T&V

While inaugurating a seminar on "Reorganisation of Agricultural Extension" at Hyderabad in July 1978, the Union Minister of State for Agriculture and Irrigation remarked: "The village level extension worker is reported to be a multi-purpose worker with maximum emphasis on agricultural extension. It is however well-known that he is used on all kinds of miscellaneous duties and very little time is being devoted to agriculture. Though circulars have been issued that he should devote 80 percent of his time for agriculture, I doubt very much whether he spends even 50 percent of his time on productive programmes, leave aside agriculture". (*Quoted in Rural Development Digest, Vol I, No. 4, Oct. 1978, p.273)*

Introduction of the T&V was seen by senior officers, who were mostly generalists, as a successful attempt by the SADs to break off from the integrated administrative setup under BDO. It is important to appreciate the deep ideological commitment of the GOI and many of its finest officers to the CDP, which is still seen by many as the hallmark of India's strategy for rural development. Most of the officers in the Centre and States, who held senior positions when T&V was introduced, were, at the beginning of their careers, directly involved in the implementation of the CDP. The main feature of the CDP, namely, all rural development activities being integrated through a single point of contact between the government and the people, remained deeply imbedded in the thinking of many of these officers. They did not like the new developments. T&V also did not live up to its reputation. The system was expected to ensure more effective utilisation of the existing staff, with only marginal additions. But recruitment of a large number of staff became necessary in many States, with attendant delays. More importantly, sudden transition from multi-purpose extension, with no linkage with research, no regularity of visit and practically no training at all, to a highly structured system, involving close field supervision, required orientation of extension personnel, found many of them unable to adjust to the rigours and discipline of the new system. The new system was field-oriented and required a new outlook. In several States, the extension staff continued to be burdened with heavy paper work and non-extension duties, because of a number of subsidy-oriented schemes, many of them CSS, involving subsidies to individual farmers. These drawbacks of the operation of the system, made it very unpopular among the senior officers. Instead of trying to fix the implementation drawbacks, there was a tendency to blame the system for many of the ills of agricultural development administration.

Present role of the BDO

The block setup under the BDO still continues to function, and is occupied mainly, with the implementation of Centrally sponsored anti-poverty schemes (social safety net programmes) and in the administration of Constitutional amendments. There has been a clear separation of the production aspects of rural development from its social aspects.

Box 6.5: GOI's Anti-Poverty Programmes

Since the publication of Poverty in India by Dandekar and Rath in 1971, there have been many attempts in India to (i) define poverty and (ii) measure poverty. These have been summarised in NIRD (1999:7-27). Those identified as below the poverty line in the survey conducted in 1997 are eligible for benefits under the GOI's anti-poverty programmes (which are the same as the poverty alleviation programmes). Since April 1, 1999, these programmes, which had been specifically designed as "safety net" programmes, have been lumped under JGSY and SGSY, wage employment and self employment programmes, respectively.

The objectives of JGSY are similar to those of the CDP, namely to use the rural manpower for the development of rural infrastructure. The major difference between the two is that in JGSY wage employment is given only to the identified rural poor families.(India 1999a: 1 paragraph 2(ii)). According to the above "Guidelines", JGSY contains an individual beneficiary component, that is, for the benefit of individual families. This component is available only for SC/ST, and 22.5 per cent of the annual allocation under the programme is earmarked for this component. The primary objective of JGSY is the creation of 'demand driven' community village infrastructure, including durable assets at the village level, with a view to enabling the rural poor to have more opportunities for sustained employment. The secondary objective is generation of wage employment for the unemployed poor in rural areas. (India 2000:27-28).

SGSY has been formed by amalgamating various individual beneficiary programmes which evolved over the past twenty years. (India 2000:40). It is described as a holistic programme covering all aspects of self-employment such as organisation of the poor into self-help groups, training and credit. The objective of the programme is to bring the assisted poor families above the poverty line in three years. Details of the programme are given in India 1999b and India 2000. Both JGSY and SGSY constitute the GOI's poverty alleviation programmes.

Developments of the 1970s: beginnings of re-centralisation and the decline of PRIs

Three major factors were responsible for reversing the trend of decentralisation which began in the First Plan and continued till the mid-1960s.

Indira Gandhi

The first factor was the political development. Jawaharlal Nehru believed in the development of rural institutions and decentralisation, but not so his daughter Indira Gandhi. In mid-1960s, she was consolidating her political power, and it suited her to reverse the pattern of decentralisation and introduce centralisation.[4] She did not believe in the institutions, in which her father Jawaharlal Nehru had great faith, such as the Judiciary and the Legislature. She used the Parliament to provide legitimacy to her personal rule as she had the charisma and people

Box 6.6: Institution and organisation

> A distinction is often made between an institution and an organisation. The issue is discussed in Binswanger and Ruttan 1978. Some examples will illustrate this distinction. Government is an institution; it has its own rules and adherence to rules assumes over-arching importance, even if it means its getting an image of not caring for the client. Individual public sector bodies are organisations. Marriage is an institution; individual marriages are examples of organisations. Judiciary is an institution and individual courts are organisations. CDP is a good example of institutional development; individual projects in the various states are examples of organisations. To quote from Binswanger and Ruttan: "Institutions are stable, valued, and possess recurring patterns of behaviour. Organisations and procedures vary in their degree of institutionalisation….. Institutionalisation is the process by which organisations and procedures acquire value and stability" (Binswanger and Ruttan 1978:328).

supported her. They voted for *her*, and not for *her party candidate*. She became an icon, and did not believe in sharing power with politicians. As a result MPs and MLAs held office at her pleasure, and they knew that. Such a situation had not existed at the national level before she came to power and has never existed since then. This has been described as "plebiscitory" politics, where personal charisma catches the votes and democracy suffers casualty. In fact, she played a major role in transferring some subjects from the "State" list[5] to the "Concurrent" list[6] in the Constitution. State politicians (particularly of the ruling party) increasingly spent more time in Delhi than in their own constituencies. State level ministers (learning from the Delhi example) did not want to share power with district level politicians; in Maharashtra (as we saw earlier) some of them were jealous of the growing power and influence of the ZP presidents. They preferred to "rule" through bureaucracy. The result was that very few politicians looked "below" at the electorate and they were all the time looking "up" towards Mumbai or Delhi.

Bureaucracy

The second factor responsible for reversing the process of decentralisation was bureaucracy. Bureaucrats would seek every opportunity to increase their power and importance. At the Central level, this translated into having a number of CSS in areas which were predominantly State subjects. At State level, this tendency of leaning heavily on bureaucrats, rather than on elected politicians at the district level and below, translated into having a number of programmes planned and implemented directly from the State secretariat, by-passing locally elected bodies. In Maharashtra, these were called State sector schemes, and ZPs increasingly came to be mere agencies to implement programmes finalised at the State level, mostly by officials. There were of course many other reasons why CD movement petered out, but the combination of the political and bureaucratic forces were the main ones.

International organisations

The third factor was the role of international organisations, particularly the World Bank. In the 1970s, the experiments of the World Bank as related to rural development and poverty described in Chapter 2, represented administrative decentralisation. When these, on the Bank's own admission, failed, it turned towards national programmes, implemented by line departments, thereby by-passing BDOs. This resulted in the emergence of the so-called "parallel structures". T&V was the earliest such programme, and it was soon followed by other national programmes. During the 1970s, three powerful forces which matter in any country, namely, political development, bureaucracy and international opinion, joined together and exerted the pull towards increased centralisation, the nascent 'decentralisation' framework became a casualty.

Notes

1. The original report was published by the GOI in April 1959. It was reprinted by Arno Press in 1976 and published in the U.S.A.
2. A detailed account of the run-up to this report and its effects are given in Taylor *et al* 1965:245-260.
3. For a discussion of the T&V system of extension see Venkatesan and Kampen (1998) and Dandekar and Wadia (1989).
4. For political developments during this period see Brass 1994, Hart 1976, Kohli 1990, Jha 1980.
5. The term "State List" was explained in Chapter 1. See also Chapter 10.
6. Item no. 25 in the Concurrent list of the Constitution of India, relating to education, is one such example.

CHAPTER 7

The Revival of the Panchayat Raj Institutions in the Late 1970s and 1980s

The pull towards centralisation which was seen in the late 1960s and the first half of 1970s coincided with the rise and fall of Indira Gandhi as a major political force in electoral politics. India passed through a period of emergency between 1975 and 1977, when fundamental rights guaranteed by the Constitution were suspended. After the end of emergency, Morarji Desai's government was installed at the Centre in 1977. This government was in favour of decentralisation. This chapter describes the efforts made by the Centre during this period to introduce decentralisation and the successful decentralisation experiments in West Bengal and Karnataka.

Asoka Mehta Committee on Panchayati Raj Institutions

After the promise of the CDP, and the encouraging note of the Balwantray Mehta Committee's report, the history of PRIs in India is one of gradual decline. We saw the reasons for this in the previous chapter. In 1977, after Morarji Desai's government came to power at the Centre, there was a revival of interest in PRIs. In order to reverse the process of centralisation of Indira Gandhi's era, the new government appointed "a high powered committee under the chairmanship of Asoka Mehta" (India 1978d: 6). The Committee was "to review the existing situation regarding democratic decentralisation in the States and the Union Territories (UT), and the working of PRIs from district to village levels so as to identify shortcomings and defects" (*ibid*: 6). The Committee submitted its report in August 1978. After surveying the performance of PRIs in many States the committee observed:

> "The story of *Panchayati Raj* has been a story of ups and downs. It seems to have passed through three phases: (a) the phase of ascendancy, 1959-1964; (b) phase of stagnation,

> 1965-1969; (c) the phase of decline, 1969-1977" (India 1978a: 3).

On the role of bureaucracy in the decline of PRIs, the Committee observed that, "Bureaucracy had probably its own role in dissociating the PRIs from the development process" (*ibid:* 3). The Committee bemoaned the fact that only "minuscule programmes... were assigned to Village Panchayats ... the few items of work which were part and parcel of the CDP were handed over to the newly elected PRIs" (*ibid*: 4).

Recommendations of Asoka Mehta Committee

The Committee recommended a two-tier structure, comprising ZP at the district level, and Mandal Panchayat[1] for a group of villages, with a population of 20,000-30,000, (Meenakshi-sundaram 1994:61) below the block level, the ZP being the key level. It also recommended that district should be the first point of democratic decentralisation (as in Maharashtra), and favoured official recognition of the participation of political parties in all panchayat elections.

The Committee was aware that the main problem with most PRIs, is the absence of funds that they could call their "own" to be spent on development programmes which their electorate want. What they want is "untied" funds; what they get is mostly funds that are tied to specific schemes. The report of the committee had this to say on the role of "tied" funds in hamstringing PRI:

> "Entrustment of developmental responsibilities to *Panchayati Raj* institutions in general, and ZP in particular, would remain an exercise in administrative decentralisation or may remain only partial decentralisation unless the authority for deciding what they execute is vested with them. Hence the second function to be decentralised to the district level should be planning." (India 1978a:61)

There is a lot of argument as to whether the Committee erred in recommending a uniform pattern to be followed by all States. The important point is not so much whether the first point of decentralisation is district level or block level, or whether there should be a uniform pattern throughout the country, as whether the Centre and States are keen on enabling

PRIs to function in the manner which the people want. Arguments such as the ones that have been mentioned above, are likely to deflect the attention of the policy makers from the main issue, which is to give to PRIs funds which are not "tied" to specific schemes.

The Report of Asoka Mehta Committee was discussed at the Conference of Chief Ministers on May 19-20, 1979. The Chief Ministers agreed to delegate more financial and administrative powers to PRIs, so that the latter could function as effective instruments of development. The Conference did not accept the recommendations of the Committee regarding Constitutional amendments for delegating more powers from States to *panchayats* and said that the State legislatures would take appropriate action in the matter. The Conference decided to set up a committee of Chief Ministers to frame guidelines for a model legislation for the purpose. But no tangible results followed. Ironically, after 1977, the decline of PRIs in most states was even more rapid. In this rather gloomy background two States stood out, namely, West Bengal and Karnataka. The developments in these two States are discussed below.

Other committees

Observers of the decentralisation scene in India are aware of the Balwantray Mehta Committee and Asoka Mehta Committee, as these are landmarks. There were other committees also during the 1980s notably *Hanumantha Rao Committee on District Planning* (India 1984) and *G.V.K. Rao Committee to review the existing administrative arrangements for rural development and poverty alleviation programmes* (India 1985). These committees echoed the sentiments of Asoka Mehta, lamented the fact that PRIs have been rendered ineffective, and recommended that they should be strengthened. The former concluded that for decentralised planning to make headway, institutional mechanisms had to be made more broad-based with active involvement of local representatives and that "PRIs and other local government institutions should play a crucial role in the district planning process" (India 1984, Vol I: 1). The latter said:

> "The States have been generally lukewarm to the process of democratic decentralisation. In most states the Panchayat

Raj bodies have been allowed to languish without powers and resources. ... The inevitable need to transfer power of the State to democratic bodies at the local level has to be recognised...." (India 1985:44).

West Bengal [2]

The West Bengal Panchayat Act, 1973 provided for a three tier system consisting of GP, PS and ZP (at District level). *Gram Panchayats,* at village level had between 5 to 25 members who were directly elected. No constituencies were reserved for SC/ST (see Glossary) or women; but the State Government, on the recommendation of the GP, had the power of nomination of the members of the SC/ST or women, upto two in each category. The structure, functions and the key features in West Bengal are shown in Annex 1. The Act of 1973 remained on paper till the Left Front Government (LFG) came to power in the State in 1977. In 1978, elections to all three tiers were held, on party basis; the LFG had agreed with the Asoka Mehta Committee's recommendation that the participation of political parties at elections to all levels of PRI should be allowed. This, in practice meant that the candidates could use the party symbols while contesting elections. The State Government, however, decided to continue the three tier structure as against the two-tier structure proposed by the Asoka Mehta Committee. West Bengal was a pioneer in introducing direct elections to all the three tiers of PRIs, as according to the State Government, this would make the representatives of elected bodies directly responsible to people. It was the first state to activate PRIs and introduce decentralisation following the Asoka Mehta Committee report. Since then it has been one of the two (the other has been Gujarat) states to have conducted panchayat elections every five years without fail. Some organisational changes were brought about as a consequence; perhaps the most significant is making BDO, the executive officer of the PS, and stipulating that he report to the chairman of the PS. The political will to increase the prestige of PRIs in West Bengal is obvious.

Flood of 1978

It was a chance event that determined the path which West Bengal's panchayats were to follow in the years to come. Immediately after the first panchayat elections of 1978, West Bengal experienced a devastating flood driving a large number of people to destitution. The State Government entrusted the newly elected PRIs, with the task of providing relief and executing various reconstruction schemes. PRIs performed the job so creditably that the usefulness and potentiality of this institution became clear to the ruling parties. Thereafter, the State Government started giving more and more responsibility to *panchayats*, beginning with the implementation of the rural work programmes of the GOI, such as the National Rural Employment Programme (NREP), and the Rural Landless Employment Guarantee Programme (RLEGP). Very soon PRIs became an indispensable part of the State's delivery system. They were involved in most target group-oriented schemes and any scheme which required mass mobilisation of the rural people.

Operation 'Barga'

At this time, along with the institutionalisation of panchayats, West Bengal undertook a major programme of land reform. Distribution of "ceiling surplus" lands which were vested in the government, and registration of sharecroppers (known as "operation *barga*") were the two main thrusts of the programme. Though the programme was implemented by the bureaucracy, the *panchayats* did give their input, particularly in the matter of distribution of vested lands. Under "operation *barga*", till Sep. 1998, 14.86 *lakh* sharecroppers obtained security of tenure. Small and marginal farmers had come to own nearly 70 percent of the total agricultural land. West Bengal achieved a remarkable growth of 4.3 percent in agricultural production between 1980-81 and 1997-98 one of the highest among States.

PRIs stike roots

By 1983, when the first term of the new panchayats was over, the system had struck firm roots. Holding of regular panchayat elections helped substantially in this process. But still, panchayats were essentially discharging 'agency functions', that is, implementing certain specific schemes of the GOI and the State Government. This problem was solved in two steps: first, giving PRIs planning functions as envisioned under Articles 243G and 243ZD of the Constitution, and second, to give them "untied" funds. The State Government recognised that introducing integrated administration ensuring "convergence" as in the BDO setup, is a pre-condition for entrusting planning functions to PRIs. This was done in 1985-86, when DPCs, and Block Planning Committees (BPC) were formed. Both these were headed by chairpersons of the *panchayats* at the respective levels. Budget provisions of line departments for the district concerned were given to the DPC. Similar exercises were done regarding BPCs and municipalities. Within the budget envelope, PRIs were given authority to prepare plans.

In addition to the above, a corpus of "untied" funds was being given to DPCs to help them bridge the critical gap between the availability of departmental funds and the needs of the schemes having a high priority in the judgement of the planning committees. For example, if a particular small irrigation scheme costing Rs. 15 lakhs was considered very important and if the department provided only Rs. 10 lakhs, then the balance could be met from "untied" funds. The "untied" funds came under a new head in the State budget, called "the DPC fund". The decentralisation of planning functions and the provision of "untied" funds to PRIs were important steps, but these did not last long. With the financial crunch which the State started facing from the early 1990s, the source of "untied" funds dried up. In due course, DPCs and BPCs lost interest in the exercise and planning became routine and ritualistic as the PRIs had no resources.

The State Finance Commission (SFC) of West Bengal tried to collect data regarding the funds from all departments of the State which flowed to districts on account of district schemes, to find out what proportions of total plan expenditures were spent in the various districts. The information they got was incomplete and did not meet their requirements. But the Chief Minister and the Finance Minister orally told the Commission that about one half of the plan budget is being spent for the districts, but this was not reflected in any document of the State Government. The Commission in their report of 1995 recommended reversal of the process of "departmentalism" and pleaded for devolution of powers to PRIs. Their suggestion was to be implemented in two steps: first, to transfer all departmental schemes back to DPCs as before, and second, to give "untied" funds to all the three tiers of panchayats by diverting 16 percent of the net revenue receipts of the State to PRIs. For several years, the State Government did not implement the recommendations of the SFC. However, since 1999, things have changed. In that year, the State Government decided that funds of all district schemes[3] of the line departments would be transferred to the appropriate level of PRIs. The process started in that year is still continuing. In 2000-01, the State Government has allocated Rs 100 crores in "untied" form, to the DPC fund. The DPC fund has been allocated between the three tiers of PRIs in the following manner: ZPs 30 per cent, all PSs together 20 per cent, all GPs together 50 per cent. A fresh attempt is now being made to decentralise planning functions and ensure proper "convergence" of development programmes of line departments through PRIs and Municipalities.

Impact of decentralisation in West Bengal

One of the advantages of decentralisation in West Bengal has been the growth of small savings collection. The State Governments can borrow from the GOI up to 75 percent of the net collection of small savings in the State in a year. So it is in the interest of the State to increase the small savings collection. The net collection of small savings increased from Rs. 190 *crores*[4] in 1980-81 to some Rs. 5000 *crores* in 1999-2000. The main reason for such a sharp increase was the involvement of the elected representatives of panchayats and municipalities with small savings collections.

A survey was undertaken in 1995 (Kumar and Ghosh 1996) to ascertain the reaction of the people to decentralisation in West Bengal. The survey revealed that an overwhelming proportion of people (about 90 percent) felt that panchayat as an institution was useful and people would suffer if the institution were to be abolished. It is difficult therefore to agree with the observation of James Manor that "decentralisation should not be expected to generate significant social change" (Manor 1999b:73). The observation of Meenakshisundaram is also reminiscent of James

Manor: "...notwithstanding the unwillingness of the state-level politicians to part with their power, even the people themselves were not sufficiently educated to understand the political implications of the PRIs. If the challenge from the grassroot level was effective, probably the PRIs would have put up a better show." (Meenakshisundaram 1994:60). It is not a question of whether people are educated or not but whether a programme which the people want, is entrusted to PRIs or not. Operation *barga* was undoubtedly a programme which was what people of the State felt that they needed. It has been observed that in the 1989 panchayat elections in West Bengal, a lot of people belonging to the landless and deprived sections of society were elected to PRIs (Dasgupta 1989:91). As a contrast in Karnataka, which was one of the states where *panchayati raj* was revived in 1983 after the report of the Asoka Mehta Committee, a study on the social background of the ZP presidents came to the conclusion that caste composition of the local government leadership does not seem to have significantly changed (Ray and Kumpatla 1987).

Lesson of West Bengal

The lesson which the West Bengal example demonstrates is that if PRIs have to take roots and be vibrant, they will have to gain credibility with the people. In order to earn such a credibility they have to deliver to people what they (the people) want. People of West Bengal wanted land reforms and the State Government let PRIs play a leading role in their implementation, thereby giving them an opportunity to deliver to the people what they (the people) most wanted. Land reforms and *panchayats* supported each other.

> "The uniqueness of the West Bengal panchayat system lies in the fact that it has brought into focus the issue of land reform in the context of *panchayati raj*, so that the *panchayat* institutions do not turn out to be hunting grounds of rural elite. Accordingly, it has been claimed by the Left Front government that land reform is inseparable from democratic decentralisation and the two together are the "two legs" of the rural development programme in the state". (ital. added). (Kumar and Ghosh 1996:5).

But land reforms were not followed by other programmes which PRIs could also deliver. The needs of the people vary from one village to another; in one village, the topmost priority could be drinking water while in another village it could be a bridge. Under the present arrangements for financing PRIs they cannot respond to the varying needs of the people. An evaluation survey conducted by the West Bengal government says:

> "The innovative spirit of the early years (1978-1983) is hardly to be seen. The panchayats have become overly engrossed in routine work. Wherever we went and whichever Panchayat level we met, we were only told of activities undertaken under the JRY[5].... So pervasive is the JRY-fixation that in the event of the scheme being withdrawn, the panchayats would have little to do and may have to fold up. That at least is the view expressed by some of the panchayats we met" (West Bengal 1993:4).

We have to wait and watch the vicissitudes of the recent trend in West Bengal towards installing political decentralisation.

Karnataka

After the formation of the State of Karnataka,[6] a uniform legislation was made. The resultant Karnataka Village Panchayats and Local Boards Act, 1959, set up PRIs at the village, block and district levels. Chairpersons of GP and PS were indirectly elected, but the District Collector, who, in Karnataka called is the Deputy Commissioner, was the *ex-officio* president of the District Development Council (DDC). DDC which is a district level PRI was merely a coordinating and supervising body. Plan/non-Plan schemes were not transferred to these elected bodies; they were merely implementing bodies and not entrusted with plan formulation.

Asoka Mehta Committee report started an active political debate on the transfer of power from State Governments to *panchayats*, and the West Bengal example intensified it. Parties opposed to the Congress, such as the Left Front in West Bengal or the Janata Party in Karnataka (in the mid-1980s), prided themselves on their determination to strengthen PRIs. It was not therefore surprising that one of the first things which

Ramkrishna Hegde (as the Chief Minister) did, when the Janata Party was voted to power in Karnataka in 1983, was to introduce a legislation which sought to revive PRIs in the State.[7] The resultant Karnataka *Zilla Parishads*, *Taluka Panchayat Samitis*, *Mandal Panchayats and Nyaya Panchayats* Act, 1983 received Presidential assent on July 10, 1985.

Karnataka Act of 1983

The Karnataka Act of 1983 closely followed Asoka Mehta. It provided for only two elected tiers of decentralisation: the Mandal and the District. The framework of this new legislation resembles that of West Bengal, Maharashtra and Gujarat. Annex 1 gives the salient features of the structure of the Acts. There were some features of the Karnataka arrangement which carried the process of democratic decentralisation much farther than any other State, such as:

- The provision that no administrator could overrule a democratically elected body,
- Conferring on the ZP president the status and authority of State Government Minister, and on the deputy president, those of the deputy minister, and,
- The insistence that all development departments of the State Government in a district were directly responsible to the ZP concerned.

But though the working of this model was not tested in the field for a sufficiently long time, it held greater promise than many others.

Under the 1983 Act, for the first time in the history of *panchayati raj*, the State Government divested substantial powers and functions in favour of sub-state democratic institutions. Almost all State level schemes were transferred to ZPs. *Gram Sabhas* had the responsibility for identifying beneficiaries under the beneficiary-oriented schemes. As far as local governance and planning were concerned, the 1983 Act provided genuine centres of decentralised units. The merits of decentralisation could well be seen in the structure and functioning of DDC and Mandal Panchayats, which are described in Annex 1. An evaluation of the decentralisation undertaken by the GOK said:

"despite ..... limitations, the actual achievements of ZPs and *Mandal Panchayats* are impressive. Virtually in all districts, the operation by schools and health facilities has improved vastly. ...there has been significant progress in the area of medical and public health facilities, the supply of drugs and medicines made regularly and in accordance with local requirements" (Naidu and Naidu 1999:184).

Fall of the Hegde government

With the fall of the Hegde government the process of withdrawal of powers and functions from PRIs began, with the bureaucrats in State secretariat, enthusiastically obeying their new political masters and tearing down the edifice erected by the previous government. Administrators for DDCs were appointed in 1992. As a result, DDCs ceased to have any role in the sectors of agriculture, horticulture, and public distribution. The share of the district plan in the State plan went down. The behaviour of the departments have given rise to some comments. Typical of them is: "This tendency had been encouraged by a part of bureaucracy, specially in the technical departments which had not fully reconciled to working under local political masters" (Naidu and Naidu 1999:187).

Recent changes

Every State legislature had to pass laws to bring their existing laws in conformity with the constitutional provisions. Such laws are collectively called 'conformity legislation.' Karnataka too passed a similar law. The resultant Karnataka Panchayati Raj Act, 1993, came into effect on May 10, 1993. There have been many changes to the Act in 1997. These changes have curtailed the power of bureaucracy over elected institutions. They have also made explicit in the preamble that one of the objectives of the Act was to enable panchayats "to function as units of local self-government." A hierarchical relationship was established between the three tiers, namely the GP, the *Taluka Panchayat* (TP), and the ZP. *Zilla Parishads* have been given the responsibility to enquire into complaints regarding non-performance of duty by TPs and so on. For more details see Mathew 2000:137-144.

District Rural Development Agency (DRDA)

In mid-1970s, the GOI asked the States to set up a society in every district under the chairmanship of the District Collector for implementing the special programmes[8] for rural development which were started at various times in the past, such as the Small Farmers Development Agency (SFDA), Scheme for Marginal Farmers and Agricultural Labourers (MFAL), DPAP and Integrated Rural Development Programme which were all Centrally sponsored.[9] There were several reasons for this suggestion by the Centre. The main reason is to merge the various schemes for rural development and give them to one body for implementation. The reason for having the society format, was the Centre's justified concern that the States might use the Central funds meant for these special programmes, to finance their own "ways and means", as almost every State Government had a resource crunch and was eyeing whatever money comes from the Centre. If at the district level, there is a society such as the DRDA, the Centre can pass moneys directly to the society, by-passing the State Government. There was also another reason for this arrangement, which was to transfer money to the district in a "non-lapseable" fashion. This is the "GOI lingo" for transferring money to a body corporate, such as the DRDA, so that it will not be a part of the consolidated fund of the Centre or the States under Article 266 of the Constitution of India. The money transferred to the DRDA will not lapse at the end of the financial year.[10] So the transferring ministry can "book" its budget, and need not include the moneys so transferred when it prepares the following year's budget.

DRDSs (DRDS is the name for DRDA in Karnataka) were established in all districts in Karnataka by March 1979. Recently DRDS was merged with DDC. The main fall-out of this decision was that a bureaucrat (such as the District Collector) was no longer in charge of programmes affecting the people, but an elected person. DDC was responsible for implementing all the special programmes such as the SFDA, the NREP and the Integrated Rural Development Programme.

Annex 1 shows the situation under the Maharashtra, Karnataka and West Bengal Acts and the Constitutional provisions. The annex is selective and illustrative. The author is aware that the time frames are different but they are given here for comparison. For details of the latest situation in each State see Mathew (2000).

Notes

1. Mandal is below the Block level. The revenue administration equivalent of a "Mandal" was known as a "Firka" in the old Madras Presidency; this latter term was explained in Chapter 3.
2. This section is based on Kumar and Ghosh (1996), Choudhury and Jain (1999), Ghosh (2000a), Ghosh (2000b).
3. "District schemes" or what is the same, "District level schemes" and "State level schemes" are explained in Chapter 9.
4. A crore is 10 million. At the current exchange rate which is approximately 1 US $=Rs. 46.00 this would be US $ 874 million.
5. JRY is now part of JGSY (see Box 10.1).
6. The State of Karnataka was formed by merging the Kannada-speaking districts of the former Madras and Bombay Presidencies and some princely states, importantly, Hyderabad and Mysore.
7. Developments during this period in Karnataka are described in Meenakshisundaram 1994, and Kurian 1999. The political angle of the strengthening of the PRIs is described in Slater 1989.
8. There were separate societies for SFDA and MFAL; in some states there was also a society for DPAP.
9. The several special programmes started by the GOI are summarised in NIRD 1999:99-117.
10. It is a common practice in all bureaucracies to transfer funds to a corporate body just before the end of the financial year. I understand that the Finance Ministry has, rather belatedly, woken up to this practice.

CHAPTER 8

73rd and 74th Constitutional Amendments

There have been many references earlier in this book to these amendments and the reader is probably familiar with them. After the Asoka Mehta Committee report and the brief glory which they enjoyed in the late 1970s and the early 1980s there have been no significant developments regarding rural institutions until the above amendments in 1993. These amendments give considerable freedom to State legislatures and many of them have used this freedom to have legislation against the spirit of the Constitution. There are many books and papers[1] which describe them, and it is not intended that this chapter should include recent and easily available material. The comments of this chapter are confined to the adequacy of these amendments and on the extent of fiscal decentralisation in practice. At appropriate places, the Constitutional provisions are described.

Gram Sabha

The basic tier is the *Gram Sabha*. According to Article 243 (b) this consists of all persons registered as voters in the electoral roll relating to the village concerned. Article 243 (g) defines a "village" as the one "specified by the Governor by public notification to be a village" for the purposes of the Constitution and "includes a group of villages so specified." The Constitution makers have not specified how often the GS should meet and what should be reserved for decision by the GS. The Constitution should have specified how often the GS should meet and on what matters the GP can take decisions. Article 243A leaves this to States. Many States have chosen to give to the GS only an advisory role; their decisions are not binding on the GP. But the scheme of the Constitution is, administration through representative democracy, and giving more powers to GS will make it impossible for GP to function; at the same time giving too little powers to the GS will make a mockery of the concept of the GS. The skill of the legislature lies in finding a balance between the two opposites.

Madhya Pradesh

Madhya Pradesh has reportedly given to GS, all the powers of the GP and many more.[2] The new system intends to give power to the people and not to their representatives. It is reported that Maharashtra too will soon be following the M.P. example. The ostensible reason for such a decision is that an analysis of six years of functioning of Panchayat Raj in M.P. clearly indicates that PRIs could not emerge as people's institutions. Under the new structure, GS will function as decision making bodies and will constitute standing committees as necessary, making GPs redundant. Giving power to the people is no doubt a step in the right direction, and that is what the Constitutional amendments are all about. But the Constitution envisions a representative democracy and the M.P. decision replaces it by a "Roman Forum" kind of direct democracy. Before such an extreme step is taken, some soul searching is necessary on the part of the Centre, State and bureaucracy. Why have things come to such a pass? Why should an analysis of six years of functioning of Panchayat Raj in M.P. indicate that PRIs could not emerge as people's institutions? Where is the guarantee that the new, empowered GS will not go the way of PRIs? What are the reasons for the non-performance of PRIs? Are these attributable to representative democracy at the village level or to some deeper malady? Unless these questions are answered and the reasons for the present state of PRIs are analysed, the M.P. step appears to be hasty and will create more problems than it can solve. The author is aware that the State Government setup a task force consisting of renowned Gandhians who deliberated the issues involved, and also discussed them with the people; the above questions must have bothered them as well. If the newly empowered GS can do away with the existing constraining factors, namely the CSS and Central Planning, give the moneys in un "untied" fashion to PRIs, give planning functions to PRIs as envisioned by the Constitution, make all the donors work through PRIs, ensure that bureaucracy is truly a servant of the elected people, then and only then, can they be accepted as having achieved something tangible. The M.P. experiment is a bold one, but the odds are stacked against it.

Challenges to be overcome in Madhya Pradesh

The following are formidable challenges to be overcome, if the "GS-*raj*", as the M.P. experiment is sometimes called, is to be effective.

1. First is a logistical problem. In a village, there is no place where an assembly of more than 200 people can meet. In the villages, that I have visited there is generally a temple in each village where about 200 people can sit. Some religious groups may have objections to visiting a temple. When I raised this point with the writer of the M.P. report (see endnote 2) the reply given was that the assembly can gather under a tree. I thought this reply was the result of not thinking through a problem. I have visited several villages where there is not single tree in sight big enough to accommodate the quorum for the GS.
2. It is easy for a leader to pack the assembly of GS with one's own followers, who have adequate lung power, and such a situation will lead to "street politics" reminiscent of the Indira Gandhi regime.
3. If two rival groups emerge in a village and each group has its own followers shouting slogans, no orderly business can be transacted in the meetings of the GS. I envision serious law and order problems here.
4. Assuming that the meeting proceeds in an orderly fashion and there is a quorum for the meeting (these are very optimistic assumptions), sheer group dynamics will prevent any useful decisions from being taken. Some people see in this provision a ruse to legitimise the rule by the "upper castes"; after all, the only way to maintain status quo, is to ensure that no decision is taken to upset the "apple cart!"
5. The scheme of the Constitution is based on representative democracy. Direct democracy at the village level is a very romantic idea, but there is a writing on the wall that it may not work in practice. It is very tempting to extend the same logic which has been advanced regarding GS, also to the State legislatures, and recommend direct democracy at all levels.

6. In a representative democracy there is always a secret ballot and this healthy practice is more conducive to the representation of the views of backward classes. Otherwise, in the proposed method, on every issue, it is widely known to everybody as to who voted for which side. It will muffle the voices of the marginalised persons.
7. All over the world the concept of representative democracy has been accepted, even in mature democracies like the U.K. and the U.S.A. If the GS has to meet more often, the remedy is not what M.P. has chosen to follow but to have a provision in the Constitution, laying down how often GS should meet and the powers it can exercise.

Non-implementation of mandatory provisions by some States

Some States have not even implemented the existing mandatory provisions of the Constitution. Some examples are given below.

- The constitution of DPC is mandatory, under article 243ZD of the Constitution. But still (as of January, 2001) the following major States have not constituted DPC – Andhra Pradesh, Arunachal Pradesh, Assam, Bihar, Gujarat, Orissa, Punjab. Maharashtra constituted DPC in 1998, five years after the Constitutional amendments. In some States, such as Maharashtra and Madhya Pradesh, minister has been made the chairperson of the DPC, making it one of the "parallel organisations", which are described in Chapter 11.
- Article 243E(3) makes it mandatory for States to hold an election to a *Panchayat*, every five years. But many states, including Gujarat, have not held elections. So the first responsibility of the Centre is to make States follow the Constitutional provisions, and ensure that its own Ministries follow the Constitution in letter and sprit.

District list – is it a solution?

There has been a suggestion to amend the Constitution and provide for a district list (Meenakshisundaram 1997: 555). But this will not solve the problem of giving to PRIs "untied" funds, making them function as institutions of self-government, and enabling them to carry out local planning. We shall see in Chapter 10 how despite the existence of the State list, the CSS have proliferated, most of dealing with State subjects, and how the Centre has prescribed a number of schemes to be implemented at the village level, by-passing State Governments. The existence of the district list is no solution to the basic problem of the State and Central politicians not trusting the local politicians and the people.

Financial decentralisation[3] and State Finance Commissions

The Constitution lays down transparent financial relationships between the Central and State Governments. But there is no such clear cut demarcation of the responsibilities and financial relationships between States and PRIs. In practice, the taxes and duties devolved by States to PRIs are very inelastic, including, as they do, land revenue, taxes on lands and buildings etc. Consequently, while expenditure responsibilities of PRIs increase, there is no way of ensuring that taxes increase correspondingly. The only income of PRIs, other than taxes and duties, are the grants from State Governments. But this would make PRIs depend upon State Governments for their survival, and would not contribute to the healthy growth of PRIs. In fact, one of the most important objectives of the mention of SFCs in the Constitution is to make PRIs as independent of the temporary whims of State Governments as possible, but, as observed below, the Constitution has to go further along the road to achieve that objective. As required by the Constitution, most States have constituted SFCs, (some for the second time) which submitted their reports in less than two to almost four years. Terms of reference of SFCs are common across States and they are required to recommend financial support from States and principles for determination of taxes, toll and fees that could be assigned to or appropriated by PRIs. While SFCs generally have recommended increased devolution to PRIs, State Governments have not accepted SFC's recommendations. One of the ideas behind providing grants to local bodies is to enable them to manage functions entrusted to them, which could not otherwise be undertaken, because of the limited taxation capacities. Since State Governments have not accepted the recommendations of SFCs, PRIs in most States act mainly as executing agents for the Central and State Governments and have become chattels of the Central and State Governments, which was not the intention of the Constitution. At present the financial picture of PRIs looks rather grim. They are not able to undertake programmes which people want, as most of their grants are tied to specific schemes. There is no firm statistics regarding PRI revenues, particularly, the percentage of own revenues to total revenues; it has been calculated that this varies from 6 per cent in Rajasthan to 19 per cent in Madhya Pradesh. One cannot but conclude that there is only a minimal fiscal decentralisation even eight years after the Constitutional amendments. It is significant to observe here that Balwantray Mehta Committee was aware of this problem and in its report has stated "that all Central and State funds spent in a block area should invariably be assigned to the panchayat samiti to be spent by it directly or indirectly." (India 1957c:13).

Constitutional status of SFC

While Article 243I makes the constitution of SFC every five years by the State Governments mandatory, there is no provision laying down the deadline for the receipt of the report, nor any mention of the period within which the recommendations of the SFC will be accepted by the State Government. Even though the Eleventh CFC has submitted its recommendations, and the Centre has accepted the recommendations, many States are yet to take decisions on the first SFC. In some States, such as A.P., the first SFC was setup on June 22, 1994, but its report was received only on May 5, 1997, but not acted upon by the State Government, by the time the State constituted the second SFC on December 8, 1998. In Bihar, there has been a tremendous delay in the submission of the report of the first SFC. In Goa, the report of the first SFC was submitted on June 5, 1996 but is still under the consideration of the State Government. In Gujarat, the report of the first SFC, which was submitted on July 13, 1998, is still under examination by the State Government. In the meantime, the time for the constitution of the second SFC has come.[4] Critics will point out that the Constitution does not speak of the time limit for the acceptance of the recommendations of the CFC either (Article 281). But a healthy convention has developed at the Centre for the decision of the GOI to be announced soon after the submission of the report by the CFC. In the absence of a similar convention in all the States, it is necessary to have an amendment of the Constitution, laying down the deadline for the submission of the reports by the SFC and for the acceptance of the recommendation by the State Governments. There is also a need to amend the Constitution to make the setting up the SFC synchronise with the constitution of the CFC, such that the action taken by the State Governments on the recommendations of the SFCs are available to the CFC.

Study of the status of rural services by the World Bank

In rural India, the quality of the public services is generally poor. Financial decentralisation to PRIs will enable the latter to provide services in respect of 29 subjects mentioned in Eleventh Schedule of the Constitution, with minimum leakage, and vastly increased efficiency. The World Bank (World Bank 2000b) recently undertook a study of the provision of rural services in seven selected states namely, A.P., Karnataka, Kerala, M.P., Maharashtra, Rajasthan and Uttar Pradesh, comparing the public (PRI level) with private expenditure from the national sample survey (NSS) data. The study noted that the total PRI expenditure including capital expenditure as a percentage of private consumption expenditure, is highest for Karnataka (23 per cent) followed by Maharashtra and A.P. (10 per cent). The remaining four states have a ratio of 5 percent or below – Rajasthan, 5 percent Kerala 1.23 percent M.P. 2.2 percent and U.P. 1.87 percent. The experience of Kerala, where the per capita PRI spending increased by almost 5 times between 1995-96 and 1999-2000, shows that it is possible for decentralisation efforts to succeed in improving these ratios. One of the reasons, besides prevention of leakage and increased efficiency, is the availability of voluntary contributions, once people are convinced that the amount will be spent in their own locality.

Notes

1. For example, see Meenakshisundaram (1997) and Mathew (2000).
2. Economic and Political Weekly, March 09, 2001.
3. In this section the terms "financial decentralisation" and "fiscal decentralisation" are used interchangeably.
4. This information has been obtained from the Ministry of Rural Development, GOI on March 22, 2001.

CHAPTER 9

District Planning

When we talk of district planning, we hear echoes of the Balwantray Mehta Committee. The Planning Commission said in its Sixth Evaluation Report on the working of the CDP (India 1959b:6) that a distinctive feature of the Balwantray Mehta Committee Report, was its emphasis on democratic planning and execution, and that this presupposed (a) building of Plans from below and (ii) associating people with their formulation and implementation. The 74th amendment of the Constitution talks about district planning. Article 243ZD which deals with the DPC, says:

> "There shall be constituted in every State at the district level a District Planning Committee to consolidate the plans prepared by the *Panchayats* and the Municipalities in the district and to prepare a draft development plan for the district as a whole." (India 1999c:99).

District is a well recognised administrative unit. The Collector is located at the district headquarters, and so are the senior representatives of almost all sector departments. It may not have a natural boundary as a watershed has. On the contrary, in many cases, a river is a boundary of the district, and it may have one part of its watershed in one district, and another part in the neighbouring district. But despite this imperfection, a district is generally taken as the unit of planning because of the other advantages which it has, the most important of which is the administrative infrastructure.

Arguments have been put forward for using a "watershed" as a unit of planning. These arguments depend on the fact that a viable watershed,[1] unlike a district, has natural boundaries. But in practice, a typical watershed is small enough, to fall entirely within a block or even a village. During my field trips, I have seen watersheds having an area of only a few hundred acres. So, by having district as a unit of planning, one is not sacrificing much technical requirement. It may be recalled that the initial pilot community projects of the CDP cut across administrative boundaries, but later, it was found administratively feasible, even at the cost of technical refinement, to confine each project within the selected district.

District planning has many facets, such as removal of regional imbalances, which is a political requirement, and association of peoples' representatives with planning. This chapter mainly deals with district planning from the point of view of decentralisation, that is, the association of peoples' representatives with planning. As Maharashtra was the first state where all the districts were covered by district planning, and as the subsequent district planning models, particularly in Kerala and Karnataka, were based on the Maharashtra model, let us examine it in some detail. The objective of this chapter is to apprise the reader of the practical difficulties in implementing any scheme of district planning, as long as it continues to be "top down", like in Maharashtra. The arguments of this chapter supports the observation of Nirmal Mukarji (1989:467), who feels that planning has become so out of touch with ground reality that it is in danger of losing credibility. This chapter also gives suggestions regarding the harmonisation of national and state priorities, with the Constitutional imperatives regarding district planning.

The origin of the concept of district planning in Maharashtra

The origin of district planning in Maharashtra had its roots in politics, as is inevitable in a democracy. Maharashtra has four regions-Vidarbha, Marathwada, Konkan and Western Maharashtra, each with its own distinct history. The politicians of the first three regions claim that their region has been neglected in development. They refer to the "Nagpur Pact" of 1961, when a promise was given to them that the chief ministership would go by rotation to a representative from each of the regions. Yeshwantrao Chavan who was from Western Maharashtra, was the chief minister of the State till 1962, when he went to Delhi to take over as the Union Defence Minister (after the Indo-Chinese War). The incoming chief minister was Kannamwar from Vidarbha, who was a chief minister for a very short period before he died; he was succeeded by Vasantrao Naik (also from Vidarbha) who had a long innings as chief minister. In the early 1970s, S.B. Chavan, who was then the Irrigation Minister of Maharashtra and who later became the Finance Minister at the Centre in 1989 and the Home Minister in 1993, emerged as the leader of the Marathwada region of the State, and for a long time was the chief minister-in-waiting since the next chief minister was to be from Marathwada. The regional feeling was very strong and there was a feeling that Chavan was playing the regional card. Regional plan was prepared and reviewed, even though it was nothing but an aggregate of the Plan schemes of Marathwada. The concept of the district plan was introduced by V.P. Naik to counteract the emerging regional feeling. He also introduced the concept of an objective distribution of the total pool of resources available for the District Plan, among the various districts in the State, according to a formula similar to the Gadgil formula.[2] This objective division of the total pool of resources for district level schemes (DLS) has been adopted by many States, starting with Karnataka in 1985. The criteria for the division of the pool of resources for DLS among all the districts, followed in Maharashtra and Karnataka, are given in Annex 5.

Box 9.1: Indira Gandhi replaces Naik for political reasons

Vasantrao Naik was replaced by Indira Gandhi during emergency, and S.B. Chavan was made the Chief Minister. The reason given was (if she needed any reason at all) that during the stewardship of Naik, Maharashtra's agricultural production did not increase. I was present at the meeting convened in Pune in circa 1975 by Indira Gandhi in which she expressed her displeasure at Naik's handling of Maharashtra's agriculture. All the important officials from the Union Ministry of Agriculture were present at the meeting.

After the meeting, I enquired with some of the officials present as to what was the immediate provocation for the meeting, as after all, the real reason for Maharashtra's dismal performance on the agricultural front was the absence of technology (till mid- 1960s) and the acute drought all over the state during 1969-1970. The answer I got was that Indira Gandhi had already made up her mind regarding Naik. Perhaps he was too independent and had a political following of his own, both of which were anathema to her.

Even if it did not go far enough, Maharashtra's experiment with District Planning was a big step at that time, and was well liked by the people. It is a good example of how an idea, born out of regional politics, becomes a very popular step among the people, and thereby derives its support from all political parties, eventually finding its place in the Constitution. In the initial years, when the author was associated with the working of the scheme, there was tremendous enthusiasm among the elected persons and the intelligentsia. An idea to take deep roots, requires careful nurturing in the initial years by representatives of the people and administration, and such nurturing was provided to the programme by both.

Maharashtra's experience with district planning

Under Section 100(4) of the Maharashtra *Zilla Parishads and Panchayat Samitis* Act 1962, a statutory obligation has been cast on the ZPs to promote planned development of the districts by utilising, to the maximum extent possible, local resources, and in order to achieve this, prepare annual and long term plans having regard to the plans prepared by the PSs. The first step towards decentralisation of planning functions was taken by the State Government in 1972 when District Planning Boards were constituted, with the District *Palak Mantri*[3] as its Chairperson and the Divisional Commissioner as the Vice-Chairperson. This was followed by the introduction of district planning in 1974. The State Government constituted a District Planning and Development Council (DPDC) for each district, and initially the President, ZP was its Chairperson, and the CEO, ZP its Secretary. From the planning period of 1975-76 the setup changed. Under the changed setup, the *Palak Mantri* for the district became the chairperson of the DPDC, with the Collector as its Secretary. Since then, the Chief Planning Officer of the District who is an officer of the State Government on deputation, has been with the Collector, and planning has remained outside the purview of the ZP. This was a blow for decentralisation. When the *Palak Mantri* did not belong to the district for which he was in charge, there was a feeling that he had not been elected from a constituency in that district, but all the same he was the Chairperson of the DPDC, whereas the ZP president, MLAs and (sometimes) MPs were elected from that district and they were only members. The ostensible reason for this change was that there had to be a balance between the urban and rural areas of the State, and having the ZP president, as the Chairperson of the DPDC would tilt the scales very much in favour of the rural areas. If this were the only problem one could think of other solutions, to do justice to both the urban and rural areas. It is generally believed that the real reason was different and that the State level politicians deliberately brought about the change, to curb the power and authority of the ZPs.

Earlier DPDC becomes the Constitutional DPC

This setup essentially continued even after the recent Constitutional amendments. DPCs were constituted in 1998 by the Maharashtra Act No. XXIV of 1998, called the "Maharashtra District Planning Committees (Constitution and Functions) Act." As observed in Chapter 8, this enactment came five years after the Constitutional amendments. This Act nominated the *Palak Mantri* of the district as the Chairperson and the Collector as the Secretary. There was no substantial change from the earlier position, and the earlier DPDCs continued under the new name. The ZP president is now one among the members and is often overshadowed by other political leaders. Before DPCs replaced the old DPDCs, an assurance was given to PRIs on behalf of the State Government that the ZP president would be made be made the Chairman of DPC, but this assurance was never fulfilled. Under the Act, the State Government can issue directives to DPCs.

The mechanics of district planning in Maharashtra

Among the gamut of activities which are relevant to the State, some can be meaningfully planned only at the Central level; examples of this are the Central sector agricultural research centres and big thermal or hydro power stations, serving more than one State. They are all part of the Central Plan.[4] There are activities which can be meaningfully planned at the State level, such as the State agricultural universities (SAU) or major irrigation or power projects (generation and transmission); these are projects of importance for the State as a whole, and whose benefits cannot be localised. Then there are activities which can be meaningfully planned at lower levels, either at the district or block or even village levels. These are schemes whose benefits can be attributed to the district concerned, such as individual beneficiary schemes, minor irrigation projects, school buildings, primary health centres, and rural roads. The last two categories of schemes are called State level schemes and DLS respectively. They are part of the State plan, and finalised by the Planning Commission. CSS are also classified as district or State level by applying the above criteria. If any matching provisions are required to be made in the State plan for any CSS which is classified DLS, the DPCs concerned need to make the requisite provisions in the Plans of their districts.

Out of the total outlay for the State plan, about 40 percent[5] used to be set apart for DLS, when the district planning was started, according to policy of the Government of Maharashtra (GOM). As mentioned earlier, the total quantum of the district level plan outlay is distributed among the different districts on the basis of a formula similar to Gadgil formula. Thus every district gets a financial allocation, within which the DLS of that district should be planned. Funds also flow for developmental purposes from donors and institutional sources, such as the commercial banks, LDB and the World Bank. They are not part of the State Plan, but they should, all the same, be taken into account while formulating the district plan, as complementary funds need to be provided in the district plan as required. For instance, let us suppose loans for minor irrigation are given by the LDB or commercial banks, to farmers; these loans themselves are not reflected in the State Plan. It is however, necessary that adequate provisions are made in the Plan for rural electrification (which is a district level scheme) so that investments made by farmers out of institutional funds can be made use of Loans are also given for purchase of milch cows and they should get the necessary infrastructure support such as rural roads and chilling plants. Most of such complementary provisions fall under district plans, and should be provided for in the plan of the district concerned.

Box 9.2: Meeting at the Zilla Parishad office, Pune

On May 7, 2001 the CEO, ZP, Pune invited me to attend a meeting in ZP organised by the President, ZP, in which all the PS Chairpersons participated. The subject under discussion was the rural drinking water supply programme. The President, ZP had announced that from its own resources, ZP would be spending Rs. 2 lakhs per village for strengthening the source of the drinking water supply scheme in each village. This was a very popular programme but does not fit in within the norms announced by either the State Government or the Central Government, who would prefer to have big piped water supply schemes. The advantages of the village well were explained by one of the meeting participants. She said that people (generally womenfolk) gather around the well each day and the occasion provides social interaction; and if there is only one well (normally there are two wells in a village, one for the so-called "upper castes" and the other for the "scheduled castes"), the caste system will, in due course, disappear. She was a "scheduled caste" woman. On the other hand, big piped water supply scheme will provide house connections to well-to-do people, who are the elite, and such schemes will perpetuate the caste system apart from depriving the womenfolk of the valuable social interaction. This is a clear example of how human and technical aspects of a programme are often in conflict with each other.

A unique feature of this scheme is the 10 percent cash contribution which each participating GP was expected to deposit with ZP, as a condition to participation in the scheme. I was reminded of many government and donor assisted schemes where such a popular cash contribution was not forthcoming. An inducement for GP to participate in the programme is the 5 per cent of the cost of the work going to GP fund.

The technical aspects of the scheme are by now well known. But what struck me as unusual and novel about the scheme, are the human and institutional aspects. I could not help feeling how remote the bureaucracy in Delhi and Mumbai were from the scene of action. Unfortunately even the Central and State Ministers who are supposed to be in touch with the "masses" also seem to be in the hands of bureaucracy.

Other popular schemes which the people want, as articulated by the PS Chairpersons, included construction of bus station (two or three villages were prepared to come together for this purpose) and expansion of burial/cremation grounds.

This is a good example of planning from below. Planning means action in the field, not writing *tomes* about it, sitting in remote offices in Delhi or State capitals.

Limitations of District Planning

While in theory every district is expected to prepare a plan for its area, in practice, there are many problems in doing so. First, the DPC cannot introduce a totally new scheme not in the approved list of schemes prepared by the State Government, except with the ZP's own funds. For example, if the State Government has prepared a scheme for increasing the production of a particular crop by using a certain package of measures, the DPC cannot alter that package or suggest any change in the pattern of assistance provided in the scheme.

Second, there is very often a conflict between DPCs and sector departments, arising out of sector allocations by the DPCs. The departmental allocations tend to be rather rigid. One would have thought that these allocations are merely indicative, the details being worked out by the DPC. But it is not so. For example, if the sector is agriculture, the district had no say on whether to spend the allocation for the sector on agricultural extension or on setting new agricultural research station. Even such intra-sectoral diversion of funds was not permitted, not to speak of inter-sectoral diversion, such as from the agriculture sector to the health sector, without the concurrence of the departments concerned of the State Government and the planning department. In effect, the role of the DPC in departmental schemes was confined to the choice of location and in the case of "individual beneficiary schemes", to the selection of beneficiaries. To illustrate this, a DPC cannot, for example, say that, people want more rural roads and therefore in the district plan there is no money for agricultural extension, which is also district level scheme. This is an example of the priorities of the sector departments conflicting with those of the DPCs. One way of dealing with this conflict is to hear the sector department representatives before a draft plan is prepared and not to involve representatives of sector departments in the subsequent planning process, both at the district and at the state levels. At present, at the district level, the DPC meeting takes place initially with the district planning officer and later on, with the District Collector and the *Palak Mantri.* At these meetings the representatives of the sector departments at the district level, and the MPs/MLAs/MLCs are present, and the district and panchayat level elected representatives are overwhelmed by them. At the State level, where the district plans are given a final shape before being sent to the Planning Commission, the Minister for Planning presides over the DPC meetings, and the *Palak Mantri* of the district concerned is present, along with the MPs/MLAs/MLCs and the State level officials (including some secretaries). At these meetings the officials plead for more allocations for their sectors and the MPs and MLAs for projects in their constituencies. Again the elected representatives of district and panchayat levels are outnumbered by these heavy weights.

Third, some districts have climatic factors favouring the cultivation of a particular crop. For example, let us take the case of scheme of intensive programme of oilseed production. In consonance with the national policy, the State Government decided that the production of oilseeds should be stepped up substantially, and for this purpose, liberal incentives were given to farmers to produce oilseeds. The outlay on this scheme was a district level scheme. Since not all districts are suitable for the production of oilseeds, the few districts selected for intensive efforts were required to bear the provision for the scheme. The DPCs concerned often are very reluctant to do so. But the sector departments concerned pressurise them to provide adequately for the scheme.

Fourth, district planning encounters a problem stemming from the planning calendar. Discussions with the Planning Commission to finalise the State plan are held in the months of December-January to adhere to the budget deadline (which is generally in February or March). Prior to that, the district plans are finalised. When the district plans and the State plan are given final shape, the State's share of the CSS to be provided in the State's plan and the consequent provisions in the plans of the districts are not known, as these outlays are indicated by the Centre very much later. It then becomes very difficult to make adjustments to the Plans of the State and of the districts. The districts are often reluctant to make complementary provisions in their plans, which at this stage would mean cutting the outlay somewhere after talks with the peoples' representatives and the local sector department officials are held. What actually happens is that the State planning department finalises the district plans, in consultation with the District Collector, as there is not enough time to call meetings of all the DPCs.

Fifth, Planning Commission is constituted by sector and it often mirrors the ministries. There is an advisor for education, one for power and so on. There is also a multilevel planning division alongside these sector divisions and it is responsible for district planning. During Plan discussions, the Advisor of the Planning Commission for each sector has a detailed discussion with the sector Secretary concerned, of the State Government. The plan is finalised by sector and the district planning then becomes a matter of exhibition of the sector plan by district. In theory, a district plan is supposed to be finalised taking into account the wishes of the people, and the State plan should be nothing but an aggregate of the district plans and the plan allocations of the State level schemes. But, in practice, it is the other way about; the plan is finalised by the Planning Commission and the State Government by sector, and flows down to the districts.

Sixth, there is an informal assurance by the Chief Minster to the MLAs and MPs that 40 percent of the State plan resources will go to the districts and will constitute district plan schemes. The districts are aware of this, and rightly demand greater transparency from the Planning Department of the State Government. When almost 50 percent of the State plan resources go to the power and major and medium irrigation sectors, and 40 percent to the DLS, the other State level schemes have to be accommodated within 10 percent-an almost impossible task. There have been many attempts to undertake planning of even DLS at the State level and exhibit them as DLS. Medium irrigation projects and some dairy plants are examples of this. The outlay in respect of these schemes are skimmed before the ceilings for the DLS are communicated to the districts. Some districts with a large urban centre have a genuine problem- the demands of the urban centre are more than the resources which the district gets on account of the urban population. Such outlays which are charged to the District Plan but kept at the State level are called State Pool schemes and they have increased to 35.61 percent of the State Plan.

Parallel state level schemes

While discussing the Maharashtra model of decentralisation in Chapter 5, we had described the gradual erosion of the power and authority of the ZPs. We had explained how certain schemes were transferred from the ZP (i.e. local sector) to the state sector. What this means is that many schemes which were originally implemented by the ZPs, are transferred to the line departments. For example, minor irrigation schemes with a culturable command of more than 100 hectares were transferred from the local sector to the state sector. But they remained as DLS, in theory, to be planned by the DPC. Certain activities pertaining to agricultural development were retained with the state sector, such as soil conservation schemes and they were classified as DLS. The distinction between state sector schemes and local sector schemes are not congruent to the distinction between state level and district level schemes. The former classification is based upon who gets to implement the scheme, and the latter upon who benefits from the scheme. In theory the DPC, which has the responsibility of indicating the allocations for DLS, can refuse to provide outlay for some state sector projects. But, in practice, this rarely happens; the state level officials, and the ministers who attend the DPC meetings at the State headquarters ensure that this does not happen. So the line departments can have the cake and eat it too. In bureaucracies everybody wants to be in a position to spend other person's budget. Line departments are no exception. They want to be able to execute as many schemes as they can, and expand their bureaucracies, at the expense of the district outlays. The districts do the planning at the bidding of the line departments, and the latter execute the plan. This matter came up for discussion when the NDC took up the Eighth Plan (1992-97) for consideration. It appointed a committee under the chairmanship of Chimanbhai Patel to make recommendations on micro-level planning and involvement of people at the grassroot level. The Committee observed: "Even when powers and functions are given up, often something is held back for parallel implementation by competing agencies, creating situations of potential conflict." (India 1993, and Sundaram 1997a:326). But nothing has been done so far to correct the situation.

Recently, Maharashtra has transferred many schemes, which were earlier transferred from local sector to state sector, back to ZPs (i.e. back to the local sector). But the limitation is, that the State Government circulars effecting the transfer, say that sectoral allocations are as decided by the planning process, that is, the Plan allocations for the State level schemes and the DLS will remain as they are, and only the implementation of these have been transferred. This means that PRIs will be the implementing agencies of a larger number of schemes than hitherto. What the State has given is not the substance, but only the shadow. This is against the spirit of the Constitutional provisions. Though the analysis of district planning given in the foregoing paragraphs relates to Maharashtra, the problems dealt with are present in most States. If it has not come to the fore in some States, it is because district planning is a relatively new experience for many States.

Developments at the national level - reports of Dantwala and Hanumantha Rao committees

After the change of Government at the Centre in 1977, there was a renewed interest in multi-level planning involving PRIs. In November 1977, about the time when the Asoka Mehta Committee was setup, the Planning Commission setup a Working Group on "Block Level Planning" with Prof. M.L. Dantwala as Chairman. At that time, many States did not have functioning PRIs, and the institutional mechanism to undertake block level planning, was weak. The group could not recommend planning responsibilities being entrusted to institutions that are yet to be developed. In fact, there was insufficiently developed institutional mechanism to undertake planning even at the district level, not to speak of block level. Many States did not have competent statistics departments, and district planning was impossible without strong and competent statistics departments. The group therefore observed:

> "First, in a large number of states, Panchayat Raj Institutions were either non-existent or were in a moribund state…This reality had to be reckoned with in making any recommendation which was meant for immediate implementation. Secondly, there was a widespread feeling

that, by and large, the Panchayati Raj Institutions did not reflect the interests and needs of the weaker sections of the rural community." (India 1978b:9).

The idea of multi-level planning again surfaced in 1982. By then, many more States had experience with PRIs and district planning. In September 1982, the Planning Commission setup a working group with Dr. C.H. Hanumantha Rao as Chairman to prepare guidelines for planning at the district level. The group submitted its report in May 1984. (India 1984). As we have already seen, the group remarked that for decentralised planning to make headway, institutional mechanisms had to be more broad-based with active involvement of local representatives, and endowed with greater degree of autonomy in local decision-making. The Committee emphatically said that ultimately district planning would have to be taken over by PRIs. The Hanumantha Rao Committee was more positive than the Dantwala Committee about the role of PRIs regarding district planning. It recognised that the States differed widely in all respects, particularly in their performance of district planning. Some States have better planning capacity at the district levels than others. Therefore it recommended a three stage approach:

Stage 1 – Phase of initiation: During this stage the States will establish planning procedures, and determine the manner of inter-district allocation of outlays. The objective of district planning at this stage, is to ensure equitable allocation of resources to all the districts of the State.

Stage 2 – Decentralisation: Bringing within the purview of district planning certain activities, such as the MNP.

Stage 3 – Final: District planning will encompass all district level activities.

Importance of "untied" funds to PRIs

After the Constitutional amendments, the following key steps need to be taken by the Centre and the States to bring multi-level planning in accordance with Constitutional requirements. These steps are: PRIs should be,

- given sufficient resources to enable them to fulfil their obligations under the Constitution.

- given "untied" grants to be spent on schemes which the local people want and not, as at present, grants tied to specific schemes.
- allowed to function as institutions of self government and should be able to prepare a plan for the district rather than, as now, used as mere implementing agencies for plans prepared at the State or Central levels.

So far none of the above have been realised. As an observer of the *Panchayati Raj* put it:

> The post-1992 panchayats are waiting passively for the concerned State Governments to assign to them a significant share of powers, authority and functions beyond what has been transferred to them in the three or four decades before the conferment of constitutional status by the 73rd amendment" (Mathur 1997:715).

"Untied" funds represent funds which PRIs can spend on development activities of their choice, as against grants from the GOI and the State Government which are tied to specific schemes. This concept of giving "untied" funds to PRIs has been tried in Gujarat, Karnataka and West Bengal. Gujarat started a new phase of decentralised planning on Nov 14, 1980 (Jawaharlal Nehru's birthday), which was an improved version of the Maharashtra model, and consisted of "untied" funds to PRIs to the extent of 20 percent of district outlays, of which one-third was set apart as incentive funds to match local resources mobilised at the district level. Karnataka has made a lump provision to each district, under the "matching fund category". (Isaac and Franke 2000:24). We saw that this has recently been introduced in West Bengal. These "untied funds" have evoked popular enthusiasm.

Planning functions that can be given to PRIs

Planning functions consist of: planning (or allocation of resources to various schemes), implementation, coordination, and review and that it is not necessary that all these are carried out by the same body (Vithal 1979). These functions are separable and can be assigned to different levels. For each activity, the Centre or State can decide at which level, what function can be exercised. For instance, in respect power generation projects involving more than one state, all the four functions are best carried out by the Central ministry concerned. The development of industrial areas by the State Industrial Development Corporations can be planned and implemented at the State level, and the coordination and review functions can be carried out at the district level. In respect certain activities such as rural roads, rural water supply, primary health and elementary education all the four functions are best carried out at the district level. Thus PRIs can carry out all the four functions in respect of some schemes implementation in respect of certain other schemes, mostly DLS; and coordination and review in respect of some schemes. Thus district planning consists of preparation of plans, implementation, coordination and review. Annex 4 shows the manner of exhibition of the responsibilities of the Centre, State and District, of different functions in respect of various hypothetical schemes.

When programmes are implemented through a decentralised setup, the role of the Central and State Governments changes from one of formulating the programme to one of monitoring its implementation and giving technical guidance. We have already seen in Chapter 4 that such monitoring has to be done in field. This is much more difficult and requires familiarity with the field where action takes place, and the power it carries is purely the power of knowledge and capacity, and such qualities are often missing at the Central and State levels.

Harmonisation of national, state and district planning

Planning has many dimensions. The most important of them is the political dimension. The political party which comes to power at the Centre should be able to translate its election promises into action. It cannot plead helplessness by saying that because most of the activities are planned at the State and district levels, the national planning strategy is the sum of the planning strategies of the States and districts. In effect this would mean that there is no national planning strategy, after all. What is true of the Centre is also true of the States. The plans prepared by districts should reflect States' priorities. After the Constitutional amendments, it is no longer a matter of choice whether PRIs can be entrusted with planning functions or not. It is a constitutional requirement, and it is expected of the policy makers to harmonise the national and State planning goals with the imperatives of multi-level planning, as envisioned in the Constitution.

Need to correct the present situation

The following steps are needed to correct the present situation so that the planning process can recognise the need to make the Plan conform to the national priorities, and at the same time satisfy the Constitutional requirements regarding district planning.

1. It is necessary to demarcate the functional domain of the various tiers of PRIs by identifying the functions which can be planned and implemented at each of the levels - district, taluka and village level – and transferring to PRIs these functions and the funds for carrying out the associated activities. Kerala, for instance, has done such a transfer directly to the different levels of PRIs statutorily. Funds transferred to them should match the responsibilities assigned to them. This will give to PRIs a sense of participation in planning. The kind of demarcation which is referred to above can be illustrated. Taking the rural water supply as an example, if the rural water supply scheme lies within the area of a *panchayat samiti,* then it can be entrusted with the planning and implementation of the scheme; coordination and review can be with the ZP at the district level. Such a demarcation will have to be done in respect of every scheme and the results exhibited in a matrix, a sample format of which is shown in Annex 4.
2. A plan will have to be prepared for each activity and then broken down by scheme. For example, suppose the objective is to increase the production of oilseed in the district. A strategy will then have to be spelt out consistent with the objectives. This strategy can consist of better extension, more relevant research, and better prices for oilseed. Once the strategy is decided, it can be broken down into schemes: such as, a scheme for training of extension staff, more operating budget for research and extension personnel, and loans to farmers for the construction of on-farm storage. An operational plan will then have to be

prepared, which will include the components of the chosen strategy. This operational plan will contain some Plan items and some non-Plan items. This concept is elaborated in the next chapter. The Plan items will form part of the development Plan for the district. Every district should be required to prepare such a development Plan, taking into account the resources, constraints and opportunities. At present neither the objective nor the strategy is clear from the district plan. Only a list of schemes along with the financial provisions is exhibited.

3. The term "planning" used in the context of PRI should include the operation and maintenance expenditures. The traditional distinction between "Plan" and "non-Plan" expenditures should not be invoked while talking about entrusting functions and giving funds to them. For example, in Kerala, both the "Plan" and "non-Plan" funds have been transferred to PRIs. Forty percent of Plan funds have been transferred to PRIs at all levels together, and these correspond to the planning functions assigned to them; in addition, the "non-Plan" funds needed by them to operate and maintain the assets are also transferred to them.
4. Plans of higher levels of government (block, district, and state, national) should be the aggregation of plans elaborated at the next lower level of government. According to this principle, the block plan should be the aggregate of the village plans and so on.
5. The horizontal distribution of funds between the various districts should be governed (as in Maharashtra, Gujarat, Karnataka and Kerala) by an objective formula; the "vertical" allocation of funds between PRIs of different tiers, should be done by the State Government, and the funds should go to the PRI concerned directly from the State Government (as in West Bengal and Kerala).
6. Funds which PRIs are allocated should be known to them in advance to enable them to plan their investments and services.

Box 9.3: Decentralisation and maintenance of community assets

We have seen how, in India, the maintenance of the assets created under the Plan has always posed a problem. The problem is more acute in community assets, such as, minor irrigation or drinking water schemes. It is here where decentralisation can be very effective. People do not prefer to maintain these assets, as they were not involved either in their planning or in their execution. Governments cannot maintain them either, as the non-Plan funds of the departments are insufficient for the purpose. People are also reluctant to bear the cost of government's delivery of services, which includes the cost of maintenance, as they find them too high and the services not satisfactory to justify the high costs. The governments are therefore forced to sell their services below cost. This results in a vicious cycle: Central Planning resulting in the creation of assets which the governments cannot maintain and people do not want to maintain for reasons mentioned earlier; governments ending up selling these services below cost as the beneficiaries do not want to pay for the full cost of these services which they find too expensive for their quality; the quality of service deteriorating further as the governments default on the maintenance of assets created. Decentralised Planning and the involvement of local people in planning and implementation of schemes of local importance will convert this vicious cycle into a virtuous one.

'Carrot' and 'Stick'

There are two ways of making PRIs provide adequately for certain schemes of National or State importance. One way is to require them to make necessary provisions. This is the "stick" approach. Another, and a more sustainable way is to persuade them to make adequate provision for schemes which reflect National or State priorities. This is the "carrot"` approach, and this approach consists of offering PRIs financial incentives, through the principle of co-financing, which can operate somewhat as follows:

- when any PRI desires to take up a programme in accordance with the National or State priorities, the contribution of the

Centre or the State, as the case may be, could be as high as 95 percent.

- when any PRI wants to take up a scheme not in the priority sector, more contribution from the PRI concerned can be insisted upon.

In this co-financing arrangement, it is also possible to have a graded Central or State contribution which varies according to the number of BPL persons, or the number of people belonging to SC and ST. Such a co-financing matrix should be well-publicised and transparent, so that all PRIs can understand the principles governing co-financing arrangements. In most CSS there is a State contribution, and it is a means of making States contribute from their Plans for schemes considered by the Centre to be of national importance. The principle of co-financing is already implicit in respect of CSS and MNP. There are, therefore, precedents to the principle of co-financing. It is only an extension of a principle, already in operation, to district plans to bring the planning process in line with the Constitutional requirements, and at the same time to make the plans prepared by PRIs, reflect the national and State priorities.

Situation in Kerala

It is difficult to write an account of district planning and decentralisation without citing the Kerala example.[6] The following paragraphs outline the factors which make the district planning in Kerala unique. The Kerala experience is described here after visiting the State and having discussion with a cross section of people, some in State Government, some at different levels of PRIs, and some NGOs. Like most other states, Kerala also has embarked on democratic decentralisation after the Constitutional amendments. Government of Kerala (GOK) enacted the Kerala *Panchayati Raj* Act which became effective in April 1994. A three tier structure was setup and elections to PRIs were held in September, 1995. There are 14 DPs, 152 BPs and 990 GPs. A DP has about 20-22 members, a BP about 8-10 members and a GP about 9-11 members. Organic linkage between different tiers is sought to be established by making the elected presidents of the lower tiers ex-officio members of the next higher tier, with full rights of voting except in elections to various offices and in no-confidence motions.

"Non-Plan" funds are also transferred to PRIs, in addition to Plan funds. These "non-Plan" funds include, funds for the maintenance of the assets created under the previous plans, funds for the continuation of non-Plan schemes,[7] salaries of the staff borne on non-Plan schemes.[8] By transferring these funds to PRIs, the GOK has set the stage for PRIs telling the GOK at some future date, that they could manage the maintenance of these assets, provided the cost of the staff (at present borne by the State Government) is also given to them in cash, in addition to maintenance grants.

"Untied" funds for PRIs in Kerala

"Untied" funds of PRIs in Kerala consist of (i) grants-in-aid from the State Government, and (ii) own funds of PRIs, and are estimated at 25.35 percent of the total plan outlay. Kerala is the only State in India in which "untied" funds of PRIs are of this magnitude. The own funds of PRIs in Kerala in 1997-98 for 14 districts are estimated at Rs. 70.88 crores, an average of about Rs 5 crores per district; as a contrast the own funds of Pune ZP which is one of the richest ZP in Maharashtra is only about Rs. 2 crores (Vithal and Rao 1997:706). The following Table gives the figures relating to the total Plan outlay and the GOK grants to PRIs. GOK has developed some guidelines for spending by PRIs of the "untied" funds: out of total funds, the panchayats can spend up to 40-50 percent on productive sectors, such as agriculture, animal husbandry, fisheries, and small industries, 30-40 percent on social sectors such as health, education, water supply, sanitation, and 10-30 percent on infrastructure such as rural roads. There is a ceiling on subsidy, and the scale of subsidy should conform to limits laid down by the GOK.

Statutory transfer of funds to PRIs in Kerala

State Government's grants to PRIs are statutory. Annex 4 of Kerala's budget shows the amounts allocated to each panchayat by name. This transfer is therefore not by a government order, but by law, and therefore can be reversed only by the State legislature. Earlier it was possible for any sector department to re-appropriate funds from one minor head to another and also from one district to another, without the knowledge of the local people.

Table 9.1: Table showing the total State Plan outlays and grants to PRIs

(The upper figures are Rupees (in crores) and the lower figures are US Dollars (in millions) at the exchange rate in 1998 which was about 1US$=Rs 42.00)

Year	Total State Plan Outlay	Grants to PRIs	Percentage
1997-98	2855.00 679.76	653.12 157.50	23.00
1998-99	3140.50 747.73	827.23 196.95	26.34

Source: The figures in this Table are calculated from "People's Campaign for Decentralised Planning" (April 1998) and "Panchayat Raj in Kerala: A Status Report" (May 1998); both have been brought out by GOK

This is no longer possible. Another feature of the Kerala pattern of funds flow, is that funds are transferred directly by the State Government to the GP, BP or DP concerned; this ensures that each tier of PRIs is financially independent of the one "above." Moreover, PRIs at the higher level have only an advisory role *vis à vis* PRIs at the "lower" level. Thus, district and block level PRIs have only an advisory role as opposed to a clearance function, *vis-à-vis* schemes prepared by PSs and GPs respectively. While the block level panchayat, that is, the PS, can advise on the technical feasibility of a proposed investment, it cannot overturn the decision of the lower level GP. And the same applies to a DP *vis-à-vis* a BP in the same district. Therefore the right to comment and "clear" any proposal emanating from a "lower tier" is an honour to be earned by the "higher tier" PRI.

The scale of voluntary contribution

The sustainability of decentralisation depends upon the extent of beneficiary and voluntary contribution to the capital costs of the local works. In 1997-98 these were estimated at 30.20 percent of the total plan outlay of the GPs; for BPs and DPs the percentages are much less, as can be expected, being 12.13 percent and 11.67 percent respectively.

The essential features of Kerala's experience with decentralised planning is given in Box.9.4.

Box 9.4: Essential features of Kerala's experience with decentralised planning

- planning takes place close to the people.
- the neighbourhood groups[9] provide a forum for the people to express their priorities in a peaceful and democratic manner.
- the people are conscious of the fact that they have the resources to fulfil their dreams and ambitions.
- the very process of decentralised planning ensures transparency and provides a good safeguard against corruption and improper utilisation of funds.
- the process encourages the association of volunteers not only for conducting neighbourhood group meetings but also for preparation of technical aspects of projects; more than 4000 technical experts have so far been enrolled as volunteers.
- the system is a very powerful instrument for social change; SC people and those belonging to the "upper" castes use the same water supply facility, planned by local communities.
- through active association of local people with planning, the process facilitates local governance by villagers, including settlement of boundary disputes (a quasi-legal function), replacing of street lights (a civic duty) and protection of medicinal plants (an economic and environmental initiative).

Notes

1. A watershed can be as small as the area commanded by a rivulet or as large as a river basin. We talk of a small size "viable" watershed where it makes sense to plan.
2. This is described in Chapter 10. Briefly, it is an objective formula, which is used by the PC, to distribute among States and UTs, the divisible pool of Central resources for the Plan.
3. In Maharashtra, there has been, the practice of appointing a Minister (not necessarily elected from that district) as the Minister for the district. In local language he is called *Palak Mantri*.
4. Some of them concerning more than one State can be CSS (see Chapter 10), in which case the Central share will be part of the Central Plan.

5. This percentage has in 1998-99 come down to 35.35 percent of the total State Plan outlay.
6. For a detailed account of the decentralised planning in Kerala please see Isaac and Franke (2000).
7. Plan schemes are generally converted into non-Plan schemes at the end of the Plan period.
8. Salaries of staff are still actually paid by GOK but the amounts of such salaries are shown against the respective *panchayat*.
9. This is one level below GS. It denotes a community.

CHAPTER 10

Centrally Sponsored Schemes

We saw in Chapter 5 that the Balwantray Mehta Committee recommended that all aspects of development work in rural areas should be transferred to *panchayats.* More specifically, the recommendations of the committee included: (a) the State, when it wants to operate in matters in the State list, has to go through the PS concerned, and (b) the Centre should not act in State matters. As the team was more concerned with ensuring that the plan programmes, particularly, the CDP and the NES, are implemented properly, it did not go deeply into the various aspects of decentralisation but the thrust of the recommendations is obvious. The Committee was not in favour of the increasing number of CSS.

CSS are those Plan schemes which are formulated and funded, either fully or partly, by the Central Ministries and implemented by the States or their agencies. They represent administrative decentralisation. They are about the implementation of activities and the delivery of services at the local level, and not about the transfer of political power or authority. It is about shifting administrative responsibility to local officials, rather than devolving decision making power to local elected representatives. In this chapter we shall describe what these schemes are, and why they are so difficult to get rid of despite the efforts of the NDC, and despite the fact that they are antithetical to the concept of local level planning as contained in Article 243G of the Constitution.

The meaning of "planning" in the context of the Indian Plans

The term "planning" in the context of India's Five year (or Annual) Plans has a very specific meaning. It denotes either a new investment, or a substantial augmentation of an existing investment or a new service. For example, a new irrigation project constitutes a new investment; so does a new power project. They are therefore parts of the Plan. Suppose a power generating station has four generators and two more are proposed to be added; this addition is an augmentation of an existing project and is therefore part of the Plan. The CDP was a part of the Plan as it amounted to a new service. Subsidies given to farmers for various developmental purposes, such as subsidy on fertilisers or wells, also figure in the Plan. The anti-poverty programmes are also part of the Plan. So a Plan contains a series of decisions, oriented towards development, from investments to subsidies. The distinction between an operational plan and the components of the Plan is explained below. The former is categorised as "non-Plan."

State Plan and Central Plan

Every State has a Plan (called the State Plan) and so does the Union Government (called the Central Plan). Both Plans are finalised by the Planning Commission. After finalisation, these are reflected in the budgets of the State and Union governments respectively, and voted by the legislature of the State or the Parliament, as the case may be. The budgets contain things other than the components of the Plan, namely, non-Plan. In fact the budgets of the States and the Union governments contain more money for non-Plan than for Plan. The major non-Plan components are "Defence" and "Police" representing the external and internal security respectively. Operation and maintenance of assets is also classified as non-Plan.

"Investment Plan" and "Operational Plan"

To illustrate how a Plan component is drawn up and incorporated in the Plan, let us take the case of oilseed production as an example. Any decision taken by the State or Union Government with the end objective of increasing oilseed production, would get reflected in the Plan to the extent to which it falls under any of the categories mentioned earlier, namely, new investment, or a substantial augmentation of an existing investment or a new service. Some aspects of the decision may not fall under any of the above categories and they would not then find a place in the financial aspects of the Plan. There are many ways in which the objective of increasing oilseed production, can be achieved, such as the appointment of special government staff with a responsibility to increase the production of oilseeds, or curtailing the release of water from the irrigation project for *rabi* irrigation, and carrying over the water so saved, for providing farmers with irrigation water for growing summer groundnut, or restricting the sanction of water for sugarcane and pre-monsoon cotton so as to give priority to meet the demands for water to irrigate the summer groundnut crop, or better research and extension on oilseeds, or a combination of the above. All the above measures would not necessarily be reflected in the Plan. The manner of operation of the irrigation system would not be a part of the Plan, for instance. The policy decision involved in curtailing of water release for sugarcane crop would not be a part of the Plan. But all the same, all or some of the above measures might constitute a "plan" to increase the production of oilseeds. The term "plan" is used here in a generic sense. In this sense of the term, planning would connote not only the components which would find a place in the "Plan", but also how administration plans to function in relation to achieving the given objective, and operate the instruments and facilities provided in the Plan or the assets created thereunder.

Planning for development would thus comprise: (i) preparing a Plan for new investments, provision of new facilities and services, setting up new institutions, strengthening the existing ones and provision of various kinds of production incentives to farmers, all of which require financial provisions to be made in the Plan; for the sake of convenience, we shall call this the investment Plan; and (ii) preparing an operational plan, which would call for certain policy decisions, but which is essentially a blueprint for administrative action in order to attain the objectives. Thus operational plan makes use of the investment Plan and also the provisions of what is known as non-Plan.

Plan scheme

One often comes across the term "Plan scheme" or sometimes simply "scheme" in Plan documents. The word has occurred earlier in this book. The term "scheme" stands for those components included in the investment Plan, and which are reflected in the financial aspects of the Plan. In the illustration given above, the components of the investment Plan would be referred to as a "scheme to increase oilseed production". Sometimes the word "scheme" is dropped from the title of the scheme, and it is referred to as "oilseed development programme". A Plan comprises a number of schemes, each scheme representing a certain objective.

Centre State Financial Transfers

Often, the finances of the States are not sufficient to meet their commitments regarding Plan and non-Plan expenditures. If such an eventuality arises, which has happened many times in the past, the Centre comes to the rescue of the State concerned. Even though efforts are made to make the process of Central financial transfer to the States transparent and objective, it is not possible to keep out the element of politics altogether. There have been instances where, objectively, a State should not get any Central assistance, but it does get the assistance eventually, for political reasons; on a number of occasions, the opposite thing has happened, that is, a State which deserves Central assistance is denied the same. India is a democracy and different political parties are often in power at the Centre and the States, and it is difficult to eschew the role of politics in this area completely. But, by and large, transfers from the Centre to the States are objective and transparent, and particularly so, after the Fourth Plan when the earlier, largely subjective, mechanism of Plan transfers to the States, was replaced by an objective formula known as Gadgil formula.

Centre-State financial relationship in India is a very complex subject and it is not possible to do justice to it here. The relative roles of CFC and Planning Commission are particularly complex. Only the bare essentials are given here to enable the reader to understand the meaning and role of CSS, and the extent to which these impact on decentralisation and rural development. Interested reader is referred to books on Centre-State financial relationship such as Gulati (1987).

Mechanisms for the flow of Central funds to States

There are several mechanisms for the flow of Central funds to the States. Four of them deserve special mention here.

1. Grants-in-aid received by the States, the quantum and mode of which are determined by the CFC appointed according to

Article 280 of the Constitution, generally once every five years; these are called statutory transfers, because CFC is a Constitutional body.

2. Transfers based on the recommendations of the Planning Commission (sometimes called Block Plan transfers), according to a formula known as Gadgil formula. Central assistance to States, comprises both grants and loans, generally, in the ratio of 30:70.
3. Transfers based on the recommendations of the Planning Commission on account of externally aided projects.
4. Transfers by the various Central Ministries, which are rather arbitrary and not governed by any objective formula;[1] these include, prominently, Central Plan assistance to the States under CSS.

The States get Plan assistance from the Centre essentially in two modes: Block Plan transfers as per Gadgil formula, and transfers from the Ministries under CSS. As stated above, the former is decided, from the IV Plan onwards, according to formula known as Gadgil formula (or its modified form) which was approved by the NDC. But the inter-state allocation of discretionary assistance, to which category the CSS belong, is still decided largely by the Central Ministry concerned, in consultation with the Planning Commission, without reference to the NDC. States prefer block grants as they are "untied", whereas Plan assistance attached to CSS are "tied" to specific schemes. This is one of the reasons for the State chief ministers, who are members of the NDC, arguing for the reduction in the number of CSS. The shares of Plan transfers, which are discretionary and non-statutory, i.e. the financial transfers mentioned in (2) and (3) above, have, in the recent past, exceeded the transfers made on the recommendations of the CFC. Some people are uncomfortable with the fact that the non-statutory transfers exceed the statutory ones. The following table shows the amounts transferred to the States and Union Territories under the different categories.

Table 10.1: Table showing the amounts transferred to the States and UTs under different categories

(Rs. in crores)

Mode of Transfer	Details of Transfer	1999-2000	2000-2001
Eleventh Finance Commission	Sr. No. 1 above	Nil	52,418
Gadgil Formula (i.e.,block plan assistance	Sr. No. 2 above	16,500	15,560
Other central Assistance	Sr. No. 3 above	Nil	21,000
CSS	Sr. No. 4 above	19,500	20,000

Transfer of funds from the Centre to States under CSS

According to the Planning Commission,[2] the CSS had a total budget allocation during 1999-2000 of Rs. 19,500 crores. Of these, about Rs. 13,000 crores relate to items on the State list; this as a percentage of the total outlay of the CSS comes to 66.66 percent. This percentage goes up to 92 percent if primary education and family welfare, which are now on the concurrent list, are included. This shows the extent to which the CSS have proliferated in items pertaining to the State list. Both in 1999-2000 and in 2000-2001, the Gadgil formula assistance is less than the amount which has flowed to the States from the Centre under CSS. In 2000-2001 the non-statutory transfers exceeded the statutory ones, in spite of the fact that the Eleventh Finance Commission is far more generous towards the States than its predecessors. In the earlier years, the non-statutory transfers exceeded the statutory ones by higher margins. One of the reasons for the proliferation of CSS is that Central Ministries prefer the arbitrariness in the allocation of funds among States through CSS and are averse to an objective formula, as this would transfer the planning functions to States.

CSS in agriculture and rural development

Agriculture, under the Indian Constitution, falls under the State list. The entry 14 in List II of the Seventh Schedule read with Article 246 makes this clear. Entry 14 reads: "Agriculture, including agricultural education and research, protection against pests and prevention of plant diseases." Rural development (as we have already seen in Chapter 1) also falls under the State list (Item No. 5 of List II of the Seventh Schedule) reads: "Local government, that is to say, the constitution and powers of municipal corporations, improvement trusts, district boards, mining settlement authorities and other local authorities for the purpose of local self-government or village administration." According to Article 246, States alone are competent to legislate in respect of matters falling under the State list, but nothing prevents the Centre from formulating a CSS in that functional area. The GOI is accountable to Parliament for the CSS; the GOI share is subject to parliamentary scrutiny by the Public Accounts Committee (PAC). CSS amount to neither political decentralisation, nor financial decentralisation, as the assistance is tied to specific schemes; they represent only administrative decentralisation, as the Centre is using States and PRIs as agencies to implement them.

Earlier Central initiatives in agriculture and rural development

Despite the fact that agricultural and rural development fall under the State list, the important initiatives in both have, in the past, mostly come from the Centre. For example, CDP, IADP and HYV strategy were mostly the result of Central initiative. When the Centre takes such an initiative, a CSS is formulated and it then becomes the vehicle through which money flows from the Centre to the States for implementing the initiative. There are some reasons why in respect of matters falling in the State list, the initiatives in the past mostly came from the Centre. First, the skill and expertise required for evolving a strategy such as the CDP or the HYV were more with the Centre than with the States. In fact, until the Fifth Plan, the States did not have full-fledged planning departments. Second, many of these initiatives required access to foreign currency which was (and still is) tightly controlled by the GOI. Third, in the initial years of planning, there was a strong political leadership at the Centre, and the same party was in power at the Centre and in most of the States. The Nehru era lasted till 1964. The States, both at the political and at the administrative levels, were willing to abide by the prescriptions of the Centre in the matter of planning and implementation of agricultural and rural development programmes. Fourth, there was, till the onset of Green Revolution, an urgent problem of stepping up foodgrain production. It was both necessary and convenient to adopt a country wide strategy to address the issue.

The present changed circumstances

Many of the above factors changed during the 1970s. The country and most states became self-sufficient in foodgrain. The political equation changed, with some states having strong chief ministers, such as, Messrs V.P. Naik (Maharashtra), R. Mirdha (Rajasthan), Dr. B.C. Roy and Jyoti Basu (West Bengal). Later on, starting from early 1970s, the States having a party in power, different from the party in power at the Centre, increased in number. Centre no longer had the monopoly of expertise; on the contrary, some of the programmes were started by the States and these were later adopted by the Centre. The much celebrated JRY was patterned on Maharashtra's EGS, which was introduced in the State in mid-1970s, and later on adopted by other states such as Karnataka (Employment Assurance Scheme). District Planning was introduced in Maharashtra and Gujarat and now it has found a place in the Constitution. The States no longer needed Centre's expertise.

Definition of CSS

To repeat the definition of CSS given earlier, CSS are those Plan schemes which are formulated and funded, either fully or partly, by the Central Ministries and implemented by the States or their agencies. Financial transfers from the Centre to States under CSS fall under the fourth category mentioned earlier. In this chapter, we are more concerned with this category of transfers. Such transfers are normally made by each Central Ministry making such a transfer, to the corresponding State Government Department. For example, the CSS of the Central Ministry of Labour is generally implemented through the State Labour Department, the CSS of the Ministry of Rural Development is implemented by the State Rural Development Department and so on. They figure in the Central budget as far the Centre's share is concerned, and the State budget for the entire amount. Sometimes money goes from the Centre to a corporate body, such as DRDA (see Chapter 7), and in such cases, the Central transfer is reflected in the Central budget but not in the budget of the State concerned; the State budget contains only the State's share. For instance, JGSY (earlier JRY), which is implemented through DRDAs and PRIs, figures in the Central budget to the

Box 10.1: EGS, JRY and JGSY

Maharashtra's Employment Guarantee Scheme started in 1972 as part of the State Plan. Between 1972 and 1974, EGS was suspended as the State went through severe drought which necessitated the starting of a large number of drought relief works. It started again in the year 1974-75. The State Government gave statutory backing to the guarantee of employment, through the Maharashtra Employment Guarantee Act, 1977, which came into force from January 26, 1979. After the starting of the National Rural Employment Programme (NREP) and Rural Landless Employment Guarantee Programme (RLEGP), October 1980 and August 1983, respectively, as CSS, the operation of the EGS stood virtually suspended. The GOI decided to merge the NREP and RLEGP into a single rural employment programme, known as JRY.

JRY was launched by Government on 1st April 1989. This was also Centrally sponsored programme (like NREP and RLEGP) with the primary objective of generating additional gainful employment for the unemployed and under-employed, both men and women, in rural areas. JRY was merged with JGSY effective April 1, 1999. JGSY is implemented through PRIs.

extent of the Central share, and figures in the budgets of States concerned, as far as the States' shares are concerned. If the Centre's money passes through the State Government and becomes part of the consolidated fund of the State, then it will figure in the State budget; otherwise not. In many CSS there is a State component, which is part of the State Plan and budget. Annex 2 shows the CSS of the Department of Rural Development, in the Ministry of Rural Development. It is seen from this annex that the percentage of the total outlay on CSS that is borne by the State is not constant, but varies from scheme to scheme. For example, the CSS "Rural Water Supply Programme", has a budget allocation for 1999-2000 of Rs. 1800 crores, and it is shared by the States and Centre in the ratio 50:50. JGSY has a budget allocation of Rs. 1665 crores and it is shared by the States and the Centre in the ratio 75:25. Sometimes a scheme stipulates that the beneficiaries contribute a certain minimum percentage; for example, the scheme of rural sanitation says that the beneficiaries contribute 20 percent towards any project taken up under the scheme.

The historical development of CSS

From the beginning of the First Five Year Plan, there have been two issues relating to CSS. These are: (a) the pattern of Plan transfers from the Centre to the States, and (b) the character of the schemes themselves. We saw how in the beginning of the planning era, there was a strong Central presence in most matters pertaining to the States. At that time, what was important was the character of the schemes; the transfers of Central funds that were attached to the schemes were incidental. For instance, in the case of CDP, what was important was the character of the CDP, and discussions in the national forums focused on this issue. The States did not question the desirability of the schemes, nor demanded that the schemes may cease to be CSS and the equivalent money be passed on to them. The same was the case with the HYV strategy. But gradually as the States developed the capacity to plan for programmes which they considered relevant to them and also politically appealing, the CSS came to be seen as imposition from the Centre and fetters on their freedom to plan. They would rather have the Central funds, than the schemes. They were helped in this regard from the change in the determination of Plan assistance to the States from the IV Plan (1969-74) onwards.

Change in the pattern of Plan assistance to States from the beginning of the Fourth Five Year Plan

Prior to the IV Plan much of the Plan assistance to the States was tied to specific schemes which the States were required by the Centre to incorporate in their Plans. Sometimes the States also took the initiative to formulate schemes and sought financial support from the Centre; such schemes were called "Centrally Assisted Schemes"; there were not many such schemes, and they practically ceased to exist after the IV Plan.

In respect of CSS either the Centre would offer to bear the entire cost or would require the States to bear a certain percentage, generally ranging from 25 to 50 percent. The CSS, and the fact that they constituted a source of Plan assistance from the Centre to the States has acted as an effective financial leverage in the hands of the Centre to make the States fall in line with the Centre's thinking, and take up schemes considered by the latter to reflect national priorities. If the States did not adopt CSS as suggested by Centre, they would stand to lose Central assistance tied to these schemes.

During the formulation of the IV Plan, the relevance and the limitations of the CSS came up for intensive discussion in various forums particularly the NDC. The subject of CSS came up for discussion in the NDC meeting in May, 1968. The States were generally in favour of reduction in the number of these schemes. To quote from the proceedings of the meeting:

> "Many States have suggested that the number of Centrally sponsored schemes should be considerably reduced and those that might continue, be financed with 100 per cent Central assistance. There should be flexibility in regard to pay scales, staffing pattern, design of buildings etc." (India 1968c:45).

It is interesting to note that all Central ministries, with the exception of Ministry of Labour and Employment, suggested the continuation of the CSS; Ministries of Food and Agriculture, Health, and Works, Housing and Urban Development suggested additions to the number of these schemes. Following the recommendation of the NDC, it was decided to curtail the number of CSS during the IV Plan.

Administrative Reforms Commission (ARC) in its recommendation stressed "the need for full initiative and freedom of action to the States" (India 1967b:34) in the matter of planning and also suggested that CSS should be restricted to a "minimum number" having "basic national importance" (*ibid*:30). With a view to giving effect to this recommendation, the Planning Commission placed the issue before the NDC, recommending a reduction in the Centre's role in the formulation of the States' plans. The NDC said:

> "These were far reaching proposals which at one stroke, sought to abolish the practice of tying Central assistance with Centrally *approved* schemes and envisaged the allocation and flow of Central assistance pre-determined on the basis of certain broad socio-economic considerations, irrespective of the sector allocations or the nature of the schemes adopted in the Plans of the States. These measures, it was felt, *would enable the States to evolve their own Plans without any dictation from the Centre* either about the contents or the nature of the Plan schemes, of course within the overall availability of Plan resources." (Italics added). (India 1970:4).

Along with the decision to curtail the number of CSS, the pattern of flow of Plan assistance from the Centre to the States was altered substantially. As mentioned earlier, till the IV Plan, there was no fixed pattern or objective formula governing the allocation of Central assistance to the States, and the quantum of Central assistance was not predetermined. This quantum was largely decided in the light of the gap in the resources of each individual State for financing the Plan, in the light of the Plan outlay decided upon during the discussion between the Chief Minister of the State concerned, and the Deputy Chairman of the Planning Commission. This gave a lot of discretion to the Centre in deciding the size of the State's Plans and the quantum of Central assistance.

From the beginning of the IV Plan, this arbitrariness was replaced by a formula, known as the Gadgil formula, the details of which are described in the next paragraph. The replacement of the pre-IV Plan pattern of Central assistance, a substantial part of which flowed to States through a large number of schemes which States were prodded by the Centre to adopt, by a block assistance, shifted the Planning initiative from the Centre to States to a considerable extent. To quote from the IV Plan document:

> "In order to simplify the procedure for release of Central assistance, to avoid adoption of standard schemes unsuited to local conditions and needs, as well as to ensure equity among States in regard to the grant assistance for the Plan, it has been decided that in future there will be no schematic

patterns of assistance. Central assistance .... would be given to the States through block grants and block loans" (India 1970:55).

The Gadgil formula together with the new pattern of Central assistance is perhaps the most important development in the history of Centre-State financial relationship in planning. The formula has largely endured, with some minor modifications[3], till to-day, mainly because of its simplicity, and the appeal of the concept. It is based upon easily understandable and measurable criteria such as the state's population. This formula was modified in 1980 and the modified formula was the basis of allocation of central assistance during the Sixth and Seventh Plans. According to the modified Gadgil formula (Guhan 1987: 291), the States' shares are determined in terms of: (a) 60 per cent according to population; (b) 20 per cent to States having per capita income below national average; (c) 10 per cent on the basis of per capita tax levels, and (d) 10 per cent to take account of special problems. Since then, it has been further modified, but the components remain essentially the same.

Initiatives to reduce the CSS

Despite the decision of the NDC in 1968, the CSS gradually increased in number and outlay.

NDC Meeting on March 18-19, 1978

The large number of CSS once again came up for discussion in the meeting of the NDC held on March 18-19, 1978. NDC felt that except those CSS which have inter-state character and those which have bearing on national security, the rest can be transferred to the States along with the resources. After the 1978 NDC meeting CSS increased in number and outlay. Since 1978 there have been two major initiatives by the NDC to reduce the number of CSS; one was the NDC meeting of November, 1985 and the other was the NDC meeting of January 1997.

Box 10.2: NDC meeting on March 18-19, 1978

As the Planning Secretary, Maharashtra, I attended the NDC meeting on March 18-19, 1978. The meeting was presided over by the then Prime Minister, Morarji Desai. I remember that when the Chief Ministers asked for more funds to the States "untied" to specific schemes, he said that (half jokingly) the Centre might put a condition that the States extend to the districts (in the form of "untied" funds) what they wanted from the Centre, and that those who "receive" something should also be prepared to "give". Very prophetic words, they were, coming from an elder statesman. He said that while States want to wrest more power for themselves from the Centre (the discussion was on the role of the CSS in areas, such as agriculture, falling predominantly within the purview of the States) they were not willing to decentralise their powers to local bodies.

Following the meeting the NDC appointed a committee consisting of the Union Planning Secretary (Dr. Ajit Mazoomdar) as Chairman, and the State Planning Secretaries as members. This committee was charged with the responsibility of identifying those CSS which should continue as such. I attended the meetings of this committee as Planning Secretary of Maharashtra. The Union sector secretaries appeared before this committee and pleaded their "case", which was, why the CSS should continue as CSS. The bureaucratic line up was clear; the Union sector secretaries and the secretaries State sector departments wanted the continuation of the CSS. This would make the latter independent of their planning departments, and in Maharashtra, also of the DPDCs (see Chapter 9). The State planning secretaries wanted to have the final say (along with the DPDCs in Maharashtra) on the State plans without the intervention of the Union Ministries. Ultimately the committee nominated by the NDC identified many CSS which can be transferred to the States along with the corresponding outlays. In effect the States got "untied" funds of the order of Rs. 2000 crores, which was divided among the States by a formula akin to Gadgil formula.

NDC meeting on November 8-9, 1985

At this meeting, NDC decided to setup a committee under the chairmanship of P.V. Narasimha Rao,[4] the then Minister for Human Resources, consisting of three Central Ministers and 11 Chief Ministers. In its first meeting held on November 3, 1986 the Rao Committee (as it came to be called) approved the following criteria for the initiation of new CSS:

- The fulfilment of an important national objective such as poverty alleviation or achievement of minimum standards in education, or
- The programme has a regional or inter-State character, or
- The programme is in the nature of a pace setter or should relate to demonstration, survey or research.

As for the retention of existing CSS, the Committee expressed the view that schemes of national importance, such as, anti-poverty, rural water supply and family welfare programmes, and programmes for promoting human resource development and sustained improvement in the quality of life like education, may be retained as CSS and schemes other than these may be considered for transfer to the States. It will be noted that the above criteria were broader than the ones approved by the NDC in 1978. In fact the 1985 NDC criteria for transfer and retention were so broad, that almost any scheme which any Central Ministry wanted to continue as CSS or start as CSS could be justified. It is therefore small wonder that, after almost six years, when the NDC met in December 1991 to consider the matter (43rd meeting of the NDC), it decided to transfer only 6 out of a total of 262 CSS. The Centre had decided to retain many schemes, many had already been transferred or closed. The breakdown of these schemes is given in Annex 3.

NDC meeting of January 1997

At this meeting, the Chief Ministers were generally of the view that: (a) the CSS should be transferred to the States along with the resources, especially those coming in the State list under the Constitution, and (b) the retention of the CSS with the Centre should be limited those with an inter-State character, matters impinging on national security, selected national priorities where Central supervision is essential for effective implementation, and multi-State externally financed projects, where Central co-ordination is necessary for operational reasons.[5] The Planning Commission elicited views of the Central Ministries concerned and States. Most of the Central ministries/departments were in favour of retaining the CSS, and Chief Ministers and State

Planning Secretaries were in favour of transfer of a large number of schemes along with funds, to States. In view of the lack of unanimity among the key players in the national Planning scene, the issue was placed before the NDC meeting held in February 1999. The NDC decided to setup a committee under the chairmanship of the Deputy Chairman, Planning Commission, with members drawn from Central Ministries and States to examine the issue of transfer of CSS to the States. The members of this committee included: the Union Ministers of Finance, Human Resource Development, Agriculture, Consumer Affairs & Public Distribution and the chief Ministers of A.P., Gujarat, M.P., and West Bengal. The terms of reference of this committee were: (a) To identify the CSS for retention by the Centre and those for transfer to the States/UTs and to classify all the CSS accordingly, (b) for those CSS which will be identified for transfer to the States/UTs suggest the modalities of transfer including earmarking,[6] the funding pattern, the time frame for the transfer and the monitoring mechanism, and (c) in order to avoid future proliferation of CSS, lay down the criteria for the introduction of new CSS.[7] The Committee has met only once since its formation in 1999.

Limitations of CSS

Despite the fact that the Centre has travelled a long way since the days of CDP when States could not change any aspect of CSS without reference to the Centre, and has given a lot of discretion not only to States but also to PRIs, some rigidities still remain and cannot go away unless schemes are formulated at local level. The field observations (see Box 10.3) in Maharashtra confirm the observations in several villages in many States.

All the above observations regarding CSS apply, *mutatis mutandis*, also to State sponsored schemes. We saw in chapter 2 that whenever a programme is formulated at a higher level (at State headquarters or the Centre) and given to PRIs only for implementation (on agency basis) the problems of vertical and horizontal coordination increase. This is another serious limitation of the CSS and State sponsored schemes.

Box 10.3: Observations during field trips

The writer undertook field visits in Maharashtra in August 2000. He attended the Gram Sabha meetings in many villages. In the village described in this box, the *Sarpanch* was a woman, and a Master's degree holder. In all other respects, the village is a typical Indian village. The visit brought out graphically, that despite the fact that the *Sarpanch* was a highly educated woman, she found it difficult to convince the villagers why the schemes, which are implemented in their village, could not address their problems. Some examples are given below.

- There were a lot of demands for repairs to existing houses from BPL population. They were told, that, there were schemes for house sites and new houses, but, there was no scheme for repairs to existing houses.
- There were no demands for funds under some schemes. But still, the GP does not have the authority to divert them for other purposes for which there was a demand.
- CSS define SC according to the Constitution. But the State Government has its own scheme parallel to CSS covering some more castes and tribes, which are specific to the State.[8] In order to cover them, the State Government has devised its own scheme as CSS would not cover them. Similarly the ZP concerned has its own scheme, covering some categories of population not covered by the CSS and the State Government scheme. These schemes, namely, the CSS, the State Government schemes and the ZP schemes, differ in their eligibility criteria and the contributions from the beneficiaries. It is also very difficult for villagers to understand why they cannot be given assistance under CSS when the budget allocation under State Government and ZP schemes is finished. It is far better to amalgamate all the schemes to make the whole process simpler. Actually the *Sarpanch* needed the help of the BDO to explain to the assembly, the bureaucratic niceties of the various schemes. They were not convinced.
- There was a problem of female infanticide in that village; it sounds not very convincing, when funds are being surrendered under one scheme, to say that funds are not available to tackle this problem.

The visit underscored the importance of:

- "Keep it simple" (KIS) principle. Villagers have a lot of common sense and cannot find their way through the bureaucratic jungle. They, justifiably, feel that bureaucrats, in their own interests, tie them (the villagers) into knots.
- doing away with CSS altogether and having a more flexible co-financing arrangement described in the previous chapter.

Some key reasons why the NDC initiatives failed to produce results

There are several reasons why so many NDC initiatives regarding curtailing CSS have failed to produce the desired results.

Political factors

The most important among them is the political factor. The national political equation has changed since the early 1950s. Apart from the factors mentioned earlier, namely more and more States having a party in power at the State level, different from the one in power at the Centre, there is a new dimension in the political scene since mid-1980s. The State and Central ministers are interested in keeping themselves in power and are not bothered about mundane things like CSS. There are far more politically charged things to engage their attention. This is borne out by the fact that the Rao Committee took almost six years to finish its task and at the end of the six year period only six schemes were transferred to States. The present Committee under the Chairmanship of the Deputy Chairman, Planning Commission, going into the issue, has been on the job for nearly four years and has not found time to complete its job. The priority assigned to the CSS is obvious.

Bureaucratic factors

While the political executives are busy otherwise, the Delhi bureaucracy has been busy consolidating its power. Administrative leadership is no longer what it was during the early days of the CDP. In the early days of the CDP and even till the mid-1960s, the ICS officers who were occupying top positions at Delhi did not have to deal with the forces which confront the IAS officers to-day. Apart from the increasing political interference in administration[9] the present day IAS officers have to contend with the many problems which impinge on their official behaviour.[10] For instance, in many States, life in the capitals has become intolerable; cities, such as Patna, and Bhubaneshwar, have become by-words for decreasing quality of life, increasing political interference and more frequent transfers of IAS officers. Officers from these States want to get to Delhi at any cost. They find in Delhi a fairly stable career (the tenure of a Deputy Secretary is 4 years and that of a Joint Secretary is 5 years) and a bigger lake to swim (and hide oneself when chased). Once an officer comes to Delhi and sorts out his personal problems, such as, Government housing, schools for his children and jobs for their spouses, which may take up to one year (if one is lucky or has good contacts), the officer does not want to get back to his "parent cadre".

There is yet another reason for this pattern of behaviour of IAS officers, and that is the increasing competition for jobs in Delhi. Postings in the Central Secretariat used to be the almost exclusive preserve of the ICS, the Central Secretariat Service and some Central Services. Increasingly, the postings in the Central Secretariat is open to personnel belonging to other services and to personnel obtained on contract basis, who do not belong to any organised service, or who were in State services. All this introduces a great deal of desirable diversity into the Central bureaucracy, and adds expertise to the GOI, which IAS officers might lack, but it also makes the environment more congenial for the proliferation of the CSS. It makes jobs in Delhi more difficult for IAS officers to get, and therefore once they are in Delhi, they do not want to leave their jobs. The above observation regarding IAS officers also apply, *mutatis mutandis,* to officers obtained by the GOI on contract, or on deputation to Delhi from other services. Politicians are quick to exploit the situation facing bureaucracy.

Every CSS has a liberal sprinkling of Central component, with financial provisions for staff in Delhi. This gives officers who get posted to the Central Secretariat, in Ministries dealing with State subjects, the needed incentive to formulate new CSS or expand the existing CSS. They therefore give many reasons for holding on to CSS. Many of them brief Central Ministers in NDC meetings. It proves the observation made in Chapter 6, that the combination of political and bureaucratic forces is very formidable. We shall see in Chapter 11, how the international financial institutions and donors have tended to define decentralisation in their own way.

Notes

1. See in this connection, D.T. Lakdawala (1979).
2. From unpublished Planning Commission papers.
3. The formula was slightly changed by the NDC in 1980. This is called the modified Gadgil Formula.
4. He later on became the Prime Minister in June, 1991 and was the Prime Minister i.e. for a full term of five years, till May, 1996. It was during his tenure as Prime Minister, the 73rd and 74th Constitutional amendments were passed by the Indian Parliament.
5. These criteria were mentioned in the Ninth Five Year Plan 1997-2002 (India 1997).
6. This refers to the practice of transferring funds and schemes to the States with a condition that the State concerned earmarks funds in the State Plan for the purpose covered by that scheme.
7. From unpublished Planning Commission papers.
8. In Maharashtra there are what are known as "*Vimukta Jathis*"(VJ) and "*Nomadic Tribes*"(NT) and VJs and NTs have always been given the same treatment as SC under many State Government schemes.
9. The IAS officers' predicament during this period has been well chronicled by Potter (1986) on pages 212-245. But this account ignores the human and family side of the officers' lives and their impact on their official behaviour.
10. There are many problems which to-day's administrators face. But this account is confined to how the present day environment in which they officers function, is congenial to the growth of CSS.

CHAPTER 11

Parallel Structures which exist alongside Panchayat Raj Institutions

Ever since CDP, there have been many successful attempts to implement programmes directly through sector departments, even in States such as Maharashtra, Gujarat and Karnataka, where PRIs have been in existence for a long time. We saw in Chapter 5, how in Maharashtra, there have been many instances of transfer of schemes from the local sector to the State sector. Direct implementation of schemes by line departments represent the earliest examples of what may be called "parallel" organisations. An organisation is said to be "a parallel organisation" if it works directly with beneficiaries at the grass root level, which is not accountable to a PRI and whose funds are not channelled through a PRI. In this chapter, we shall see the proliferation of such organisations in the recent past.

These organisations are antithetical to decentralisation, but still are supported by the GOI and State Governments and are funded by international organisations. World Bank has to take the clearance of the Department of Economic Affairs, Ministry of Finance for funding any project in India, including those implemented by NGOs. And if it is a rural development project, that department generally take the views of the Ministry of Rural Development. Other international organisations are not obliged to even seek the clearance of the Ministry of Finance. This has created a situation where many NGOs knock at the doors of donors,[1] both Indian and Foreign, and obtain finance from them for their rural development projects without the knowledge of PRIs. Many PRIs come to know of the project, only when the NGO concerned starts operations in the project area.

The main issues discussed in this chapter are:

- The growth of such "parallel organisations" in rural areas has led to a segmented approach to development. Instead of an integrated District Plan, there are as many plans as there are schemes of line departments, and programmes of NGOs, which are generally donor funded. A situation is created where donors decide what development activities are to be pursued not people's representatives.

- Whereas, the programmes of line departments (which are examples of "un-integrated" administration, described in Chapter 2), have at least managerial sustainability, those of NGOs, are not firmly anchored in sustainable institutions, such as PRIs, and are not therefore managerially more sustainable than a PMU, which was described in Chapter 2.

What constitutes a "by-pass"

The term "by-pass" in the sense in which it is used in this book, and in which it is commonly understood, requires elucidation. That institution is said to be by-passed when funds are not routed through it. In this sense, the Centre by-passes State Governments as far as anti-poverty schemes are concerned, as the Centre gives moneys directly to DRDAs, and these moneys are not reflected in the consolidated fund of the State concerned. Many donors have told me: "After all, we do not by-pass State governments, as we keep them in the picture as to our activities in the State concerned." What they mean is that they have a discussion with the Secretary or the Minister of the State Government Department concerned, but their funds do not pass through State governments. They probably do not by-pass State governments according to their definition but they certainly do according to the commonly accepted meaning of the term in government circles.

Some examples of "Parallel Structures"

The following types of parallel organisations exist in most districts (Mathew 2000: 16):

- *Line departments:* Earlier we had occasion to comment on their behaviour. They are the earliest examples of "parallel" organisations.
- *DPC:* In those States, in which the ZP president is not the chairperson of the DPC, (e.g. Maharashtra) and the ZP is not given the freedom to plan for all DLS, DPC is a "parallel structure.

- *DRDA:* We have seen that the moneys for DRDAs do not pass through PRIs in many States, except in Karnataka, Kerala and M.P. who have merged the DRDA with ZPs.
- *NGOs, beneficiary groups and community based organisations (CBO):* Joint Forestry Management Committees fall in this category.

In this chapter we shall confine our discussion to the last type mentioned above.

Recently, after user committees[2] became more fashionable there have been more examples of parallel structures. In several development projects, drinking water, health, watershed development and primary education, Government has relied upon user committees, which are independent of PRIs. Very often in the same region, such as the hill region of U.P., the World Bank has promoted different committees, one for forest, the second for drinking water and the third for education and so on and all these committees by-pass PRIs.

World Bank and Rural Development

Among the rural development initiatives of donors, those by the World Bank deserve special mention. First, no bilateral donor can match the funding strength of the World Bank. Second, the World Bank has been using its financial clout to initiate dialogues with countries regarding institution building. Some of the lasting institutions, such as, T&V system of agricultural extension, Water and Land Management Institutes (WALMI) were created under World Bank-funded projects. The World Bank used to work with the departments concerned of the Central and the State governments for building sustainable institutions, such as the ones mentioned above.

Earlier attempts by the World Bank to tackle rural poverty were not successful as the institutions chosen for the purpose did not work as expected, as we saw in Chapter 2. Recently, the World Bank has returned to rural development and poverty after nearly 25 years, and this time, it had undertaken a programme of research that has synthesised experiences of various countries to identify mechanisms and strategies most likely to succeed. The research found that all the three elements of decentralisation namely, political, administrative and financial (see Box 1.1), need to be in place for decentralisation to work successfully. But it would appear that the World Bank is not following the conclusions of its own research.

Present situation

The recent World Development Report (World Bank 2000a) deals exclusively about poverty. The President of the World Bank, Wolfensohn (like McNamara) promises to eradicate poverty, some kind of a universal *Garibi Hatao* slogan (see Glossary). But it appears that the World Bank has not devoted sufficient thought to the institutions to be setup to carry out poverty alleviation programmes, if one goes by the recent first cohort of anti-poverty projects of A.P. and Rajasthan,[3] and is repeating the past mistakes. These projects are setting up institutions which are not sustainable after the project ends. (see Box 11.1)

Interaction between NGOs, donors and PRIs

We have seen above, how bureaucracy tends to by-pass PRIs by getting more and more schemes implemented through line departments and how the World Bank also tends to by-pass them by creating parallel project-specific organisations. There are many more organisations who tend to create parallel structures by-passing PRIs. Many of them are implemented by NGOs, often with donor finance. One can see in them, the gradual emergence of a sector, which is project specific, not managerially and financially sustainable, not statutory (let alone being Constitutional), which claim to have more resources than PRIs.[4]

The term "NGO" seems to open many doors nowadays. The term evokes visions of organisations driven by beliefs, compassion, altruism, voluntarism, the absence of profit or religious motive and headed by "larger than life" persons whose names are legendary. A typical NGO used to be a value-based organisation which depended mostly on voluntary charitable donations. The term now refers to any non-profit organisation, which is independent of government. As suspicions over governments in third world countries increase, NGOs often tend to be looked upon as the preferred alternative.

Box 11.1: World Bank funded District Poverty Initiative Projects in A.P. and Rajasthan

World Bank is funding the District Poverty Initiative Projects in A.P. and Rajasthan. If these first cohort of such projects are any indication, they are unlikely to setup sustainable institutions. A scrutiny of these projects reveals the following features.

- World Bank proposes to have its own definition of rural poverty line. It does not seem to have any faith in the democratically arrived at definition of poverty line of the GOI and State Governments.
- In both States the projects are being implemented as if the 73rd and 74th Constitutional amendments did not take place at all, and that the World Bank is writing on a clean slate, ignoring the rural development efforts that have taken place in the past 50 years. For instance, there is no mention of DRDA in the Staff Appraisal Report,[5] when the managerial arrangement at the district level is discussed.
- The past mistakes (mentioned in Chapter 2) are being repeated, and it is proposed to have PMUs accountable to State governments by-passing local elected governments. The PMUs which these projects setup will go the way of the earlier PMUs setup under IRDPs. Both the projects side step PRIs, the A.P. project more blatantly so.
- There is no beneficiary participation at the district level.
- Extra staff positions are being created at the State and district levels. It is indeed ironical that these projects by-pass elected bodies and recommend an increase in bureaucracy.
- The projects are silent about the involvement of line departments.
- The World Bank proposes to work through a set of NGOs selected by State Governments. The credibility of such NGOs selected by the government is questionable.

The responsibilities of NGOs are described in many books and articles (Cheema and Rondinelli 1983a: 203-209). It is very difficult to classify NGOs into convenient typologies: they vary from relief oriented organisations, to organisations who merely act as middlemen providing contacts with government, donors or international financial institutions. But, functionally, they can be classified into (a) advocacy groups, and (b) operational groups. The latter fall into three main categories: (a) community organisations which work closely with CBOs which vary in size, quality and integrity; (b) national organisations and (c) international organisations such as Oxfam, Greenpeace, Technoserve. In this chapter, we shall talk about NGOs mentioned in category (a) above.

Box 11.2: Planning Commission's Task Force

The Planning Commission had appointed a Task Force on PRIs to study, among other things, the interface between NGOs and PRIs. The Task Force submitted its report in March 2001. It has expressed concern over the fact that the Ministries are increasingly implementing their programmes through NGOs which are expanding rapidly in social sectors. But despite the existence of parallel structures created by the Central and State Governments in the districts, such as the Joint Forest Management Committees, DRDAs, and Watershed Committees, the Task force did not categorically say that funds for the above schemes should be routed through PRIs and that NGOs should work as subordinates to PRIs. The recommendations of the Task Force are ambivalent and will be flouted by NGOs and those who fund them, with impunity.

Community based organisations

CBOs (or user committees) are grass root or peoples' organisations. They are not intermediaries, but are "membership" organisations. Members having a common interest join these organisations to further their own interests. Examples of this kind of organisations are: women's groups, watershed committees, joint forestry management committees and water users' committees. But in practice, there is very often an intermediary, a local NGO, between the CBO and the donor concerned. Unorganised beneficiaries become a CBO only when they are organised and that is one of the jobs of the NGO. The NGO is generally contracted by the external donor to deliver services, such as organisation of beneficiaries, training, designing projects and implementing them. That is why such NGOs are called "development intermediaries."

NGOs and their supporters argue that, granting the inevitability of an intermediary between the CBO and the funding agency, NGOs have many advantages over big-sized governments. First, due to their small size and flexibility they can be risk-taking and innovative. They can demonstrate the usefulness of an approach, which can then be "scaled up". Second, a local NGO can elicit participation by beneficiaries in project design and implementation. We have seen how one of the negative features of the CDP, was the fact that bureaucracy was expected to elicit people's participation which, by temperament and training, it is not equipped to do. Third, a good NGO has more credibility with people, and can be a useful vehicle to carry messages from the government to them, regarding various aspects of the project. They can articulate local needs and demands and can play a useful role in mobilising local resources. Fourth, NGOs can ensure that the benefits of the project reach those who need it most, and can be a useful tool for preventing "leakage". Fifth, they can create political awareness.

All the above advantages, which a good NGO enjoys over government, are obvious. But they do not apply automatically in all cases. In India many NGOs are either religious organisations or caste-based ones. One has to be careful while selecting an NGO, particularly if the NGO is to be entrusted with the responsibility of providing services, project implementation or working closely with people. NGO selection is best done, not by the State or Central Government, in which case, it will have a low credibility, nor by the international financial institution or the foreign donor concerned, but by a non-political body, staffed by eminent persons known for their integrity and political neutrality.

Donor-funded watershed development projects

Some examples of donor funded watershed development projects are given below, to help the reader appreciate the connection between user groups or CBOs and NGOs on the one hand, and the latter and donors on the other. Indian agriculture is largely rainfed. Therefore watershed development, which includes water harvesting, is very important. Very few CBOs are funded directly by donors without the intermediation of an NGO, and the practice started long ago, with donor supported watershed development projects. In watershed development, there is a greater role for PRIs, than in other sectors such as health and education, for the simple reason that watershed development and rural development are handled by the same ministry at the Centre. But the role assigned to PRIs even in these projects does not go far enough.

Indo-German watershed development project (IGWDP)

IGWDP is often cited as an example of collaboration between government and non-government organisations that seeks to "scale up" the success of small micro-watersheds. This project is mostly implemented in Ahmednagar district in Maharashtra. There are NGO intermediaries in the project, who provide Technical Assistance support (TA) to the CBOs, participating in the project (Farrington and Lobo 1997). As of the end of 1997, the IGWDP covered about 100,000 ha in 90 villages, involving of some 55 NGOs. Under IGWDP, investment in the development of physical capital, begins only after evidence of social organisation suggests that people will work together to maintain the investments on both private and community land. There is a strong emphasis on developing the village's social capital as well as its natural and physical capital. Accordingly, the villagers must submit to several strict social conditions, including ban on free grazing and cutting trees; reducing livestock population; banning cultivation of water intensive crops; undertaking *shramdan* (voluntary labour) and contributing to a maintenance fund for watershed development. An important early project activity under the IGWDP is to plant trees and grass in the catchment area of the watershed. This is done prior to building water harvesting structures, in order to enable the villagers to demonstrate that they can enforce social fencing to protect natural vegetation. Following the demonstration of such social discipline, the project invests in new watershed structures.

Swiss Development Cooperation (SDC)

SDC projects are implemented by Karnataka and Rajasthan, the former through Karnataka Dry Land Development Board (DLBD), and the latter through the Rajasthan Directorate of Watershed Development and Soil Conservation (DWSC) and participating NGOs. Five NGOs are involved in Karnataka and one in Rajasthan. SDC passes the project funds directly to the NGOs. There are a range of intermediaries between the State government and the beneficiaries, namely, the SDC and its participating NGOs. The main job of the NGO is in motivating farmers to join the programme, organising them and preparing plans for the watershed selected for the programme. There is considerable emphasis on beneficiaries' contributions, which is 10 percent in Karnataka and 25 percent in Rajasthan.

DANIDA aided watershed development projects

The DANIDA assisted projects are implemented in Karnataka, Rajasthan and Orissa by the respective Soil Conservation Divisions in the Directorates of Agriculture. There is a government appointed Project Director (PD) in each project who is responsible for its implementation. In all the States, the projects include a salary component for the government staff working on the project. In addition there is a TA for each project which is paid by DANIDA. In all the States, NGOs have been obtained by DANIDA on contract to train and organise beneficiaries. Technologies are evolved by external consultants in discussion with NGO and government staff, and input by beneficiaries into the planning of land treatments is minimal. Staff are required to collect detailed information on villages, at the beginning of the project, but this is ritualistic and the information does not seem to have adequately been used for planning the programmes under the project. In the early stage of the project, beneficiary contribution was not insisted upon, but now that the project has started to yield benefits, contribution from beneficiaries is insisted upon, which can be either cash or in the form of labour.

Interaction between NGOs and PRIs

It is clear from the above survey of donor funded watershed development projects, that, in most cases, there is an NGO. The issues relating to the interaction between NGOs and PRIs, are mainly the following:

- Should NGOs be accountable to PRIs? More specifically, since most projects of the kind we are talking about, fall within a village, should they be accountable to the GPs concerned?

- Should project funds be routed through PRIs, in this case the GPs?

These issues are discussed further (see also Box 11.3).

Box 11.3: Diagram showing the interaction of NGOs with Beneficiaries and Donors

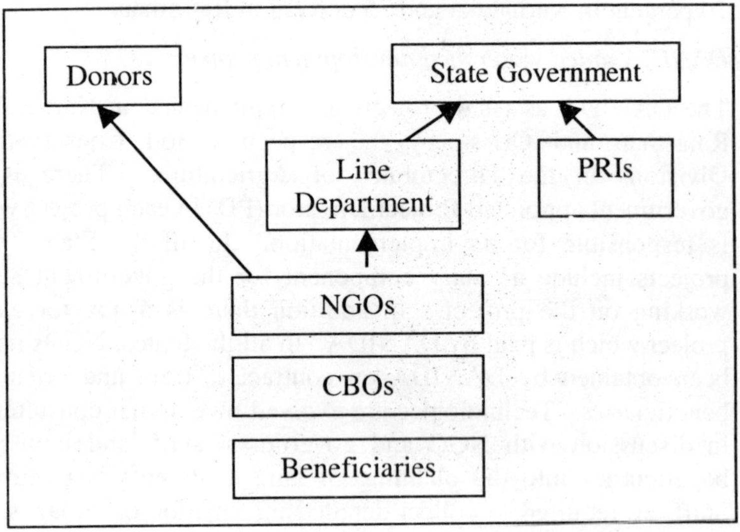

The success of PRIs in broadening and deepening democracy

There is no doubt that PRIs have been enormously successful in broadening and deepening democracy. There are now over 500 district level PRIs (DPs or ZPs), 5100 block level PRIs (BPs or PSs), and 225,000 village level PRIs (GPs) in India. Together with municipal bodies they now elect over 3 million representatives. (Mathew 1994:37). The reservations for SC/ST and women increase the representation in grassroot institutions, of hitherto marginalised groups. There is a growing respect for democratic institutions at all levels, and an increasing understanding of democratic processes and power structures. Political participation is based less on caste alliances than often assumed, and more on party affiliations or political factors. There are many and growing instances, where PRIs have challenged the dominant political group, through the active participation of women and SC in politics. In fact, at the State level, the reservation for SC and women is hardly questioned.

Arguments against PRIs

While all these virtues of PRIs are readily conceded by those who support "parallel structures", it has been argued, not only by NGOs, but also by line departments and donors, that PRIs:

- are political bodies, and that the villagers come together and form user groups, such as watershed committees, to meet an economic objective, and that
- they have to address several issues, unlike user groups which are more focused. Focusing on specific issues, be it education, health or forest management, these user groups would be able to attend to the specific needs of the programme and serve their members better.

For these reasons people would want their user groups to be distinct and separate from PRIs.

Arguments for PRIs

On behalf of PRIs it is often argued, and this argument has considerable force, that:

- If there are watershed committees for rainfed areas, water management committees for irrigated areas, common interest groups (as in the A.P.) for the poor, and similar groups for primary health and education, each having its NGO, then PRIs will have only "the shell without contents." This could not have been the intent of the Constitution makers, who had provided for 29 subjects of the Eleventh Schedule to be transferred to PRIs by the States. In no democracy in the world, is there such a separation of economic factors from the political.
- CBOs representing watershed users etc. present a homogeneous group which are often caste-based. Only PRIs represent the entire electorate which is heterogeneous, embracing all castes and religions, and all economic strata.
- Parallel structures are not sustainable, a point made earlier. After the source of funds dries up, the assets created under the projects, such as plantations, disappear, committees are disbanded or abandoned, and the livelihood base of the poor

remains only marginally improved, if at all. Perhaps, in some cases, they create some sustainable social capital by raising the awareness amongst the poor. However, evidence suggests that most of the social capital which projects create, is held by the rich, and that in fact most projects have contributed to a further entrenchment of their powers, as the author learned recently from informal discussions with a senior secretary of the GOI.

- Many CBOs are not democratic bodies. A representative of an NGO from A.P., said that there are a few villages in which user committees have the capacity to become partners of PRIs, but 60 per cent of these former institutions are not democratically elected.

Thus the present approach of the GOI, State Governments and donors raises several questions about the links that exist, and should exist, between them and PRIs. There are strong arguments on both sides, that is, PRIs on the one hand, and CBOs/NGOs funded by donors, on the other. What clinches the issue in favour of PRIs, is the fact they are democratic bodies, and it is in the interests of institutional development in rural areas that they be strengthened. Further, they are the only bodies in rural areas with heterogeneous electorate, and will therefore contribute to the gradual whittling down of caste barriers, whereas the user committees would re-inforce these.

Need to route funds to NGOs through PRIs

As mentioned at the beginning of this chapter, deconcentration without devolution will lead to a situation where the NGO will have a *carte blanche* to spend funds without being accountable to democratically elected persons at the local level. The very purpose of democratic decentralisation is to ensure local accountability and that is sought to be nullified by the arrangement whereby funds are not routed through PRIs. Though NGOs have successfully involved people in decision-making, there has to be "institutional anchoring" in a body which is sustainable. Thus the twin goals of accountability and sustainability will be met, if funds are routed through PRIs. It can then and only then, constitute genuine decentralisation.

Another area of conflict between NGOs (who are development intermediaries) and PRIs relates to the funds that they (NGOs) would access. Many NGOs are afraid of losing control over the money, and accuse PRIs of not having sufficient integrity and honesty, for being entrusted with project funds. They often argue that, when the GOI and the State governments do not trust PRIs, how could they (i.e. the GOI and the State governments), lecture to NGOs, with clean conscience? They point out, justifiably so, certain standing monuments of lack of trust in PRIs, such as, DRDAs, CSS, and State sponsored schemes.

Association of NGOs with donor assisted projects

The rules for the association of development intermediaries, such as NGOs, with rural development projects vary with the external donor concerned. There is no central clearing house for the projects funded by donors. Donor funds (except those of International Financial Institutions) do not have to pass through any Ministry of the GOI. NGOs who desire to access foreign funds need only the clearance of the Home Ministry under Foreign Contribution Regulation Act. NGOs are very reluctant to reveal the source of their funds. Considering that foreign funds are involved, one would have thought that the flow of these funds is centrally monitored by the GOI and is transparent. The author learnt during his field trips, that there is no easy way in which one can collect information about the financier of a donor assisted project, and the amount of money which has come into the country through the project. The following are the steps which an NGO has to take to get the project funded through a donor agency.

- Identify the user group and the activity (whether it is watershed management etc.).
- Give details of the project.
- Send the project report to the various foreign donor agencies, many of whom have their offices in New Delhi.
- After it is approved and the amount of money is indicated, apply to the Ministry of Home Affairs for clearance.

Informal links exist between the field staff of donor agencies and these development intermediaries. First, English is a common language for both of them. Second, many local employees of donor organisations come from the same background as the NGO executives-English educated, urban middle class background. The representatives of many donor agencies and NGOs, prefer to deal with district collectors and senior State government officials (many of them belonging to the IAS) rather than with unsophisticated, rugged villagers. In India , social workers and activists are also more at home with their own class in bureaucracy, than with the villagers. It is not therefore surprising that donor agencies prefer to deal with NGOs than with PRIs. Sector departments also would prefer to deal with NGOs as they feel that the association of NGOs with the development process will bring in more funds.

Interaction between NGOs and CBOs

CBOs and NGOs have a symbiotic relationship. Each requires the other for its existence. It would appear that bureaucracy is the main reason for the proliferation of NGOs. The main reason is that line departments do not trust PRIs. They feel that it is better that CBOs associate with NGOs rather than with PRIs, as NGOs are more amenable to bureaucracy than PRIs. The relationship between PRIs and user committees is important because in many development projects, such as drinking water projects, government has relied upon committees which are independent of PRIs. Many World Bank assisted projects involve committees for different purposes, one for forests, another for drinking water, and the third for education and so on, and they are all independent of PRIs, forming parts of the increasing number of parallel organisations.

Accountability in donor funded projects

The term "accountability" can be used in a broader sense (Binswanger 1999) to include, besides adherence to financial propriety, also political accountability. In CDP, accountability to the moneys entrusted, which is what financial accountability means, was almost taken for granted, as accountability in government mostly consists of adherence to financial propriety. CDP sought to embrace accountability in a broader sense of being "accountable to beneficiaries", and in order to achieve this, democratic decentralisation was introduced. In due course, the broader concept became the exclusive focus, and those who questioned the financial probity were dismissed, rather derisively, as "bean counters". But accountability in a narrow sense, of being accountable for the moneys entrusted, and adherence to financial propriety are equally important. In this narrower sense, accountability is a necessary condition for any successful programme, but not a sufficient condition. It is likely to be overlooked, in the concern for a broader concept of accountability, which is very fashionable now. Where public funds are involved, circumspection is called for. There are instances of misappropriation of funds by office bearers of co-operative societies and of NGOs. The surest safeguard is to have accountability both in the narrow as well as in the broader senses. In the euphoria of the times, certain time-honoured safeguards are likely to be forgotten. For instance, in the World Bank assisted DPIPs in A.P. and Rajasthan, there is little scope for financial audit, as project funds are proposed to be given to beneficiary groups, which have no legal entity, and there are no safeguards against misappropriation of funds by the office bearers of these bodies. PRIs are subject to Local Fund Audit, much of which is concerned with the narrow definition of accountability, mentioned above; democratic decentralisation will make them accountable to people in a broader sense also. NGOs on the other hand, is accountable to the beneficiaries of the projects, in a broader sense, but they do not have the kind of rigorous financial audit which PRIs have.

GOI guidelines regarding watershed projects

The GOI has issued guidelines (India 1994b) for the implementation of watershed projects by CBOs. These guidelines apply only to watershed projects, which are funded by the GOI through CSS and do not apply to externally funded projects, where money can flow directly from the external donor to the NGO concerned. They envision an institutional structure with strong association with PRIs and is therefore managerially more sustainable than a PMU. At the district level, the DRDA or the ZP are responsible for implementation. They select Project Implementing Agencies from among the departments, NGOs or corporations interested in implementing the projects. The Project Implementing Agency is responsible for 10 to 12 watersheds and is expected to appoint a multi-disciplinary Watershed Development Team. At each watershed, a

Watershed Committee implements the project under the guidance of the Watershed Development Association. The funds for the project are to be released directly to the Village Implementing Organisation or the Watershed Development Team, as the case maybe. People's involvement is to be initiated through Self-Help Groups which receive financial support from the project. The representatives of these groups are brought together to form the Village Watershed Association.

Watershed projects are planned and implemented by the Watershed Development Association, comprising all adult members of the Gram Panchayat and a Watershed Committee, which is a nominated body of the Watershed Development Association, with the help of the Watershed Development Team. After completion of the watershed project, the Watershed Committee would continue to function for the maintenance of assets and for this purpose, a Watershed Development Fund would be setup through contributions from User Groups and Self-Help Groups. The duties of the Gram Panchayat would include:

- implementation of the programme, especially organisation of rural communities and training programmes;
- support to the formation of Self Help or User Groups;
- the operation and maintenance of the assets created; and,
- monitor and review the programme to ensure that departmental norms for the cost of works and guidelines under Watershed Development schemes are strictly followed.

As far as possible the decisions of the Gram Panchayat should be taken in the full meeting of the Gram Sabha so that transparency and wide acceptability are ensured. The ZPs, PSs and the GP*s* are also entitled to take on the responsibility of implementing a cluster of watershed projects in the capacity of Project Implementing Agencies.

The guidelines require a seasoned bureaucrat to understand them. Bureaucracy derives its power through its capacity to interpret the maze of rules (which are themselves the invention of bureaucrats) that often constrain the freedom of elected leaders. As can be seen, the guidelines are extremely complicated. They acknowledge the fact that different programmes have different levels of subsidy and different funding pattern. There are at least five programmes concerned with watershed development – DPAP, Desert Development Programme(DDP), Integrated Wastelands Development Programme(IWDP), JRY and Employment Assurance Scheme(EAS). The last two programmes have been merged with JGSY. The guidelines say that:

> "Attempts have been made in the past to dovetail different schemes/programmes in order to achieve greater impact at the implementation level. However, it has been found that coordination and convergence of different programmes to a single area, suffers from several administrative problems."(India 1994b:3).

These guidelines envision:

- PRIs only as implementing agencies,
- That ZPs /DRDAs will receive funds directly from the GOI, and.
- The existence of project implementing agencies, which can be an NGO (whose role is that of a development intermediary).

These guidelines are definitely a step ahead of similar CSS of the GOI. They have given the monitoring and review functions to the Gram Panchayats, and have increased the accountability of line departments to PRIs. (India 1994b: paragraph 34, p.14). They however, suffer from two fatal flaws. First, they do not give the freedom to PRIs to decide where the money goes. This is a serious limitation. For example, the PRI concerned cannot decide that it would increase the provision for Integrated Rural Development Programme, now part of SGSY, with a view to utilising the benefits of watershed development. Second, there is no association of beneficiaries in the Watershed Development Team. Paragraphs of the guidelines which speak of Watershed Development Team, envision that agency as yet another bureaucracy interacting with beneficiaries. Training envisioned under the guidelines do not involve beneficiaries in identifying the areas where training is needed.

CAPART

Council for Advancement of People's Action and Rural Technology (CAPART) was formed in 1986 by merging two organisations, namely, People's Action for Development India (PADI) and Council for Advancement of Rural Technology (CART). Since 1999-2000 this organisation has been funding NGOs for implementing various projects in the rural sector. Some of the issues funded by CAPART are, empowerment and training in capacity building. Actually if the States operate decentralisation properly, there is no justification for CAPART. PRIs, if they feel the need for entrusting any matter to an NGO, can do so. CAPART is example of a scheme which can be entrusted to PRIs for implementation as they choose to, but is now being implemented by the Centre.

Notes

1. In this chapter the term donor includes international financial institutions, such as the World Bank.
2. "User committees" or "user groups" is also called community based organisations (CBO), which is defined later in this chapter.
3. See Venkatesan (2000).
4. There is no official estimate as to how much money flows to rural development through NGOs. One unofficial estimate is that about Rs.12,000 crores ($2.5 billion) are received each year by NGOs from foreign sources alone. In addition they also get money from local sources including the GOI.
5. This is the report which sets out the details of the project. A.P. report is Report No. 20089-IN and Rajasthan report is Report No. 20203-IN.

CHAPTER 12

Conclusions

This chapter brings together the arguments of the previous chapters and summarises the conclusions of our enquiry.

Coordination and democratic decentralisation

In India, the probability of coordination is higher in integrated administration than in un-integrated administration. The CDP instituted integrated administration in the rural areas in the form of the BDO's establishment. This is more managerially sustainable than project-based institutions, such as, for example, those set up under the World Bank assisted rural development projects described in Chapter 2. But because it amounted only to administrative decentralisation, the BDO's establishment did not deliver to the extent expected. Balwantray Mehta Committee tried to reverse this trend. The democratic decentralisation experiments in Maharashtra and Gujarat in the early 1960s, following Balwantray Mehta Committee report, grappled with the problem of coordination and proposed District as the first point of decentralisation. This was never given a chance to prove itself, as the task of coordination was given by the State Government to the District Collector, which (s)he was not able to perform well, since people's representatives were not associated with administration. India is very much seniority conscious. That was why it was proposed by Naik committee, on whose report the Maharashtra model of decentralisation was based, that the CEO, ZP would be senior to the District Collector, but this never came about. So the problem of coordination remained to be systematically tackled by a democratically decentralised administration.

The role of sector departments in decentralisation

We have seen how the sector departments have been responsible for stifling any efforts at democratic decentralisation and how they should transform themselves from agencies to provide funds to PRIs, and plan their programmes, to agencies to monitor the implementation of programmes and provide technical guidance to PRIs. During the visit of the author to Kerala this attitudinal change was discussed. There was strong evidence that the State government has already thought of this and is taking steps to address the issue. The Kerala Health Secretary explained the role of the Health Department in providing technical advice to the gram panchayats, taking the control of malaria as an example. According to the Secretary, if the local people feel that malaria should be controlled, the health department can lay down the technical options before the gram panchayat, and advise it on the most cost-effective option. In every field, this new role of the sector departments needs to be explored, if they are to play a useful role supporting decentralisation.

The impact of political factors, bureaucracy and international organisations on decentralisation

Following Balwantray Mehta Committee report, democratic decentralisation was introduced with great fanfare in A.P.and Rajasthan and later, in Maharashtra and Gujarat in 1961. It was soon realised that the bureaucracy, which never looked kindly at the integrated setup under the BDO, joined hands with Central and State level politicians in ensuring that the democratic decentralisation did not work. Following the Ford Foundation Report, the line departments, starting with State Agriculture Departments, broke away from the integrated administration represented by the BDO's establishment. The introduction of T&V cemented this trend. At the Central level, a number of CSS in areas which are predominantly State subjects, came to be formulated. At the State level, a number of programmes came to be planned and implemented directly from the State secretariat by-passing locally elected bodies. This reinforced the emerging tendency of the Central and State level politicians of leaning more on bureaucrats, rather than on elected politicians at the district level and below. Donors also joined the decentralisation-avoiding group. The result was the gradual decline of the CDP and democratic decentralisation.

Democratic decentralisation – the result of evolution

Democracy is deeply entrenched in Indian politics, and I have often sat in the officer's gallery of Central parliament or the

State legislature with a sense of pride, that I was witnessing democracy at work, in spite of all the unseemly happenings in the House. The careful nurturing of democracy after Independence, by leaders, such as Jawaharlal Nehru, has indeed paid off. The progress of democratic decentralisation in India, culminating in the 73rd and 74th Constitutional amendments indicate an evolutionary trend. The major milestones are shown below.

Independence	August 15, 1947
First Five Year Plan	1951-1956
CDP Pilot Projects	November, 1951 – May, 1952
Lauching of CDP	October, 1952
Second Five Year Plan	1956-1961
Balwantray Mehta Committee Report	1957
Ford Foundation Report and the Intensive Agricultural Districts Programme	1959
Third Five Year Plan	1961-1966
Democratic Decentralisation in Maharashtra and Gujarat	1962
West Bengal decentralisation	1978
Report of the Dantwala Committee on Block level planning	1978
Asoka Mehta Committee Report	1978
Karnataka decentralisation	1987
Hanumantha Rao Committee on District planning	1984
G.V.K. Rao Committee	1985
L.M. Singhvi Committee	1986
Patil Committee (Maharashtra)	1986
Constitutional amendments	1993

The recent Constitutional amendments have given a shot in the arm of decentralisation. So far democratic decentralisation was brought about by the State legislatures, and the States could indefinitely postpone panchayat elections. But giving a Constitutional status to panchayats is a definite step towards greater democracy. Now the time has come to make Gandhiji's dream of village democracy come true.

The return of the triumvirate

But the triumvirate consisting of politicians, bureaucrats and international organisations, would not give up easily despite Constitutional amendments. The State and Central politicians have used every excuse to postpone panchayat elections, keep the State Ministers as Chairpersons of DPCs, and keep the panchayats away from important aspects of rural administration, such as, disaster management. In the recent Latur and Gujarat earthquakes, PRIs were not entrusted with the rehabilitation work. The interim report of the National Committee on Disaster Management, which consists mostly of politicians, does not make any tangible reference to PRIs. Bureaucracy and international organisations have not exhibited that they have any beliefs, and have played the tune which the politicians called. Bureaucrats have responded enthusiastically by neutralising PRIs, and the number of CSS will bear testimony to this fact. PRIs do not have the facility of having "untied" funds with which to plan and implement programmes which local people, and not those sitting in Delhi or State capitals want. Many donors have, under the pretext of encouraging CBOs, systematically demolished the fragile rural institutions set up under the Constitution. Their motives are highly questionable, and it is not clear whether they believe in democracy at the grassroot level at all.

Parallel structures and NGOs

In the area of rural development, donor funds and those of international financial institutions, are substantial. International organisations by-pass the democratic institutions represented by PRIs and fund NGOs, and through them, CBOs, directly, resulting in the creation of parallel structures. Many NGOs fall for the lure of the foreign money. While there are NGOs who are engaged in self-less work, the presence of big money attracts undesirable NGOs, who bring discredit to the good ones. The fact that the GOI and State governments also by-pass PRIs is no justification for the anti-democratic behaviour of donors. The local bureaucrats of many donors want their projects to be successful in the short term. Never mind the long term sustainability of the projects. They therefore opt for an institutional arrangement that will result in "show pieces" to be exhibited to their masters "back home." It is doubtful if the Minister in charge of overseas development (in the case of bilateral donors) knows that the activities of "donor" bureaucracy are not congenial to the growth of democracy of the recepient country at the grassroot level. The redeeming feature is that the bilateral donor community consists of democratic countries, and this cannot be said of many other international organisations, which are mostly driven by their own bureaucracies.

Box 12.1: Short term vs. long term developmental goals

Comparisons are often made between the approach of the World Bank and that of Rockefeller foundation in the area of Indian agricultural research. The former by its statutes cannot have a long term time horizon. The development of a country's agricultural research system is a long term effort lasting more than fifteen years. Ralph Cummins (Sr) of the Rockefeller foundation was in Delhi for a long time, as against the frequent transfers of the personnel of the World Bank. While analysing the causes of the slow growth of Africa's agricultural research systems, the inherent conflict between what is good in the short term vs. what is essential in the long term, is often cited as one of the main reasons.

PRIs as institutions of self-government

It is too early to judge the performance of PRIs. Even in a short time, when given a chance, PRIs have proved to be effective as the Kerala and West Bengal examples would show. PRIs in other States are not given a chance to prove themselves and have not been entrusted with decentralised planning nor given untied funds. The Constitution (Article 243G) speaks of PRIs as institutions of self-government. The problem comes when they are viewed as instruments to bring about rural development, and the Centre and States consider them as mere implementing agencies of programmes prepared in distant Delhi or State capitals. Any institution of self-government must have, at the minimum, the following:

- The delineation of functional areas where it is responsible. The 29 subjects mentioned in Eleventh Schedule of the Constitution is a good starting point.
- Wherewithal to carry out its assigned tasks. This implies that PRIs should not be required to go with a begging bowl to the State or Central government, and funds available to them should match their responsibilities. The Constitution makers were aware of this need of PRIs and have provided for the setting up of SFC (Article 243I).
- PRIs should be able to decide how much of bureaucracy they want and should be free to lay off personnel found surplus to their requirements. This implies that they have their own staff, and not those belonging to the State or All-India bureaucratic cadre, so that the district bureaucracy is accountable to the district government.

Democratic decentralisation the only way for rural development in India

Democratic decentralisation offers better coordination as it offers a combination of integrated administration and coordination from below, namely, the representatives of the clients of administration, who in democracies are the people. It combines the political and economic factors, and offers the necessary heterogeneity. It avoids exclusiveness that is inherent in the CBO-based development. It has the potential of realising Gandhiji's dream of a casteless society. A fuller treatment of the rationale for decentralisation is contained in Manor 1999b.

In spite of the obvious advantages of decentralisation why should governments not decentralise? Why is it that in India there are forces working against decentralisation? There are no easy answers. Some, at least, are apparent. First, despite more than fifty years of independence the administration in India is not fully "developmental". All that has happened is at the

Central and State levels elected persons are in command and they are effectively preventing democracy from reaching the district level and below. In order to be fully developmental, there has to be complete decentralisation. Second, the inherent conflict between technical goals and the parameters of human development and the "politics" of dealing with citizens as human beings with aspirations is not yet resolved. To give an example, there was, some years ago, a dispute between two groups in a cluster of villages, over the design of rural water supply project. Technically, it made more economic sense in the long run to have a big piped water supply scheme from a dependable source, to supply water to a cluster of villages. But the real issue involved was not a technical one. Villagers, for their own reasons, wanted ground water-based wells without house connections. The local officials were called, and they treated it as a "technical" and "law and order" problem. The Minister was not interested in such "trivial issues"as they were not going to affect his election, nor his Ministership. The PRI concerned might have solved the problem. The local Sarpanch would also have taken the credit for resolving the issue, which the State level politicians did not want. Third, despite Constitutional provisions regarding the setting up of SFCs and embarking on financial decentralisation (the third leg of the tripod, the other two being administrative and political decentralisation), the political process has still to get used to the new setup. The main question regarding financial decentralisation seems to be, "is it possible to conduct a meaningful planning process from the bottom up (as the rhetoric requires, and the Constitution demands), when it seems clear that the resources will almost inevitably have to come from the top down?" Politicians and bureaucrats are still to come up with answers which are politically feasible and bureaucratically acceptable. Cutting across all this is the caste issue. The M.P. experiment raises many interesting questions regarding the role of caste in village politics.

Other related issues are:

- Is it possible to harmonise centrally sponsored schemes and state funded and implemented activities (in education and health particularly) on the one hand, and local preferences on the other, given the political dynamics of national and state political (party) systems, and agendas, and local systems of power?

- Can elected representatives at the local level be made accountable on a continuing basis to developmental programmes at the local level, so that national and state level politicians and bureaucrats, and international organisations will not be tempted to set up parallel institutions, particularly those relying on NGOs?

Factors favouring decentralisation

Among the pro-decentralisation factors, the one which is the most important is the commitment of the leaders at the top. India was, during the immediate post independence period, blessed with such leaders. The other factors are:

- Elites at intermediate levels -e.g. Brazil and Columbia; or the opposition parties lobbying effectively for devolution- e.g. South Korea.
- The presence of intellectuals and NGOs – both national and international.
- Foreign governments and world opinion. Increasingly the force of world opinion plays a significant role. In the recent Nigerian elections for example, the force of world opinion played a significant role. Globalisation and the modern communication technology by making news travel faster has contributed to the spread of democracy.
- Combination of like-minded people from different countries to raise the awareness of the rest of the population; something akin to what the environmentalists have achieved over the past several decades.

Box 12.2: Decentralisation and Globalisation

When I was travelling in Malawi sometime back, I was asked by a coffee farmer in a remote area of the country, (actually this area on the border of Malawi, Tanzania and Zaire (as it was then known)) that he had seen the news item on the CNN, that international coffee prices had gone up and why he was not getting the benefit of the increase in prices. He was not happy with what he described as "the bureaucrats of the Coffee Board." I had a similar experience in Tamil Nadu. People there were wondering why politicians and bureaucrats sitting in distant Chennai or Delhi should have a say in what happens in their village. No wonder politicians and bureaucrats paint globalisation as something that is thrust on poor countries by the rich ones. Globalisation will inevitably lead to decentralisation, which the national and State level politicians and bureaucrats do not like.

While the presence of a liberal democracy at the national level is a sufficient condition for decentralisation it is not a necessary condition. There can be decentralisation without a liberal democracy at the national level. Uganda is a good example. For President Museveni, decentralisation to the district level and even below, is a means to maintain himself in power, as a leader to challenge them is unlikely to emerge in such a situation, as the top leader who can emerge to challenge his position is at best a district level leader. Thus the leaders of autocratic regimes have seen in decentralisation a surrogate for democratisation at the national level, and as a pathway for acquiring much needed legitimacy and grassroot support. In the eyes of the world they are very democratic, because they have decentralised! But just as their yearning for recognition and keeping themselves in power, makes them decentralise, the very process will awaken the desire for national recognition in many others, who some day may rise to challenge them. Thus decentralisation, even though driven by self-interest, has the possibility of bringing about liberal democracy at the national level.

Decentralisation – an unstoppable process

There are many factors which make decentralisation an unstoppable process. There is a growing realisation that:

- Rural development in the Third World is undergoing a rapid transformation.
- The future challenges will be different from the past ones.
- It is urgently necessary to equip the development practitioners to design and implement rural development programs which will address the key challenges, which are described below.

Key challenges

Technological: There is, in every aspect of rural development a tremendous growth of technology, with the attendant need for: (i) change in the processes of delivery of rural services; (ii) more frequent interaction between associated institutions; and (iii) providing rural population with a wider range of technological options.

Poverty alleviation: In almost every country, there is growing hiatus between the rural rich and poor, not confined to those who inhabit the harsher environments, necessitating increased focus on poverty alleviation.

Natural resources management and environment: There is an increasing concern for an improvement in the management of natural resources and environmental considerations. The environmental problems require a much longer time horizon, longer than the political life cycle of the national or local politicians.

Funding: Many governments in the South are unable to fund critical components rural development adequately and there is an increasing call for these services being funded by the users, who can afford to do so.

Sustainability: There is an increasing awareness of issues concerning the institutional and financial sustainability of rural extension systems.

Globalisation: One aspect of globalisation was mentioned earlier, namely its capacity to make news travel faster between borders. The other aspect is the interplay between technology and institutions. New technology will require new institutions. Those who are very comfortable with the old ones do not like new technology.

Role of governments: The role of governments is under close scrutiny and there is a growing support for the view that this role should change from one of provider of rural services, to one which will catalyse the provision of services by a range of institutions; this will affect the way in which governments are structured and the international institutions and donor communities operate.

Addressing the above challenges will call for a range of 're-engineering' efforts. Beneficiary participation in the design and implementation of rural development programmes, accountability of administration to beneficiaries, beneficiary assessment of services and democratic decentralisation have come up in the recent past, as important parts of the agenda of 're-engineering' rural development.

Annex 1

Table showing the salient provisions of the Maharashtra, West Bengal and Karnataka Acts and the Constitutional provisions

Criteria and Structure	**Maharashtra** (1961)	**West Bengal** (1978/1985)	**Karnataka** (1985)	**73rd and 74th amendments of the Indian Constitution** (1993)
Number of levels of democratically elected local bodies	Three – the Village, Block (i.e, PS) and District (ZP)	Three: the Village, Block and District	Two-Mandal and District	Three: the Village (GP), District and Intermediate level.
Number of effective levels	Three: the Village, Block and District	Three: the Village, Block and District	Four: Village (Gram Sabha), Mandal, Taluka (Block) and District. Taluka PS was designed to be a purely advisory body.	Three
The frequency of meeting of the Gram Sabha mentioned in the Act	Nil	Nil	Gram Sabha was the basic unit of the system. It had to meet, by law, at least twice a year, presided over by the Chairperson of the concerned Mandal Panchayat.	Left to the state legislatures.
How are the members of the GP elected. The manner of electionof its	Members are elected directly. The chairperson (called the *Sarpanch*) is	Directly. For every fice hundred voters there was one member. The	Doest not arise	Directly elected.

Criteria and Structure	Maharashtra (1961)	West Bengal (1978/1985)	Karnataka (1985)	73rd and 74th amendments of the Indian Constitution (1993)
Chairperson	elected by the members from among themselves.	Chairperson was called the *Pradhan*, and Vice-Chair was called the Upa-Pradhan. They were elected by members from among themselves.		
The next higher level of democratically elected body and the manner of election of its members and chair and vice-chair	PS. Members were directly elected. The chair and vice-chair were elected by members from among themselves.	PS. Members were directly elected, the number of members elected from each village should not exceed three. In addition the pradhans of all GPs within the PS, and the local MLAs and MPs as long as they were not ministers, were also members. The Chairperson of the PS were elected by the members from among themselves.	The first level of democratically elected body was the Mandal Panchayat. Each mandal would have roughly 30 members, who was directly elected. Its Chairperson was elected by its members. Taluka PS was a purely nomnated body comprising ex-officio memebrs. It had no powers and its role was purely advisory.	
The Constitution of the District level body (ZP)	Members of the ZP (other thanthe nominated	It was a supervisory body over the PS and GP. The	DP (or what is the same, ZP) was the second tier of	

Criteria and Structure	Maharashtra (1961)	West Bengal (1978/1985)	Karnataka (1985)	73rd and 74th amendments of the Indian Constitution (1993)
and the manner of election of its chair and vice-chair	members) were directly elected. The ZP works through a number of committees such as the Standing Committee. The President and the VP of theZP and chairpersons of the committees were elected by the members of the ZP.	members were elected directly, each block returning two members. The *Sabhapatis* of all PS were ex-officio members of the ZP.	democratic decentralisation. It was the apex body of the district development and welfare administration. Its members were directly elected. The Chairperson *(Adhyaksha)* and *(Upadhyaksha)* were elected by the members of the ZP. The *Adhyaksha* was the executive head of the ZP.	
Association of MPs and MLAs with these bodies	Associate members without voting rights.	They were members of both the PS and ZP	Organic linkage was provided by the provision that all the PS Chairpersons and one-fifth of the *Sarpanches* (by rotation) were members of the ZP. They but did not have the right ro hold any office. But had the right to vote.	The state legislatures can decide whether MLAs, MLCs and MPs should be members of District or Intermediate Level Panchayats; but if they are made members of these panchayats by State law, they would have voting rights except in

Criteria and Structure	Maharashtra (1961)	West Bengal (1978/1985)	Karnataka (1985)	73rd and 74th amendments of the Indian Constitution (1993)
				matters relating to the election of the Chairperson. (Article 243C of the Constitution)
Existence of organic linkages between different levels	Nil	Yes. The Pradhans were members of the PS and the *Sabhapatis* were members of the ZPs.		State government may by law provide for organic linkages. See Article 243C(3) of the Constitution.
Terms limits of the Chairpersons of PRIs	Originally, i.e., in 1962, two terms. After the state enacted legislation to bring the state Act in conformity with the Constitution the term of office of the President and the Vice-President was reduced to one year, and subsequently increased to two and a half years.	No mention of term limits. The PRIs have a life of five years.	No mention of term limits. The PRIs had a life of five years. Recently after the enactment of the conformity legislation, the term of office of the ZP president had been reduced 20 months.	
The extent of autonomy of PRIs	Collector and Divisional Commissioner have been given some powers	No supervisory powers were given to the State bureaucracy over ny of	State government could dissolve the ZP for abuse of their powers and	

Criteria and Structure	Maharashtra (1961)	West Bengal (1978/1985)	Karnataka (1985)	73rd and 74th amendments of the Indian Constitution (1993)
	regarding PRIs. The CEO of the ZP is appointed by the state government, is subordinate to the ZP and has to be withdrawn from the ZP if 2/3 rds. of the total number of members of the ZP so request. The President or a VP can be removed from office by the state government.	PRIs. But the State Government had retained the powers to suspend any resolution of the any of PRIs and also to supersede them.	persistent default in the performance of or incompetence to perform their statutory duties. Reconstitution by election was mandatory within six months. ZPs had similar powers vis-à-vis Mandals. No government officer could suspend a resolution of PRI.	
Planning functions	Nil. These are with another body called the DPDC (now DPC), under the chairmanship of a separate Minister (called *Palak Mantri*).	The planning work was entrusted to an outside body which functioned under the chairmanship of a separate Minister like in Maharashtra and Gujarat.	Chairperson of the ZP is the Chairperson of the District Planning Council. Subject to National and State priorities the plans prepared by PRI are final.	Article 243 ZD gives planning functions to DPCs (see Chapter 9)
Statutory resource transfers			The State government was required to make a grant at the rate of Rs.10 per person residing in the Mandal. 20% of this	Article 243-I stipulates the Constitution of SFC by the state government. As mentioned in Chapter 8, there is no mention of

Criteria and Structure	**Maharashtra** (1961)	**West Bengal** (1978/1985)	**Karnataka** (1985)	**73rd and 74th amendments of the Indian Constitution** (1993)
			amount was payable to the ZP. This grant is "untied". While Mandal could levy taxes or cesses, ZP cannot. But the ZPs could retain with them accruals from income generating schemes transferred to them by the State government. In addition the sectoral allocations for district sector schemes were provided in the state budget.	the deadline for the state government to decide on the recommendations.
The Status of the DRDAs	Exists as a separate entity and the President ZP is the Chairperson of this body.	District Rural Development Society existed as a separate entity and the Chairperson of the ZP is the Chairperson of this body.	Has been absorbed in the ZP.	

Source: Relevant Acts of Maharashtra, West Bengal, Karnataka and the Constitutional Amendments.

Annex 2

Table showing the Centrally Sponsored Schemes of the Ministry of Rural Development (Department of Rural Development and Department of Land Resources)

(Rs. In Crores)

Sr. No	Names of the CSS	Year of Starting	Patter of Funding Centre/State	Grant/Loan Component	Eight Plan Allocation	Plan Expenditure	1999-2000 Bueget Est.	Remarks
1.	Rural Water Supply Scheme	1977-78	50:50	Grant	5100.00	4141.83	1800.00	Retain
2.	Rural Sanitation	1986-87	Centre 40% State 40% Benef. 20%	Grant	380.00	232.87	110.00	Retain
3.	JGSY (earlier JRY)	1989-90	75:25	Grant	18400.00	14712.84	1665.00	Retain
4.	Employment Assurance Scheme	1993-94	75:25	Grant		5242.94	2040.00	Retain
5.	Indira Awaas Yojana	1985-86	75:25	Grant		1232.84	1710.00	Earmark
6.	Strengthening of State Training Centre	6th Plan	100% NR 50:50 recurring	Grant	15.00	16.12	4.25	Retain
7.	Strengthening of Extension Training Centre	7th Plan	100 % NR Recurring upto Rs. 5 lakhs per ETC	Grant	10.00	11.76	3.0	Retain
8.	Roads in Special Problem Areas	1985-86			20.00	7.71	0.50	Retain
9.	National Social Assistance Programme	1995-96	100%	Grant		933.83	725.00	Retain

Sr. No	Names of the CSS	Year of Starting	Patter of Funding Centre/State	Grant/Loan Component	Eight Plan Allocation	Plan Expenditure	1999-2000 Bueget Est.	Remarks
10	Drought Prone Area Programme	1973-74	50:50	Grant	500.00	442.36	110.00	Retain
11.	Desert Development Programme	1977-78	75:25 (Hot Arid Non-Sandy) 100% Others	Grant	500.00	375.89	60.00	Retain
12.	Computerisation of Land Records	1988-89	100%	Grant	48.00	60.35	33.00	Retain
13.	Strengthening of Revenue Administration and Updating of Land Records	1987-88	50:50	Grant	175.00	97.85	10.00	Retain
14.	SGSY (earlier IRDP etc.)	1980	75:25	Grant	3800.00	3540.81	1100.00	Retain
15.	District Rural Development Agencies (DRDA's) Administration	1998-99	75:25	Grant			215.00	Retain

Source: Planning Commission, Government of India.

Annex 3

Table showing the total number of Central Sponsored Schemes and those recommended by the Rao Committee for retention by the Centre and for transfer to the States

Total No. of CSS identified by the committee	**262**
CSS recommended for retention	125
CSS identified by the committee for continuation to be implemented by autonomous bodies	24
CSS recommended for transfer to the States	**113**
CSS which were discontinued/defunct/completed/ non starters	68
CSS which were reclassified as Central sector schemes	4
CSS which were transferred to the States in 1992-93	34
CSS which were transferred in 1993-94	1
CSS identified for transfer from 1994-95	**6**

Source: Planning Commission, Government of India.

Annex 4

Table showing the functional responsibilities of the different levels of government under various schemes

Name of the scheme	Planning	Impleme ntaion	Co-ordination	Review	Remarks
Central					
1	Centre	Centre	State	Centre	Functional responsibilities depend on the scheme. What are shown here are illustrative. Central and State schemes include centrally sponsored and State sponsored schemes.
2	Centre	State	State	Centre	
3	Centre	District	State	Centre	
State					
1	State	State	State	State	
2	State	State	State	State	
3	State	District	District	District	
District					
1	District	District	District	District	
2	District	District	District	District	
3	District	District	District	District	

Annex 5

Table showing the criteria for the division of the pool of resources for the district level schemes among all the districts, followed in Maharashtra and Karnataka

	Indicators	Mah. %	Kar. %
1	Population	60	50
2.	Urban Population	5	
3.	Backwardness in agriculture as measured by the value of agricultural output per ha	5	5
4.	Backwardness in irrigation as measured by the proportion of irrigated area tonet sown area	4	7
5.	Backwardness as measured by the value of industrial output	5	5
6	Backwardness in communications as measured by the road and railway mileage per 100 sq. km and per lakh of population	5	5
7.	Backwardness in financial intrastructure as measured by size of population served by each commercial and co-operative bank		2
8.	Backwardness in medical and health facilities as measured by the number of hospitals percent 1000 population/bed population ratio		5
9.	Backwardness in power supply as measured by the proportion of villages electrified		5
10.	***Problem of the weaker sections:***		
(a)	As measured by the proportion of SCs/STs in the population	5	2
(b)	As measured by the proportion of landless agricultural labourers		2
11.	***Special problems of Malnad areas and drought prone areas:***		
(a)	As measured by the area under forest	1.5	2
(b)	As measured by the rural population of drought prone areas	3	2
12.	Literacy percentage		5
13.	Performance in family planning programme		3
14.	Problems of coastal areas	1.5	
15.	Amounts retained at the State level for solving special problems	5	
16.	**Total**	**100**	**100**

Criteria for determining the share of the mandal panchayat within a district.		
1.	Population	50
2.	Area of Mandal	15
3.	Dryland area	15
4.	Agriculture labour population	10
5.	Per capita resources raised	10

References

Bagchee, Sandeep. 1987. 'Poverty Alleviation Programmes in the Seventh Plan: An Appraisal', *Economic and Political Weekly (India)*, 22:4.

Bajaj, J.L. and Rita Sharma. 1995. 'Improving Government Delivery Systems: Some Issues and Prospects', *Economic and Political Weekly (India)*, M-73 to M-81, May 27, 1995.

Bandyopadhyay, D. 1988. 'Direct Intervention Programmes for Poverty Alleviation: An Appraisal', *Economic and Political Weekly (India)*, 23:26.

__________. 1986. 'Land Reforms in India: An Analysis', *Economic and Political Weekly (India)*, 23:25.

__________. 1996. 'Administration, Decentralization and Good Governance', *Economic and Political Weekly (India)*, Nov. 30, 1996, (3109-3114).

Bardhan, Pranab. 1996. 'Decentralized Development', *Indian Economic Review*, XXXI(2): 139-156.

__________. 1997. *The Role of Governance in Economic Development – A Political Economy Approach*. Paris:OECD.

__________. 1984. *Land, Labour and Rural Poverty: Essays in Development Economics*. New York: Columbia University Press.

Baumann, Pari. 2000. *Panchayati Raj Institutions and Natural Resource Management*. London: Overseas Development Institute (processed).

Bhattacharyya, S.N. 1970. *Community Development- An analysis of the programme in India*. Calcutta: Academic Publishers.

Binswanger, Hans. 1999. 'Fostering economic growth and reducing poverty: can decentralization help?' in *Technical Consultation on Decentralization for Rural Development (Proceedings)*. Rome: FAO.

Binswanger, Hans and Vernon W. Ruttan. 1978. *Induced Innovation-Technology, Institutions and Development*. Baltimore and London: The Johns Hopkins University Press.

Bird, R.M. 1995. 'Decentralizing Infrastructure:For Good or for Ill?', in Estache 1995.

Bombay, Government of. 1959. *Manual on Community Development*, Bombay: Government Printing Press.

Bose, Nirmal Kumar, ed. 1957. *Selections from Gandhi*. Ahmedabad: Navjivan Publishing House.

Brass, Paul R. 1994. *The Politics of India since Independence*, 2nd Edition. Cambridge and New York: Cambridge University Press.

Brinkerhoff, D.W. 1994. 'Institutional Development in World Bank Projects: Analytical Approaches and Intervention Designs', *Public Administration and Development* 14: 135-141

Cheema, S.G., and Dennis A. Rondinelli. 1983a. *Decentralization and Development: Policy Implementation in Developing Countries*, New Delhi: Sage Publications.

Cheema, S.G., and Dennis A. Rondinelli. 1983b. *Decentralization in Developing Countries: A review of Recent Experience*, World Bank Staff Working Papers, No. 581. Washington D.C: World Bank.

Chopra, R.N. 1985. *Green Revolution in India.* New Delhi: Intellectual Publishing House.

Choudhury, R.C. and S.P. Jain. 1999. (Ed.). *Patterns of Decentralized Governance in Rural India.* Hyderabad, India: National Institute of Rural Development.

Crainer, Stuart. 1998. *Key Management Ideas-Thinkers that changed the management world.* London: Financial Times, Prentice Hall.

Crook, R., and J. Manor. 1994. *Enhancing Participation and Institutional Performance:Democratic Decentralization in South Asia and West Africa.* London: Overseas Development Administration.

Dandekar, V.M. and N. Rath. 1971. *Poverty in India.* Pune: Indian School of Political Economy.

Dandekar, V.M. 1979. 'Below the Poverty Line', *Economic and Political Weekly (India)*, XIV: 7&8, Annual Number 1979.

Dandekar, V.M. 1996. *The Indian Economy, 1947-92: Vol II: Population, Poverty and Unemployment.* New Delhi and London: Sage Publications.

Dandekar, V.M. and F.K. Wadia. 1989. 'Development of Agricultural Administration in India', *Journal of Indian School of Political Economy*, I (1): 1-28.

Dantwala, M.L., Ranjit Gupta, and Keith Souze. 1986. *Asian Seminar on Rural Development: The Indian Experience.* New Delhi: Oxford University Press and IBH.

Dasgupta, Biplab. 1989. 'Panchayati Raj in West Bengal', *Kurushetra,* February, 1989.

Dasgupta, Biplab. 1995. 'Institutional Reforms and Poverty Alleviation in West Bengal', *Economic and Political Weekly (India),* October: 14-21.

Desai, D.K. 1986. 'Lessons of IADP', *Economic and Political Weekly (India),* 4:26.

Devas, Nick. 1997. 'Indonesia: What Do We Mean by Decentralization', *Public Administration and Development,* 17:351-367.

Dey, S.K. 1962a. *Community Development - A Chronicle, 1954-1961.* New Delhi: Government of India, Ministry of Community Development, Panchayati Raj and Cooperation.

_______. 1962b. *Nilokheri.* Bombay: Asia Publishing House.

Dillinger,William and Marianne Fay. 1999. 'From Centralized to Decentralized Governance', *Finance and Development, December 1999,* Washington DC: IMF.

Drèze, Jean and Amarthya Sen. 1995. *India: Economic Development and Social Opportunity.* Delhi: Oxford University Press.

Drucker, Peter. 1988. 'The Coming of the New Organization', *Harvard Business Review,* Jan-Feb 1988.

Estache, A. (Ed.). 1995. *Decentralizing Infrastructure: Advantages and Limitations,* World Bank Discussion Papers 290. Washington D.C: World Bank.

Farrington, John and Crispino Lobo. 1997. 'Scaling up Participatory Watershed Development in India: Lessons from the Indo-German Watershed Development Programme', *Natural Resource Perspectives Number 17, February 1997.* London: Overseas Development Institute.

Frankel, Francine R. 1978. *India's Political Economy, 1947-1977: The Gradual Revolution.* Princeton, NJ: Princeton University Press.

Gaiha, R. 1996. *Participation and Empowerment of the Rural Poor: The Case of Panchayats in India.* Delhi, (processed)

George, K.K. 1987. 'Discretionary Budgetary Transfers: A Review' in Gulati, Iqbal Singh (Ed.). *Centre-State Budgetary Transfers.* Delhi: Oxford University Press.

Ghosh, Buddhadeb. 2000a. *Panchayati Raj-Evolution of the Concept.* New Delhi: Institute of Social Sciences.

Ghosh, Buddhadeb. 2000b. 'Land reforms: Lessons from West Bengal' in Sinha, B.K. and K. Pushpendra (Ed.). *Land Reforms in India Volume V: An Unfinished Agenda.* New Delhi: Sage Publications.

Guhan, S. 1987. 'Devolution Criteria of Finance and Planning Commissions' in Gulati, Iqbal Singh (Ed.). *Centre-State Budgetary Transfers.* Delhi: Oxford University Press.

Gulati, Iqbal Singh. (Ed.). 1987. *Centre-State Budgetary Transfers.* Delhi: Oxford University Press.

Gupta, Devendra and Anil Gumber. 1999. 'Decentralization: Some Initiatives in Health Sector', *Economic and Political Weekly (India)* 34: 356-62.

Hart, Henry. 1976. *Indira Gandhi's India: A Political System Re-appraised* Boulder, Colorado: West View Press.

Hayami, Yujiro and Vernon W. Ruttan. 1985. *Agricultural Development: An International Perspective,* Baltimore: Johns Hopkins University Press.

Holdcroft, Lane E. 1984. 'The Rise and Fall of Community Development, 1950-65' in Carl Eicher and John M. Staatz (Eds.).

Agricultural Devlopment in the Third World, pp. 46-58. Baltimore: Johns Hopkins University Press.

ICSSR. 1980. *Alternatives in Agricultural Development,* New Delhi: Allied Publishers.

India, Government of. 1951. *The First Five Year Plan: A Draft Outline.* New Delhi: Planning Commission.

_______. 1953. *The First Five Year Plan.* New Delhi: Planning Commission.

_______. 1954. *Agricultural Legislation in India, Vol. V, Village Panchayats,* New Delhi: Directorate of Economics and Statistics, Ministry of Food and Agriculture.

_______. 1956a. *The Second Five Year Plan.* New Delhi: Planning Commission.

_______. 1956b. *Sixth Meeting of the Standing Committee of the National Development Council: Summary Record.* New Delhi: Planning Commission.

_______. 1957a. *A Guide to Community Development.* New Delhi: Ministry of Community Development.

_______. 1957b. *Review of the First Five Year Plan.* New Delhi: Planning Commission.

_______. 1957c. *Report of the Team for the Study of Community Projects and National Extension Service,* New Delhi: Committee on Plan Projects.

_______. 1957d. *Report of a Community Development Evaluation Mission in India.* New Delhi: Ministry of Community Development and Cooperation.

_______. 1958a. *Annual Report, 1957-58.* New Delhi: Ministry of Community Development.

_______. 1958b. *Tenth Meeting of the National Development Council: Summary Record.* New Delhi: Planning Commission.

_______. 1959a. *Report on India's Food Crisis and Steps to Meet It.* New Delhi: Ministry of Food and Agriculture and Ministry of Community Development and Cooperation.

_______. 1959b. *Sixth Evaluation Report on Working of Community Development and N.E.S. Blocks.* New Delhi: Planning Commission.

_______. 1961. *Report of the Expert Committee on Assessment and Evaluation.* New Delhi: Planning Commission.

_______. 1962. *Third Five Year Plan.* New Delhi: Planning Commission.

_______. 1965. *Lok Sabha Debates, Third Series,* XLIX (24). New Delhi: Lok Sabha Secretariat.

_______. 1967a. *Report of the Study Team on the Machinery for Planning* (Final Report), New Delhi: Administrative Reforms Commission.

_______. 1967b. *Report of the Study Team on Agricultural Administration.* New Delhi: Administrative Reforms Commission.

_______. 1968a. *Report on the Machinery of the Government of India and its Procedures of Work.* New Delhi: Administrative Reforms Commission.

_______. 1968b. *Preparation of States' Plans: An Appraisal of the Fourth Plan Experience* (Mimeo). New Delhi: Planning Commission.

_______. 1968c. *Twenty-fifth meeting of the National Development Council: May 17, 18, 1968: Summary Record.* New Delhi: Planning Commission.

_______. 1968d. *Evolution of Community Development Programme in India*, New Delhi: Department of Community Development, Ministry of Food, Agriculture, Community Development and Cooperation.

_______. 1970. *Fourth Five Year Plan, 1969-1974.* New Delhi: Planning Commission.

_______. 1976. *Abridged Report.* New Delhi: Ministry of Agriculture, National Commission on Agriculture.

_______. 1978a. *Report of the Committee on Panchayati Raj Institutions.* New Delhi: Ministry of Agriculture and Irrigation, Department of Rural Development.

_______. 1978b. *Report of the Working Group on Block Level Planning* (Dantwala Committee Report), New Delhi: Planning Commission.

_______. 1978c. *Rural Development Digest* I(4):273. New Delhi: Ministry of Agriculture and Rural Development.

_______. 1978d. *Annual Report, 1977-78.* New Delhi: Ministry of Agriculture and Irrigation.

_______. 1981. *The Sixth Five Year Plan, 1980-85.* New Delhi: Planning Commission.

_______. 1984. *Report of the Working Group on District Planning.* New Delhi: Planning Commission.

_______. 1985. *Report of the Committee to Review the Existing Administrative Arrangements for Rural Development and Poverty Alleviation Programme.* New Delhi: Ministry of Agriculture, Department of Rural Development.

_______. 1993. *The Report of NDC Committee on 'Micro-Level Planning and Involvement of People at Grass Root level'*, New Delhi: Planning Commission.

_______. 1994a. *Annual Report 1993-94,* New Delhi: Ministry of Rural Development.

_______. 1994b. *Guidelines for Watershed Development* (mimeo). New Delhi: Ministry of Rural Areas and Employment.

_______. 1997. *Approach Paper to the Ninth Five Year Plan (1997-2002).* Presented to the National Development Council on the 16th January, 1997. New Delhi: Planning Commission.

_______. 1999a. *Jawahar Gram Samridhi Yojana: Guidelines.* New Delhi: Ministry of Rural Development.

_______. 1999b. *Swarnajayanthi Gram Swarozgar Yojana: Guidelines.* New Delhi: Ministry of Rural Development.

_______. 1999c. *The Constitution of India,* New Delhi: Ministry of Law, Justice and Company Affairs.

_______. 2000. *Annual Report 1999-2000.* New Delhi: Ministry of Rural Development.

Isaac, Thomas, T. M., and Richard W Franke. 2000. *Local Democracy and Development: People's Campaign for Decentralised Planning in Kerala,* New Delhi: Leftword Books.

Jha, Prem Shankar. 1980. *India: A Political Economy of Stagnation.* Delhi: Oxford University Press.

Khatkate, D.R. and V.V. Bhatt. 1987. 'Accommodating the Planning Dimension' in Gulati, Iqbal Singh (ed.): *Centre-State Budgetary Transfers.* Delhi: Oxford University Press.

Klingensmith, Daniel. 1997. 'The Western Aid Community and Post-colonial India: On Development's continuities with Colonialism' in Steven C LaRue, et al. (eds.): *The India Handbook*, pp. 70-86. Chicago: Fitzroy Dearborn Publishers.

Klugman, J. 1994. 'Decentralization: A Survey of Literature from a Human Development Perspective', in Human Development Report Office Occasional Papers 13. New York: UNDP.

Kohli, Atul. 1990. *Democracy and Discontent: India's Growing Crisis of Governability.* Cambridge and New York: Cambridge University Press.

Kumar, Girish and Buddhadeb Ghosh. 1996. *West Bengal Panchayat Elections 1993: A Study in Participation.* New Delhi: Institute of Social Sciences.

Kurian, George. 1999. *Empowering Conditions in the Decentralisation Process: an Analysis of Dynamics, Factors and Actors in Panchayati Raj Institutions from West Bengal and Karnataka, India.* Working Paper Series No. 288. The Hague: Institute of Social Studies.

Kurian, N.J. 1989. 'Anti-poverty Programme: A Re-appraisal', *Economic and Political Weekly (India)*, 24:12.

Lakdawala, D. T. 1979. 'Plan Finances in A Federal Economy', *Yojana*, XXIII, 9.

Lele, Uma. 1975. *The Design of Rural Development: Lessons from Africa.* Baltimore: Johns Hopkins University Press.

Lewis, John P. 1995. *India's Political Economy: Governance and Reform*, Delhi: Oxford University Press.

Maharashtra, Government of. 1961. Cooperation and Rural Development Department, *Report of the Committee on Democratic Decentralization.* Mumbai: Government Printing Press.

_______. 1966. Rural Development Department, *Report of the Team of Enquiry into the Role of the Panchayati Raj Bodies in Agricultural Production Programme* (processed).

_______. 1971. *Report of the Reorganization of Maharashtra Administration.* Mumbai: Government Printing Press.

_______. 1986. *Panchayat Raj Evaluation Committee Report* (P.B. Patil Committee), Mumbai: Government Printing Press.

Maheshwari, Shriram. 1985. *Rural Development in India: A Public Policy Approach.* New Delhi: Sage Publications.

Manor, James. 1999a. 'Promise and limitations of decentralization' in *Technical Consultation on Decentralization for Rural Development (Proceedings).* Rome: FAO.

Manor, James. 1999b. *The Political Economy of Democratic Decentralization.* Washington D.C: World Bank.

Mathew, George. 1994. *Panchayati Raj-From Legislation to Movement.* New Delhi: Institute of Social Sciences.

Mathew, George. (ed.). 2000. *Status of Panchayati Raj in the States and Union Territories of India.* New Delhi: Institute of Social Sciences.

Mathur, Kuldeep. 1995. 'Politics and Implementation of Integrated Rural Development Programme', *Economic and Political Weekly (India)* 30:41.

Mathur, P.C. 1997. 'Rajasthan State Finance Commission's Report-A Critical Analysis', *Journal of Rural Development,* 16(4).

McLure Jr, Charles E. 1995. "Comment on 'The Dangers of Decentralization' by Prud'homme" *World Bank Research Observer* 10(20):221-26.

McNamara, Robert S. 1973. *Address to the Board of Governors*, Washington D.C: World Bank.

Meenakshisundaram, S.S. 1994. *Decentralisation in Developing Countries,* New Delhi: Concept Publishing Company.

_______. 1997. 'The 73rd Constitutional Amendments: A Case for Further Amendment', *Journal of Rural Development* 16(4): 549-556.

Minhas, B.S., I.R. Jain and S.D. Tendulkar. 1991. 'Declining Incidence of Poverty in the 1980s: Evidence Versus Artifacts', *Economic and Political Weekly (India)* 26:27.

Mukarji, Nirmal. 1989. 'Decentralisation Below the State Level: The Need for a New System of Governance', *Economic and Political Weekly (India),* March 4, 1989: 467-472.

Mukarji, Nirmal. 1995. 'Self-Government and its Instrumentalities', *People's Representatives and Bureaucracy-the Interface in Panchayati Raj.* New Delhi: Institute of Social Sciences.

Mukerji, B. 1961. *Community Development in India.* Calcutta: Orient Longmans.

Mukarji, Nirmal and D. Bandyopadhyay, (1994). 'New Horizons for West Bengal Panchayats' in Amitava Mukherjee (ed.). *Decentralization:Panchayats in the Nineties.* New Delhi: Vikas Publishing House Pvt Ltd.

Naidu, K.M. and K.S. Naidu. 1999. *Rural Development and Micro Regional Planning.* New Delhi: Reliance Publishing House.

National Institute of Rural Development (NIRD). 1999. *India Rural Development Report 1999, Regional Disparities in Development and Poverty*, Hyderabad: National Institute of Rural Development.

Oechssler, Jörg. 1997. 'Decentralisation and the co-ordination problem', *Journal of Economic Behaviour and Organisation,* 32: 119-135.

Olson, Marcus. 1965. *The Logic of Collective Action.* Cambridge, Mass: Harvard University Press.

Parker, Andrew. N. 1995. *Decentralization: The Way Forward for Rural Development?* Policy Research Working Paper 1475, Sector Policy and Water Resources Division, Agriculture and Natural Resources Department. Washington D.C: The World Bank.

Pillai, Sudha. 2000. 'Empower Gram Sabhas', *Economic Times*, June 26, 2000, New Delhi, India.

Potter, David. 1986. *India's Political Administrators-1919-1983.* Oxford: Clarendon Press.

Prud'homme, Remy. 1995. 'The Dangers of Decentralization' *World Bank Research Observer* 10(20): 201-20.

Ravillion, Martin. 1999. *Monitoring Targeting Performance When Decentralizing Allocations to the Poor are Unobserved* Development Research Group. Policy Research Working Paper 2080. Washington, D.C: World Bank (Processed).

Ray, Amal and Jayalakshmi Kumpatla. 1987. 'Zilla Parishad Presidents in Karnataka' *Economic and Political Weekly (India),* Oct 17-24, 1987.

Rondinelli, Dennis A. 1989a. 'Decentralizing Public Services in Developing Countries: Issues and Opportunities', *Journal of*

Social, Political and Economic Studies (U.S.) 14:77-98 Spring 1989.

Rondinelli, Dennis A., James S. McCullough and Ronald W. Johnson. 1989b. 'Analyzing Decentralization Policies in Developing Countries' *Development and Change* 20:57-87.

Ruttan, Vernon W. 1975. 'Integrated Rural Development Programmes: A Skeptical Perspective', *International Development Review*, XVII(4): 9-16.

Ruttan, Vernon W. 1984. 'Integrated Rural Development Programmes: A Historical Perspective', *World Development,* 12: 393-401.

Ruttan, Vernon W. 1987. 'Institutional Requirements for Sustained Agricultural Development', in Davis, Ted J., and Isabelle A. Schirmer (eds.). *Sustainability Issues in Agricultural Development: Proceedings of the Seventh Agriculture Sector Symposium.* Washington D.C: World Bank.

Sab, Abdul Nazir. 1996. 'Towards a Four Pillar State', in George Mathew (ed.). *Panchayati Raj in Karnataka Today: Its National Dimensions.* New Delhi: Institute of Social Sciences and Concept Publishing Company.

SDC. 1999. 'Decentralization and Development'. No. 2 in the series *SDC Publications on Development'*, Berne, Switzerland: Swiss Agency for Development and Cooperation.

Sivaramakrishnan, K.C. 2000. *Power to the People? The Politics and Progress of Decentralization,* New Delhi: Centre for Policy Research.

Slater, Richard and John Watson. 1989. 'Democratic Decentralization or Political Consolidation: The Case of Local Government Reform in Karnataka', *Public Administration and Development,* 9: 147-157.

Sundaram, K.V. 1997a. *Decentralized Multi-level Planning: Principles and Practice.* New Delhi: Concept Publishing Company.

Sundaram, K.V. 1997b. 'District Planning Committee: Its implications', *Journal of Rural Development* 16(4): 589-599.

Tanzi, V. 1995. 'Fiscal Federalism and Decentralization: A Review of Some Efficiency and Macro-Economic Aspects', *Proceedings of Annual Bank Conference on Development Economics.* Washington DC: World Bank.

Taylor, Carl C, Douglas Ensminger, Helen W. Johnson, Jean Joyce. 1965. *India's Roots of Democracy*, New York: Frederick A. Praeger.

United Nations Development Programme. 1993. *Human Development Report*, Oxford, England: Oxford University Press.

Venkatesan, V. 1982. *Planning and Implementation of Agricultural Development in India with Special Reference to Maharashtra.* Unpublished Ph.D thesis, University of Pune, Pune, India.

Venkatesan, V. 2000. 'Experiments with Poverty in Andhra Pradesh and Rajasthan', *The Hindu*, December 12, 2000.

Venkatesan, V and Jacob Kampen. 1998. *Evolution of Agricultural Services in Sub-Saharan Africa-Trends and Prospects.* Discussion Paper Nc. 390, Africa Region Series, Washington DC: World Bank.

Vithal, B.P.R. 1979. 'District Planning in the Context of Multi-Level Planning', *Economic and Political Weekly (India).*

Vithal, C.P. and Y. Bhaskar Rao. 1997. 'Management of Panchayati Raj Finances in Maharashtra: An Analysis', *Journal of Rural Development,* 16(4).

Vyas, V.S., and Pradeep Bhargava. 1995. 'Public Intervention for Poverty Alleviation: An Overview', *Economic and Political Weekly, (India).*

Wadia, F.K. 1996. 'Panchayats in India-Approaches and Ground Realities in a Historical Perspective', *Journal of Indian School of Politcal Economy*, 8(1): 64-97.

Webster, N. 1990. *Panchayati Raj and the Decentralisation of Development Planning in West Bengal: A Case Study.* Copenhagen: Centre for Development Research.

West Bengal, Government of. 1993. *New Horizons for West Bengal Panchayats – A Report on Panchayat Raj Institutions by Nirmal Mukarji and Debabrata Bandhopadhyay* (processed).

World Bank. 1975. *Rural Development Sector Policy Paper.* Washington, D.C.

_________. 1988. *Rural Development: World Bank Experience, 1965-1986.* Washington DC: Operations Evaluation Department.

_________. 1994. *Infrastructure- World Development Report 1994.* New York: Oxford University Press.

_________. 1995. *Columbia Local Government Capacity: Beyond Technical Assistance.* World Bank Report 14085-C. Washington, D.C: World Bank.

_________. 1997. *Rural Development: From Vision to Action - A Sector Strategy* Washington, D.C.

_________. 1999a. *Entering the 21st Century: World Development Report 1999/2000.* New York: Oxford University Press.

_________. 1999b. *Decentralization – Briefing Notes,* Ed. Litvack, Jennie and Jessica Seddon, World Bank Institute Working Papers in collaboration with PREM network (processed).

_________. 2000a. *India: Reducing Poverty, Accelerating Development.* New Delhi: Oxford University Press.

_________. 2000b. *Overview of Rural Decentralisation in India-Approaches to Rural Decentralisation in Seven States* (processed).

Wunsch, James S. 1991. 'Institutional Analysis and Decentralization: Developing an Analytical Framework for Effective Third World Administrative Reform', *Public Administration and Development,* 11: 413-451.

Index

D

E

F